Small-Town Restaurants in Virginia

The Starving Artist in Abingdon

Spring House Tavern in Woodstock

The Ashby Inn in Paris

JOHN F. BLAIR, PUBLISHER

Winston-Salem, North Carolina

Toliver House in Gordonsville

Seawell's Ordinary in Ordinary

Small-Town Restaurants in Virginia

Joanne M. Anderson

Second edition, first printing, 2004

DESIGN BY DEBRA LONG HAMPTON
PHOTOGRAPHS BY THE AUTHOR

Cover photographs clockwise from top left:
*Trick Dog Café, Irvington; Château Morrisette, Blue Ridge Parkway; The Summit, Blacksburg;
Cristina's, Strasburg; Chesapeake Bay Café, Cheriton; Mario's, Wytheville*

*The paper in this book meets the guidelines
for permanence and durability of the Committee
on Production Guidelines for Book Longevity
of the Council on Library Resources*

Library of Congress Cataloging-in-Publication Data
Anderson, Joanne M. 1949–
Small-town restaurants in Virginia / by Joanne M. Anderson.—2nd ed.
p.   cm.
Includes index.
ISBN 0-89587-299-4 (alk. paper)
1. Restaurants—Virginia—Guidebooks.   2. Virginia-Guidebooks.
I. Title.
TX907.3.V8A53   2004
647.95755—dc22   2004008266

Contents

Region 2
Shenandoah Valley

Region 3
Central Virginia

Region 4
Northern Virginia

Region 5
Tidewater and Eastern Shore

Contents

Introduction

This second edition is a continuation of my interest in, curiosity about, and love affair with small towns and restaurants. Small towns because they're, well, small. People smile easily and have a strong sense of community spirit. Restaurants because they have evolved from mere places to satisfy hunger to centers of social activity and entertainment. The people who run restaurants work hard, make sacrifices, and strive to please every person who enters their doors. They are often as interesting as the restaurants.

Traveling around Virginia seven years after the earlier edition of this book was published proved as interesting as the first time. While the innovative and upscale places continue to change their menus often, the family and home-style restaurants, where everything is just the same, provide comfort with their familiarity. Lots of people like Jim and Debbie Donehey (Griffin Tavern and Restaurant in Flint Hill) have realized their dream of having a restaurant. Still others, such as Jim Wade, (Smokin' Jim's Firehouse Grill in Lexington), never dreamed of owning a restaurant.

There are a lot more crab cakes, buffalo burgers, and Key lime pies on menus. Vegetarian offerings have increased, it seems, and tiramisu is found in restaurants of all kinds, not just ones featuring Italian cuisine. I was surprised at the minimal focus on the low-carb diet, despite its current trendiness.

I interviewed more corporate dropouts this time

around, such as John O'Brien (Jake's in Manassas). Many people have left big cities for small-town America, such as Lucas and Debbie Woodruff (The Victorian Inn in Luray) and Stephanie Fretwell (Fretwell's in Front Royal).

The establishments included in these pages run the gamut from no-diamond diners to five-diamond gourmet restaurants. The major criteria for inclusion were that a restaurant be clean, the staff be friendly, and the food be good enough to eat.

I offer no critiques. What I thought too greasy, too rare, too salty—too whatever—you might love. And what I consumed with delight you might consider unappetizing. I mention many dishes that I found to be delicious, but do so merely as someone expressing her personal taste, not as a food critic.

For the same reason I don't critique cuisine, I don't rate the restaurants with a system of stars, forks, crowns, or anything else. I may think the service is slow on the same night you're enjoying a special anniversary dinner and wish to dine for the entire evening. I appreciate linens, candlelight, and classical music, but I can also enjoy twirling on a stool at an old-time diner listening to local folks chat or hearing Patsy Cline belt out a tune on the jukebox. You might not like the former, or you might be uncomfortable at the latter. Running a restaurant is not a simple job. In fairness to owners and managers, you should eat in a restaurant several times before drawing conclusions about food and service.

For the purposes of *Small-Town Restaurants in Virginia*, a "small town" is an incorporated town, an independent city, or a spot in the road with a United States Post Office and a population under 30,000. Of course, there's an exception to every rule, and I have two in this edition.

Charlottesville has a population of slightly more than 40,000, yet retains a small-town feel once you get through the traffic to the downtown mall or University of Virginia campus. The other is Manassas. Its population is less than 40,000 and more than 30,000. Many people encouraged me to consider Old Town Manassas, so I went there. It is very nice with a train track and small-town atmosphere. Restaurants not within corporate limits are listed under the closest town or the town to which their mail is addressed. The restaurants on the Blue Ridge Parkway are listed under the parkway as if it were a town.

I visited each of the new restaurants included in this edition, and dropped in on many of the ones that stayed in the book. Others from the first edition were contacted for updated information. Many of the restaurants that are not making a repeat appearance in this edition are still in business, still putting out great food, but could not be included because of size constraints on the book. I paid for all of my meals.

Some restaurants were recommended to me by patrons and townspeople, some were listed in tourism brochures, and others were discovered by just driving around. I limited the number of restaurants per town to four. In a few cases, restaurants listed with a particular town are actually outside the town boundaries, so it may appear that there are more than four.

I made every effort to assure that the information presented is accurate and current. However, restaurants change hands, serving schedules are adjusted, and menu items disappear. You should call ahead to verify hours of operation whenever you're planning to visit a particular restaurant.

Whatever your taste in dining, I hope you'll find some restaurants here that you didn't know about before and that you'll find just plain interesting.

How to Use This Book

Small-Town Restaurants in Virginia is divided into five geographical regions—roughly the same ones used by the *Virginia Is for Lovers* travel guide and the Bed and Breakfast Association of Virginia. The only difference is that I've combined the Tidewater/Hampton Roads area with the Eastern Shore in a section I call "Tidewater and Eastern Shore." Region 1 covers the Southwest Blue Ridge Highlands; Region 2 features the Shenandoah Valley; Region 3 highlights Central Virginia; Region 4 covers Northern Virginia; and Region 5 features the Tidewater and Eastern Shore.

The towns are arranged geographically within each region, and the restaurants are covered in alphabetical order within each town. The towns are noted on regional maps at the beginning of each

section. Indexes of towns and restaurants are at the end of the book.

For each restaurant, I provide basic information such as address, telephone number, website, price range, and meals served. Seasonal schedules are given for those establishments not open year-round. Reservations are mentioned only if they are required or recommended. In citing each restaurant's "style," I've tried to make the designations self-explanatory: "fine dining" is just that; "casual nice" means that a restaurant is upscale but informal; "resort" indicates that the establishment combines dining, lodging, entertainment, and activities; "homestyle" suggests that the restaurant is very casual; "family-style" indicates that it's appropriate for everyone; "diner" means that it probably has counter stools (perhaps in addition to booths and tables); "drive-in" means you can have food delivered to your car, although some drive-ins no longer offer curb service. A "pub" has a predominant bar atmosphere but also has dining.

"Full bar" means that all alcoholic beverages are served; it doesn't necessarily mean there's a bar with stools. I also provide a brief list of "superlatives." These may be outstanding features, something I ate that was great, or things for which the restaurant is widely known.

After the basic information for each restaurant, there's a brief write-up touching on things such as the history of the town and the restaurant, the restaurant's atmosphere and décor, and the variety of foods served throughout the day.

Your Comments and Suggestions, Please

Of course, one author can't know everything about Virginia's restaurant business. Let me hear from you—what you like about the book, what you don't like, what restaurants you'd like to see included in future editions. Your comments and suggestions might help keep this book accurate and ensure that it fairly represents those who work so hard at bringing good food to clean tables in small towns throughout the Commonwealth.

Please mail your letters to me in care of the publisher or send e-mail to jmawriter@aol.com.

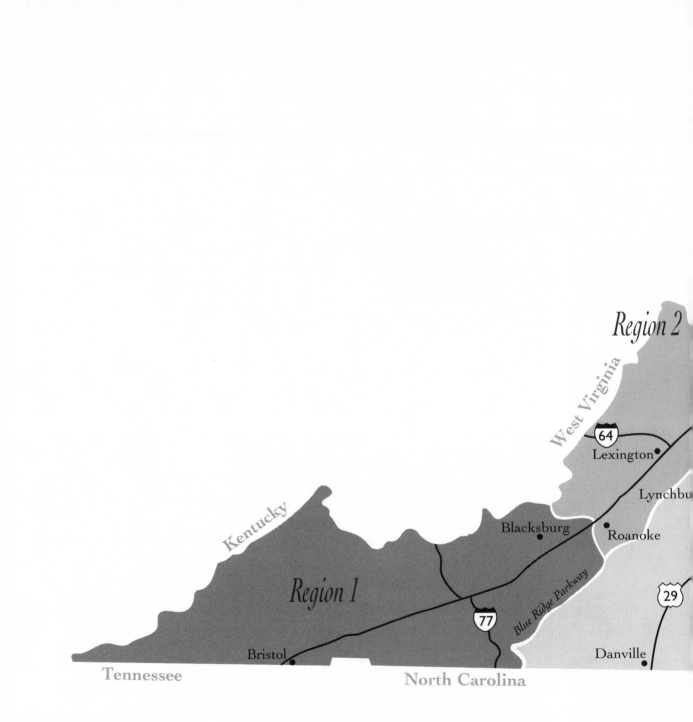

Winchester

Maryland

Arlington

Region 4

Alexandria

81

66

Harrisonburg

Blue Ridge Parkway

Fredericksburg

95

64

Charlottesville

RICHMOND

Region 5

64

Chesapeake Bay

Atlantic Ocean

Region 3

95

85

South Hill

17

Norfolk

Virginia Beach

Small-Town Restaurants in Virginia

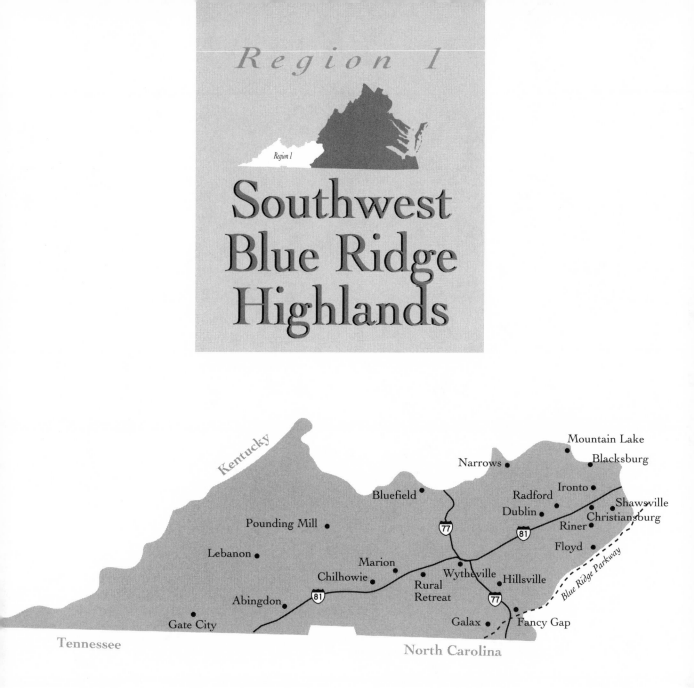

Region 1

Southwest Blue Ridge Highlands

Region 1

Kentucky

Tennessee

North Carolina

Mountain Lake
Blacksburg
Narrows
Ironto
Shawsville
Bluefield
Radford
Christiansburg
Dublin
Riner
Pounding Mill
Floyd
Lebanon
Marion
Wytheville
Chilhowie
Hillsville
Rural Retreat
Abingdon
Galax
Fancy Gap
Gate City

Blue Ridge Parkway

77
81
81
77

Southwestern Virginia was shaped by pioneers, farmers, miners, and rugged individuals like Daniel Boone, who blazed the Wilderness Trail through the New River Valley.

Half a million acres of national forest in this region offer wilderness for hiking, camping, exploring, hunting, and fishing. The area is also home to the highest mountain in the state, Mount Rogers, which rises more than 5,700 feet above sea level. And several miles of the 2,000-plus mile Appalachian Trail are located here.

Many of the small towns in the western part of the region owe their existence to the coal-mining industry, and small museums and markers pay tribute to this heritage. Other towns developed as trading posts or train depots. Some have flourished while others floundered, but each has a unique story to tell.

Cuz's Uptown Barbeque

U.S. 460 / POUNDING MILL, VA. 24637
(276) 964-9014
WWW.CUZS.US

Style	Home-style
Meals	Dinner is served from 3:00 to 9:00 P.M., Wednesday through Saturday, from March through November
Price Range	Moderate
Superlatives	Smoked prime rib, huge steaks

Cuz's comes up in southwest Virginia conversation as one of the best places to go for food, fun, and entertainment. So, here's the scoop on Cuz's Uptown Barbeque. I've quoted from their website because they can describe their place better than I ever could:

A long time ago, the mayor of Doran Bottom, Marv McGuire, the original cuz, advised me to open a honky tonk in our old dairy barn. So it started out with five tables in the bottling building with Dreyan, Margaret, Yvonne and the new cuz. We put in a little beer garden, then connected up with the barn and went big time. The pace has never let up since the first day. Our philosophy is still the same. Fresh food served quick and hot, steaks big enough to do all the advertising we would ever need, fish so fresh and varied that it seemed that the beach had come to Pounding Mill. Then we renovated the hayloft upstairs and here we are with bluegrass and crooners keeping the hungry crowd happy on the weekends. So

then come the cabins, clay tennis court, pool and who knows what's next? The thrill is still in Pounding Mill.

A long time ago was 1979, and Doran Bottom is more of a neighborhood than a real town. Marv McGuire wasn't really the mayor, but he held that locally esteemed, honorary title. Mike and Yvonne Thompson are the founders and owners, and they're still having a good time.

Two charming log cabins were built in 1995. Five years later, the restaurant burned to the ground. Soon thereafter, up went a new one, complete with a pizza oven and wood-fire rotisserie. For country folks with an adventuresome palate, Cuz's serves a popular cheese egg roll with Velveeta and an equally popular Thai seafood curry.

But, alas, it's the fresh fish and those big steaks that keep the people rolling through Cuz's. All the desserts are homemade with French silk chocolate pie and sour cream apple pie the most in demand.

Cuz's Uptown Barbeque is a unique, foot-tappin', knee-slappin' place to get a great meal and a respite from the woes of the world.

Campus Drive-In

U.S. 23 BUSINESS / GATE CITY, VA. 24251
(276) 386-3702

Style	Drive-in
Meals	Breakfast, lunch, and dinner, seven days a week
Price Range	Inexpensive
Superlatives	Pinto beans and cornbread, homemade biscuits and gravy

Gate City is the gateway to the Smoky Mountains. It's been the county seat since 1815, when it was called Winfield for General Winfield Scott. It was later renamed Gate City for its location in Moccasin Gap, through which the Wilderness Road went west. It's a nice town—not fancy but friendly.

Walking into the Campus Drive-In is like stepping into an old friend's place. People look your way. Some of them smile or nod as if to say, "Glad you walked in. Take a load off your feet."

If the customers aren't running the jukebox, the waitresses probably are, and they're not stingy with their quarters. I approached to see what they stocked for music, and a server who had just dropped in her money but not made a selection asked, "What do you want to hear?"

The restaurant was built by Darrell Dougherty in 1955. It's named the Campus Drive-In because it's right down the street from the high school. The tongue-and-groove walls are covered in plaid wallpaper. Fluorescent fixtures and ceiling fans with lights illuminate the place when the sun isn't pouring in the front windows.

Seven swivel stools, eight booths, and half a dozen or so tables provide seating. Behind the counter is an open window to the kitchen with a wire strung across it. The orders are clipped up here with wooden clothespins. The system reminded me a little of the restaurant in *Frankie and Johnnie*, with Michelle Pfeiffer and Al Pacino.

The salt-cured, country ham so popular throughout Virginia sells as fast as hot cakes at breakfast, as well as the other meals. According to Debra Dougherty, who owns the restaurant with her husband, Allen (son of founder Darrell), good country ham is one reason people come into the Campus Drive-In for any meal.

The hamburgers are good, and the chicken tenders are the least greasy fried chicken pieces I've had. The breading is peppery but not too hot. French fries, onion rings, tater tots, fried mushrooms, cheese sticks—all that stuff is here, too.

Dinners such as pork barbecue, flounder, popcorn shrimp, catfish, and chicken tenderloins come with french fries, slaw, and rolls. You can finish any meal with pie, cake (if there's any left), a banana split, a sundae, or hot fudge cake.

Then you can leave, and nod to the others on your way out.

Hob-Nob Drive-In

Hob-Nob Drive-In

DANIEL BOONE HIGHWAY (OLD U.S. 23)
GATE CITY, VA. 24251
(276) 452-4538

Style	Drive-in
Meals	Lunch and dinner, Tuesday through Sunday (open daily at 10 A.M.); breakfast served all day
Price Range	Inexpensive
Superlatives	Ostrich burgers, milk shakes

*S*omeone told me to bear left in town and "just drive for a while." Once I passed the new highway about a mile out, I wondered if there could be a real place to eat out here.

Then I spotted it on the right, a small, low, reddish building with a sign that seemed extremely short—at least in these days of 50- to 70-foot highway posts. It was packed when I drove in at 5:30. The cars included a new Jeep Cherokee, a Lexus, a Ford Explorer, a mix of mid-size Buicks and Oldsmobiles, and a few pickup trucks and small imports.

The Hob-Nob is basically red, black, and cream with fluorescent lighting. The bright, clean windows have mini-blinds, and there's an aura of friendly banter among the tables.

Ten booths and three or four tables with dark red vinyl chairs make up the inside eating area. Of course, it's a drive-in, so you can take your meal out or eat in your car—just honk and wait and you'll be tended to.

Built in 1953, this small restaurant got its name because it quickly became a popular place to eat and chat with neighbors or folks passing through.

In the 1970s, the new, improved, four-lane U.S. 23 replaced the old road, putting the Hob-Nob out of sight from travelers. A young couple who met while working here as kids took over the restaurant for several years before moving on to open their own. Once again, the Hob-Nob's demise seemed imminent. But along came a grandson of the original owner, who purchased it and continues to operate it.

Biscuits are served anytime. You can order them with gravy "while it lasts." Pancakes are around a dollar each—just order however many you want. Eggs, ham, and breaded steak are also available.

The sandwiches and burgers are run-of-the-mill—except for the ostrich burger, which isn't on the menu but is available some of the time. Ostrich farming is gaining popularity. Only time will tell if it's fad or fortune.

Besides the popular Neapolitan flavors for milk shakes, you can get cherry, raspberry, and peanut butter. Dinners include potato, slaw, and roll. And you can choose between making one trip or unlimited trips to the salad bar. Country ham, chicken, flounder, oysters, shrimp, and catfish are among the entrée choices.

If you can find a parking place, the Hob-Nob deserves your business if for no other reason than to honor its defiance in the face of progress.

Caroline's

301 EAST MAIN STREET / ABINGDON, VA. 24210
(276) 739-0042
WWW.CAROLINESLLC.COM

Style	Casual nice
Meals	Spring and summer: lunch and dinner, Tuesday through Sunday; fall and winter: dinner, Tuesday through Sunday. Reservations recommended on weekends.
Price Range	Moderate
Superlatives	Atmosphere; chocolate and strawberry mousse crêpe
Extras	Full bar

Carl Eskridge left his hometown of Abingdon, attended the New England Culinary Institute in Vermont, and then took a job as chef at a Native American casino in Michigan. There he met Jennifer. They fell in love, got married, and decided to move to Abingdon and start their own restaurant.

The charming eatery, which opened on August 21, 2002, is named for Carl's mother, who comes in quite often. It is located just a mile from The Barter Theatre, in a building constructed in 1901 for a general store. The log structure next door, known as the Crooked Cabin, is even older, and the uneven brick sidewalks outside attest to its age.

The interior is bright and inviting. One's eye is naturally drawn to the lovely staircase rising to an open second floor. Looking straight ahead across the black-and-white checkerboard floor the entrance to the outside patio comes into view. It's a great outdoor dining spot because it's covered, yet airy. The lattice-style walls built partway to the ceiling allow fresh air to circulate.

White tablecloths and napkins dress up the tables, along with John Cowan's pottery. Each centerpiece is handmade by this talented, local potter. Jennifer uses his mugs and serving dishes, and all pottery on the shelves is for sale. The art on the walls changes every eight weeks, and it's also produced by local artists and is for sale.

Caroline's signature salmon club sandwich places salmon with applewood bacon, lettuce, tomato, onion, and sun-dried tomato mayonnaise on toasted sourdough bread. Reuben, high Dagwood-style club, and Maryland-style crab cake sandwiches are just a few other options. Salads, pasta, and side dishes, such as char-grilled asparagus, are also on the menu.

Dinner is a lovely experience. Balsamic and peach-glazed chicken breast, citrus-and-herb lamb chops, trout almandine, or andouille-stuffed pork loin are just a few of the enticing entrées. The Sunday light fare includes soup and salad, vegetable Reuben, roast beef and Swiss sandwich, horseradish rib-eye, or barbecue salmon.

The desserts are extravagant in presentation, texture, and taste. Death by Chocolate Cake is amazing, but the chocolate and strawberry mousse crêpe is more amazing.

It is the mission of the chefs that every menu item is as enjoyable and flavorful as possible without compromising quality standards. The ingredients are fresh, the preparation exquisite, the experience divine.

Off I-81, take Exit 17 through the shopping section, turn right at the traffic light on to Main Street. Travel about a mile down on the left.

The Starving Artist

The Starving Artist

134 WALL STREET / ABINGDON, VA. 24212
(276) 628-8445

Style	Café
Meals	Lunch, Monday through Saturday; dinner, Tuesday through Saturday
Price Range	Moderate/Expensive
Superlatives	Vegetarian entrées, steak, seafood
Extras	Wine and beer

When artist Shawn Crookshank finished college, he found there wasn't much work for art majors in his hometown of Abingdon. So he and his wife, Kim, bought a little restaurant in 1985, renovated it, and opened The Starving Artist. The name honors all the artists who make a living doing restaurant work.

The art exhibit in the restaurant is changed monthly and often showcases unknown artists. The walls are white on the top with old pine boards on the bottom. Dark green vinyl tablecloths are dressed up with white linen napkins and fresh flowers. The carpeting and chair pads are also dark green.

Lunch appetizers range from shrimp cocktail and smoked Norwegian salmon to nachos and Cajun fries. Hot croissants, French onion soup, and a soup du jour are also offered. The salads can go with a sandwich or constitute a light lunch by themselves. The chicken, tuna, and shrimp salad may fit the latter category.

The 20 or so sandwiches are named for artists.

The Salvador Dali is billed as a surrealist tuna melt. The Jackson Pollock is piled high with thinly sliced roast beef dripping with Monterey Jack cheese. Auguste Renoir, Henri Matisse, Georgia O'Keeffe, James Joyce, Andy Warhol, Ansel Adams—they're all represented. The "Expressionist Sandwich" is yours to create from a list of meats, cheeses, and breads.

Dinner appetizers include sea scallops pesto and oysters Rockefeller. Pasta lovers and vegetarians will find salmon fettuccine, pasta primavera, vegetable stir-fry, and other entrées. Maryland-style crab cakes, filet Oscar, Cajun prime rib, Cajun shrimp, Delmonico steak, filet mignon, lemon chicken, and other seafood and beef choices are also offered.

Desserts such as raspberry walnut torte, Kentucky Derby pie, and coconut cream pie are homemade at The Starving Artist.

ABINGDON

The Tavern

222 EAST MAIN STREET / ABINGDON, VA. 24210
(276) 628-1118
WWW.ABINGDONTAVERN.COM

Style	Casual nice
Meals	Dinner, Monday through Saturday
Price Range	Moderate/Expensive
Superlatives	Historic atmosphere, stuffed filet mignon
Extras	Full bar

A few years before the first of earth's fellow planets was discovered, and almost a century before Alexander Graham Bell patented his telephone, The Tavern was open for business.

There's no record that George Washington slept here, but Henry Clay, King Louis Philippe, and Andrew Jackson reportedly did. And not a lot has changed in the interior since their visits.

Sure, there are some new support beams, and the fireplaces have been converted to gas, but as soon as you set foot on the brick floor behind the old wooden door, you'll be enveloped in the historical spirit of the place. Take the arm of a friend on your way upstairs if you're predisposed to vertigo. There's quite a pitch to floors this old. But the tilt only adds to the restaurant's authenticity and warm intimacy.

The building has a colorful past. If only these walls could talk! The first post office west of the Blue Ridge was housed in the east wing; the original mail slot is still visible from the street. The building has served as a bank, a bakery, a general store, a cabinet shop, a barbershop, a private residence, and an antique shop.

Today, The Tavern operates under the watchful eyes of Max Hermann, a United States Air Force veteran. Max is a native of Germany, and his influence can be found in the menu's continental touches.

The wine list spans the globe, with selections from Virginia, California, Washington, France, Germany, and Australia. There's a selection of imported beers, including a dessert beer served in a chilled wineglass. You can also purchase port or a cigar. And you may smoke the cigar in the smoking section.

Dinners with a German bent include Wiener schnitzel and *Kasseler Rippchen*. From Cajun country, there's jambalaya. From our own waters, there's trout. Other tempting entrées showcase lamb, steak, shrimp, chicken, and salmon.

Desserts are homemade and vary by the day. A chocolate confusion dessert and cheesecakes are usually available. Seasonal desserts with fresh berries or pumpkin come along in summer and fall.

CHILHOWIE

Riverfront Café

1449 LEE HIGHWAY / CHILHOWIE, VA. 24319
(276) 646-2233

Style	Family-style
Meals	Lunch and dinner, seven days a week
Price Range	Inexpensive
Superlatives	Apple festival chicken sandwich, certified Angus beef® steaks
Extras	Full bar

*O*wner Stan Landis came from New Jersey to southwest Virginia when he was in middle school. He worked for UPS for 15 years, advancing from driver into management. Then he started a little donut business, selling to convenience stores. When he was offered a job in food sales, he took it and sold food to hospitals, schools, restaurants—any entity that buys food wholesale.

He picked up a lot of knowledge at food shows

and in customer's kitchens along the way. People love to show you what they do and how they do it, so Stan was often coerced into kitchens. Although not with the intent to open a restaurant, he paid attention. When the opportunity presented itself to start his own establishment, he stepped up to the plate, so to speak.

On March 3, 2001, Stan opened the Riverfront Café, a family restaurant, pub, sports bar, and all-round nice dining experience. There are tables in the front across from a long bar. Lots of sports jerseys and NASCAR memorabilia create a sports bar aura. There are bar-height tables in a middle dining area. Toward the back is a more spiffy atmosphere with terra-cotta walls, floral drapes, gold frame prints, and a small bar.

Riverfront specialties on the appetizer menu are spinach artichoke dip and the nachos with salsa and cheese. Other items such as beer-battered mozzarella sticks, Cajun catfish strips, and fried mushrooms are also offered.

Salads and soups include popcorn chicken salad, Caribbean mango chicken salad, house salad, and potato soup with cheese and bacon. There are several sandwiches, including an apple festival chicken sandwich on a hoagie bun.

Stan is not a pushy kind of guy, but he's confident of the quality and preparation of his certified Angus beef® ribeye. I could see that my husband and I were not going to get away without trying it. Our reaction: juicy, tasty, melt-in-your-mouth, so full of flavor that few other steaks will satisfy again.

However, if you are just not in the mood for steak, consider sloppy chicken, grilled and butterflied pork loin, batter-dipped Alaskan white fish, hickory-smoked BBQ pork platter, Mediterranean butterfly shrimp, or another entrée. Side dishes include pineapple walnut salad, mashed potatoes, cottage cheese, peaches, green beans, and a few other things.

Eat slowly and hang around long enough to have some dessert. Peanut Butter Panic features peanut butter ice cream with Reese's Cup topping. Or try caramel pecan passion—caramel ice cream topped with caramel fudge pieces and crunchy glazed pecans. Blackberry cobbler, New York-style cheesecake, and hot fudge brownie might also be available.

Riverfront Café is between Exit 35 on the south end of Chilhowie and Exit 39 north of town. It's an easy parallel to I-81. It's a friendly spot with great food.

CHILHOWIE

Town House Grill

132 EAST MAIN STREET
CHILHOWIE, VA. 24319
(276) 646-8787
WWW.TOWNHOUSEGRILL.COM

Style	Fine dining
Meals	Lunch and dinner, Tuesday through Saturday
Price Range	Expensive
Superlatives	Atmosphere, crab cakes, fish dishes
Extras	Beer and wine

Chilhowie is easy to miss. You can glance over from I-81 going 70 miles per hour and think there's not much there except an old town left behind in the times. Well, slow down, and take a peek. *Chilhowie*, Cherokee for "valley of many deer," has a past and a present, both interesting and intriguing.

During the community's stagecoach days, the town was simply known as Town House. Only the chimneys remain from the first Town House. Constructed circa 1750, the building served as a stagecoach inn, post office, home, and gathering place for those who served in the Revolutionary War, Civil War, and War of 1812.

In present day, Tom Bishop, who was born in the clinic in Chilhowie, works in the family business, Berry's Home Centers. He and his wife, Kyra, are big fans of this little town and are playing a forward-thinking role in its revitalization by opening Town House Grill.

The restaurant is a stunning departure from commonplace eating spots. It's elegant, yet relaxed; classy, yet not intimidating. Soft sconces and beautiful chandeliers softly light a rich burgundy-and-wood dining room. Many of the old photos, prints, and paintings that adorn the walls are of old buildings in Chilhowie.

The tables are made of wood with copper edging. The floors are oak. There are generous bouquets of fresh flowers on every table and in the elegant ladies room. Tea lights on the tables provide a romantic feel.

The Town House salad, listed under "field of

greens," is a medley of Mesculin greens, sun-dried cherries, walnuts, bleu cheese crumbles, carrots, and grape tomatoes. Other salads are available, and appetizers include marinated shrimp cocktail, smoked salmon, and *Montrachet crostini*, which is warmed goat cheese on crusty bread drizzled with herbed balsamic.

Lunch sounds fabulous. Charleston cheese sandwich, Carolina crab cake, teriyaki steak stir-fry, chicken cordon bleu on a Kaiser roll, Reuben O'Grady, and a Town House garden grill are offered. You can also get a petit filet with the chef's daily starch and vegetables or other enticing items.

Black Angus rib-eye, lamb chops Dijon, black sesame-seared tuna, and chicken Marsala are some of the dinner entrées. I ate my first crab cake here, and now I'm an expert. All crab cakes must live up to the Town House standard of excellence. Wow, what a crab cake! Though I have discovered others in the state as wonderful, they are mostly in eastern Virginia.

Town House Grill is not a hurry-up place, though if you're on a schedule, tell them. If not, then leisurely hang on for dessert. The pastry chef is British, so you'll find an old-fashioned and authentically English bread-and-butter pudding. She also makes Chocolate Lava, a Belgium chocolate cake with a warm molten chocolate center, Kentucky Derby pie, and others. If Tom partakes in dessert, he's right happy with the homemade ice cream.

More of the downtown revitalization is taking place on the block with a bookstore, an art shop, and other small shops slated to open soon. Chilhowie is worth a stop.

Brenda's Hub Restaurant

89 SOUTH MAIN STREET / GALAX, VA. 24333
(276) 236-6701

Style	Home-style
Meals	Breakfast, lunch and dinner, seven days a week
Price Range	Inexpensive
Superlatives	Chicken and dumplings, chicken livers, homemade cobblers

Known as the "Home of Mountain Music," Galax has hosted the annual Old Fiddler's Convention since 1935. The town's name comes from a plant common on local mountainsides. The galax plant's waxy, heart-shaped leaves are a rich, deep green in summer and bronze in winter. Used by florists all over the country in fresh and dried arrangements, they're an integral part of the town's economy.

Speaking of names, the word hub once referred solely to the center of a wheel. Nowadays, it's taken on the broader meaning of a center of activity. This restaurant has been an unofficial hub since it opened as a drive-in restaurant for teens in the 1950s. Since August 1996, it's been Brenda's Hub.

Helen Smith has seen the changes. She waitressed the first night the original restaurant opened—just that one night to help out the owner.

Small-Town Restaurants in Virginia 11

Brenda's Hub Restaurant

About 40 years later, she returned to waitressing and has been back about 12 years now.

Brenda's is a simple place decorated with old signs and pictures. The big front windows have white mini-blinds, and the back room has wood paneling with a wallpaper border. The whole place can probably hold around 75 to 80 people.

Breakfast starts early. You can get just about any combination of eggs, ham, sausage, Canadian bacon, biscuits, grits, omelets, and hot cakes you want.

The "Hub Club" is a popular lunch sandwich. Burgers, chicken, baked ham, barbecue, tuna salad, chicken salad, and roast beef and turkey sandwiches are also served, as are assorted soups and salads.

Roast beef, turkey, rib-eye steak, veal cutlets, chicken, pork chops, flounder, shrimp, oysters, and a seafood plate are among the choices at dinner. Chocolate, lemon, or coconut pie and assorted cakes and cobblers finish the meal.

It's reasonable, it's folksy, and it's a true hub in this town. And according to Helen, Brenda's serves "real" food—"what the folks are raised on around here."

County Line Café

956 EAST STUART DRIVE (U.S. 58)
GALAX, VA. 24333
(276) 236-3201

Style	Home-style
Meals	Breakfast, seven days a week; lunch and dinner, Wednesday through Saturday
Price Range	Inexpensive
Superlatives	Homemade yeast rolls, French pie

*H*orace and the late Patsy Patton, affectionately called Papa Horace and Mama Patsy, started County Line Café in 1988 with their son and daughter-in-law, Craig and Sue Patton. The restaurant operates today under the watchful eyes of Sue and her children, Justin, Erin, and Catie.

Three white dining rooms seat 70 to 80 people comfortably. The first two rooms have dark tables and a variety of prints and photos on the walls. There's a sliding barn door between two of the rooms, and the back dining room has tables made completely from pine.

Breakfast is served until 11:00 A.M., and a wide variety of breakfast plates and combinations is available. For example, one of the country breakfasts consists of eggs, tenderloin or country ham, two biscuits or toast, and either gravy, grits, apples, or hash browns. Like most country-style breakfasts, you can mix eggs, breakfast meats, buttermilk pancakes, and gravy in almost any arrangement you want.

Grilled chicken salad, chef salad, cottage cheese salad, or stuffed tomatoes are light lunch ideas. All the soups are homemade, and the cooks put generous pieces of beef into the vegetable beef soup. Sandwiches, vegetables, cold plates, and hot roast pork, beef, or turkey are always available.

Pinto beans and cornbread are apparent staples in this neck of the woods. Vegetable plates are popular, too. Dinners include pork barbecue, fried shrimp, cold boiled shrimp, chicken nuggets, crab cakes, country ham, city ham (another name for regular smoked ham), flounder, and hamburger steak. The homemade bread and yeast rolls are yummy.

The heavenly hash served here is not a breakfast item from the flying pan. It's like an ambrosia salad—pineapple, oranges, mini-marshmallows, and cherries mixed with whipped cream. It's delicious and tastes like a dessert. Real desserts are homemade at County Line Café with Nana June's (Sue's mother's) homemade French Pie heading the list in popularity. It's a chocolate, brownie-like, fudge-like pie.

If you're not in a chocolate mood, though I cannot imagine such a thing, you can order a slice of homemade coconut or butterscotch pie or the day's cobbler.

The Galax Smokehouse

101 NORTH MAIN STREET / GALAX, VA. 24333
(276) 236-1000

Style	Family-style
Meals	Lunch, seven days a week; dinner, Monday through Saturday. Reservations are accepted.
Price Range	Inexpensive
Superlatives	Pork barbecue, smoked meats

When Barbara Jordan's parents retired in 1991, they left New Jersey for the southwest Virginia town of Galax. Barbara and her husband, Jon, visited and liked what they saw. Barbara was a teacher. Jon had a varied background, but they shared a dream of having a restaurant. They left their Nashville, Tennessee, home and relocated to Galax.

At church, the Jordans met Ron Passmore and Dan Milby, Sr., more out-of-state transplants to Galax. The foursome shared restaurant ideas. A concept was laid out, and a partnership was created, which was affectionately dubbed "Three Pigs & a Lady."

In a former corner drugstore in downtown Galax, they have established a restaurant venture that's poised for success. Ron is the general manager, and Dan serves as business office manager. Barbara handles the dining room. Jon is the pit master, the official barbecue jargon for one who prepares the meats and manages the smokers. Here, that means Jon does all the cooking, too.

The walls are painted burgundy. The wonderful black-and-white photos of Galax over the last century or so were contributed by one of their regular customers. Lighting is provided by brass chandeliers mounted next to the walls, fluorescent lighting above, and windows in front. The floor is the store's original terrazzo, and the counter with 18 stools has also survived for decades.

The Galax Smokehouse can seat about 60 in tables and booths. The faux marble tabletops hold a nice variety of the restaurant's own barbecue sauces.

The first appetizer on the menu is Smokehouse Fried Potatoes, which come covered in cheddar cheese and brisket bits with your choice of sauce. Brunswick stew and Texas brisket chili are offered by the cup or bowl. Sandwiches are reasonably priced and the selection includes beef brisket, pulled pork, smokehouse burger, sloppy joe, and Smokin Dogg [*sic*]—remember, all the meats are smoked.

Lunch specials pair a sandwich with a side order and drink for one price. Entrées include two sides and a choice of bread or Kaiser roll. You can order Texas beef brisket, pulled pork, a half rack of ribs, or chicken.

There are barbecue chef salads, combo platters, and bottomless drinks. Side items include barbecued beans, green beans, those wonderful fried potatoes, coleslaw, a house salad, hush puppies, or a slice of cheese.

My recommendation is the pulled pork. I ordered the sandwich without the bread, then smeared it with their house sauce. It was tender and tasty. If you don't have a meeting to get to or a flight to catch somewhere, mosey off I-77 at Exit 14 and travel the 15 or so miles into Galax to have yourself some mighty fine barbecue.

The Galax Smokehouse was in business less than a year when they won a "Best of the Best" award from *National Barbecue News*, an industry publication that sends people to taste barbecue anonymously. I suspect there are more awards on the horizon for this establishment.

Mountain Top Restaurant

U.S. 52
FANCY GAP, VA. 24328
(276) 728-9196

Style	Home-style
Meals	Breakfast, lunch and dinner, seven days a week
Price Range	Inexpensive
Superlatives	Breakfast and dinner buffets, homemade fruit cobblers and cakes

*T*he Mountain Top is not only reminiscent of 1950s roadside restaurants with a motel; it really is one. Run by Tommy Phillips, the 23-unit motel was built by his dad in 1953. The restaurant followed in 1959. Tommy's grandparents Ezra and Nora Phillips built and operated a restaurant with cabins a couple of miles down the mountain.

Breakfast was given a good review by a couple from Charlotte, North Carolina, I met in the parking lot. They said they often stop in the morning on their way to visit their daughter in Virginia. Hot cakes and eggs are the breakfast mainstays, served with salt-cured country ham, tenderized cured ham, sausage, or bacon.

At lunch, the names of sandwiches all end with *deluxe*. Chicken, barbecue, BLTs, and hamburgers are among the choices. French fries, tater tots, or hash browns are also available, as are spaghetti and some side orders.

Dinner comes with two vegetables and rolls. The Mountain Top offers the usual home-style meals—fried chicken, liver and onions, breaded veal, country ham, and chicken Parmesan. Seafood platters and steaks are available, as is a buffet featuring meats, vegetables, and salad.

Country ham is a special item here. You can get it at any meal, and occasionally, there will be an extra whole one that you can buy and take home.

Speaking of buying things, there's a bookcase in the center of the right-hand dining area with an eclectic collection of items for sale—plastic race cars, toys and games, big and little dolls, figurines, and what-nots. For the practical-minded, they sell thermal socks and flashlight batteries.

One thing you really should buy before you depart, however, is a slice of homemade cake or a dish of fruit cobbler.

Hillsville Diner

525 MAIN STREET / HILLSVILLE, VA. 24343
(276) 728-7681

Style	Home-style
Meals	Breakfast, Monday through Saturday; lunch, Monday through Friday
Price Range	Inexpensive
Superlatives	Stewed beef, pancakes

*T*he Hillsville Diner was founded by local fellows, Andy Howlett and Marvin Marshall, in 1946. About three years later, it was acquired by Roy McPeak and has stayed in the McPeak family ever since. Roy ran it for a while, then his brother, Dempsey, took it over. Dempsey's son, C.D. "Mac" McPeak, has had it since 1983.

Mac grew up in town and worked at the diner during high school. He went away to Concord College in West Virginia to become a teacher. After a couple semesters in the classroom, he knew this was not the career for him. He was smiling the day I walked in, so I guess 21 years in the restaurant business has agreed well with him. And he must be nice to work for because our waitress, Misty France, who was a very happy, pleasant young lady, had worked there more than two years.

It's a knotty-pine and red-checkered kind of place. The knotty pine is found on the walls, of course, and the different-sized red-checkered patterns can be found on the tablecloths, curtains, and floor. Terry Lawrence, a local artist and art teacher,

Hillsville Diner

did two of the great paintings on the wall—the one of the diner itself and the one of Mac's dad, Dempsey, serving customers a long time ago.

The front section of the diner has 18 stools, and the low-ceiling dining room in back can accommodate another 50 or more. It's a cheerful place with cheerful staff and customers.

Mac said breakfast is big, and their pancakes are incredibly popular. The menu is identical in both sections of the diner. It lists lots of combinations, such as biscuits and gravy with an egg; two eggs or one egg with ham; two eggs and sausage; bacon with no eggs—you get the idea. The prices are so reasonable, they actually seem unreasonably low.

One of the lunch specials is chicken tenders and gravy with two vegetables. The daily veggies number well over a dozen and include potato salad, pickled beets, potato wedges, and tossed salad. Stewed beef, a moist and tender preparation served with your choice of vegetables, is the house specialty.

Sandwiches, burgers, deli sandwiches, tuna salad, or chicken salad plates are offered daily. Other dinners include chicken livers, chicken tenders, veal steak, beef stew, flounder, barbecue pork, and chuck-wagon steak. Carry-out plates for leftovers cost ten cents. Pie is the dessert of the day—apple, egg custard, pecan, coconut cream, or chocolate cream.

Nostalgia never goes out of favor, and the Hillsville Diner has been noticed for its unique character. The *Richmond Times-Dispatch* published an article about the restaurant, and it was featured prominently in a story about diners in *Blue Ridge Country* magazine. It's the kind of place that can encourage you to slow down and contemplate the simple pleasures of life.

HILLSVILLE

Main Street Grill

311 SOUTH MAIN STREET
HILLSVILLE, VA. 24343
(276) 728-3363

Style	Home-style
Meals	Breakfast, seven days a week; lunch and dinner, Wednesday through Saturday
Price Range	Inexpensive
Superlatives	Hot dogs, pinto beans and cornbread

You could miss the Main Street Grill because it's quite small, not much larger than a two-car garage. The reason you won't miss it is because there are always lots of cars parked around it, and you'll wonder what's so good about it. It's the food that's so good, along with the curb service and getting called "honey" by Mildred a number of times, even in one sentence.

Mildred Turman, and her husband, Junior, worked years in restaurants, until one day they decided to give it a try on their own. Main Street Grill opened in this tiny spot in 1987, and the homemade food draws in a steady crowd from 9 A.M. until closing.

Six seats at three little tables are tightly positioned across from the counter where you bend down to place your order through a screen window. A couple of picnic tables are available outside, or you can take curb service.

Including the egg sandwiches, there are 42 sandwiches on the list. The only breakfast-type items are the egg sandwiches that come with bacon, cheese, sausage, ham, spiced ham, or plain. The other sandwiches run the gamut from burgers to fish filet, flounder, club, meat loaf, chicken, roast pork, barbecue, and turkey.

Main Street Grill is best known for its hot dogs, which come loaded with chili, slaw, cheese, or whatever else you want on one. This restaurant has been informally referred to as the "hot dog capital of Carroll County." Pinto beans and homemade cornbread are kept hot on the stove all the time, and the establishment sells lots of orders for this offering. There are also vegetable plates with one to four vegetables and homemade macaroni salad.

Dinners include oysters, chicken tenders, shrimp, flounder, hamburger steak, among others. Some of the sides are yam sticks, savory fries, onion rings, squash, chips, oysters, and waffle fries.

Ice cream and apple turnovers are offered, but I'd stick with Mildred's homemade desserts such as strawberry shortcake, coconut or butterscotch pie, blackberry cobbler, and whatever else she feels like putting together.

If you want curb service, you won't need to toot your horn or flash your lights. They're paying attention to the traffic in the little lot, and if you don't get out of your car fairly fast, someone will come out to you.

HILLSVILLE

Peking Palace

U.S. 58 / HILLSVILLE, VA. 24343
(276) 728-5539

Style	Chinese
Meals	Lunch, seven days a week; dinner, Friday through Sunday
Price Range	Inexpensive
Superlatives	House combination, moo goo gai pan
Extras	Wine and beer

Jimmy Hsu, owner of the Peking Palace, came to the United States from Taiwan in 1971. He worked in Roanoke for two decades before opening his restaurant in 1991.

The space had previously been a restaurant, and Jimmy has done a wonderful job of refurbishing

Peking Palace

the interior. It's bright, light, clean, and comfortable. Track lights and Oriental-style lamps provide illumination. There are double linens under glass at the tables and booths. About 120 guests can be seated in three dining rooms.

There's a lunch buffet every day. All the lunch specials come with soup and fried rice. Some of the options—such as curry chicken and spicy hot chicken—include an egg roll, too. Pepper steak, Chinese-fried shrimp, sweet-and-sour pork, and beef chop suey are some of the other options.

Among the hot-and-spicy dinner entrées are orange-flavored chicken, twice-cooked pork or shrimp, and chicken sautéed with bamboo shoots, water chestnuts, and vegetables in hot sauce. Milder alternatives include the house shrimp special, crispy beef, and Hong Kong chicken. The popular house combination includes beef tenderloin, sliced chicken, and fresh shrimp sautéed with Chinese vegetables in a special sauce. The moo goo gai pan is another favorite among patrons. The family dinners feature a variety of Chinese foods for a set price and can be ordered for two, three, four, five, or six people. There

are also Southern attractions such as ham steak, fried chicken, and pork chops, as well as a cheeseburger and a roast beef sandwich.

Some Chinese items—figurines, plates, porcelain Buddhas, and carvings—are offered for sale at the counter.

It's a credit to Jimmy that his restaurant was recommended for inclusion in this book by another restaurant owner.

WYTHEVILLE

Log House 1776

520 EAST MAIN STREET
WYTHEVILLE, VA. 24382
(276) 228-4139

Style	Home-style
Meals	Lunch and dinner, Monday through Saturday
Price Range	Moderate
Superlatives	Old log buildings, gift shop, pork tenderloin
Extras	Full bar

Originally called Abbeville, then Evansham, Wytheville received its present name when it was incorporated in 1839. The name honors George Wythe, a signer of the Declaration of Independence, America's first law professor, and the designer of the seal of Virginia. Wytheville is the hometown of Edith Boling Wilson, wife of Woodrow Wilson, the 28th president of the United States and a native Virginian himself.

Log House 1776 is well worth a five-minute drive off the interstate. Get off I-81 at Exit 73 and head toward town. In about three miles, you'll reach a log house on the right, which was built by a Revolutionary War soldier. Other log structures on the property were built in 1804.

During the Civil War, Joseph Chadwell, the owner, and Benjamin Steptoe, a freed slave who lived in the cabin that now houses the deli, went together to fight for the Confederacy.

The restaurant was opened by James and Pat Green during our nation's bicentennial year. They had moved their bakery into the building a couple of years earlier but weren't crazy about the early-morning hours a bakery demands.

The log walls create a nostalgic warmth. Lace under glass adorns most tables downstairs; upstairs, there's a mix of tablecloths and lace. The large, round table downstairs rests on a barrel pedestal. Kerosene lamps sit on some tables, and a beautiful old lamp hangs in the center of one room. The fireplaces have been converted to gas without destroying the warm ambiance.

At lunch, guests can use the sandwich menu or select from the dinner menu at $1.50 less than dinner prices. The "Sunshine Sandwich" is one of the most popular items. It's toasted French bread with asparagus, ham or turkey, provolone, and bleu cheese. You can also get burgers, sandwiches, salads, soup, and a variety of appetizers, such as a grape cheese cluster, egg rolls, cheese sticks, and corn fritters with honey.

Log House 1776

The chef's specialties are two varieties of pork tenderloin. The "Log House" version features pork filled with apples, celery, onions, breadcrumbs, spices, and a special sauce. The "South of the Border" pork tenderloin is filled with cheese, mildly hot peppers, and special sauce. The "Confederate Beef Stew"—as prepared for General Robert E. Lee and his troops—includes apples and herb potatoes. Two vegetables come with dinner. The house specialty is stuffed yellow crookneck squash filled with onions and crackers and topped with cheese.

The triple-layer cheesecake has chocolate, praline pecan, and white almond layers covered in a hard chocolate shell. Raspberry cheesecake, bread pudding, and coconut cream pie are some of the other desserts.

Before you leave the property, go out back and see the birds, rabbits, gardens, and gift shops. Among the birds are a type of partridge that, with training, can talk. Pat is working on teaching them to say, "Hi there, you're pretty."

Pat has a simple explanation for keeping the birds and rabbits: "Children get restless riding around."

But you don't have to have kids to enjoy this place.

Mario's

100 WEST MAIN STREET
WYTHEVILLE, VA. 24382
(276) 228-1212

Style	Family-style
Meals	Lunch and dinner, seven days a week
Price Range	Inexpensive/Moderate
Superlatives	Fresh tomato sauce, cannolis
Extras	Wine and beer

*M*ario's is on the corner of Main and Tazewell streets near the center of Main Street. The awning looks very Italian—red, white, and green. The counters behind glass on both sides of the entry are artfully decorated with vases of spaghetti pasta, bright streamers, and seasonal items. This used to be a jewelry store, which explains the counter displays.

Inside, Mario's is bright, cheery, and very clean. A wallpaper mural on one wall depicts a shore scene, and there are photos from Italy on the opposite wall. Tables are covered in red-and-white-checkered tablecloths. There are three beautiful chandeliers situated among the ceiling fans. There is a drop ceiling with every rectangle impeccably clean.

Mario grew up in Naples, Italy. He traveled back and forth between Italy and the United States several times before settling down with the Wytheville restaurant.

There are 17 tables for four in an uncrowded dining area. The staff is nice and friendly, and Mario steps out of the kitchen often to wander the dining room and visit with his customers.

There's a long list of hot submarines and cold submarines, as well as burgers and club sandwiches. The subs are offered in an 8- or 11-inch size. Pizzas come in small, medium, and large sizes, and you can choose the New York, specialty, or Sicilian style.

Non-Italian appetizers include chicken wings, fries, onion rings, and breaded zucchini strips. Bread sticks are freshly baked and served with tomato sauce for dipping. All the bread is homemade here, and it is coarse, crusty, and delicious. Regular salads such as garden, chef, and grilled chicken are offered along with antipasto over salad, calamari with salad, and a Greek salad.

All the standard pasta dishes are here—spaghetti, manicotti, fettuccini, stuffed shells, lasagna (including vegetarian lasagna), ziti, and ravioli in various combinations. There are around a dozen house specialties such as *Vitello Florentine* (fresh veal sautéed with mushrooms and topped with spinach), *pollo cacciatore* (chicken breast topped with black olives, onions, and mushrooms in a marinara sauce) and *melezane parmigiana* (battered eggplant under tomato sauce and melted mozzarella cheese).

Seafood specials come with a garden salad and garlic bread. Shrimp is served in three different ways, while fresh-shelled clams come sautéed in wine, garlic, and olive oil with white or red sauce.

The cannolis are not your standard American variety. These are real Italian cannolis, with a thick crust wrapped around a tasty filling. The filling is not at all like whipped cream, but a richer, thicker filling with tiny chocolate chips inside. The tiramisu is imported from Italy.

Mario's offers excellent, authentic Italian food in a nice, clean environment. Traveling north on I-81, take Exit 70 into town and turn left on Main Street. If you are going south on I-81, take Exit 73 into town.

The Matterhorn Restaurant and Lounge

170 MALIN DRIVE / WYTHEVILLE, VA. 24382
(888) 950-3382; (276) 223-0891
WWW.WOHLFAHRTHAUS.COM

Style	Pub
Meals	Lunch and dinner, seven days a week
Price Range	Moderate
Superlatives	German cuisine
Extras	Full bar, dinner theatre, gift shop

*P*eggy Sutphin grew up in southwestern Virginia.

She said there were enough places to eat, but not much for entertainment. Occasionally, her family went up to Roanoke, but it was quite a drive. So, later in life, she thought it would be wonderful to have theatre in Wytheville and expanded the idea to dinner theatre.

When researching the German side of her ancestors, Peggy discovered the Wohlfahrt name and decided to use it for the dinner theatre's name and theme. Peggy's business background carried her concept into reality and success, even though she had neither restaurant nor theatre experience.

Chef Richard Houser heads up the kitchen for both The Matterhorn Restaurant and Lounge and the Wohlfahrt Haus dinner theatre. There is no buffet, as traditionally found at dinner theatres, but full table service at both places. Houser makes a mighty popular crab bisque and crab cakes. For an appetizer or light appetite, there are dips, wings, nachos, cheese sticks, and chicken tenders. House salads and chef salads are offered, as well as Southwest chicken wraps.

Reubens, Cuban pork sandwiches, Wohlfahrt Haus burgers, and grilled chicken sandwiches with ham and Swiss may be accompanied by German potato salad, sweet-and-sour cabbage, or sweet potato fries.

German is the theme throughout in décor and design, so Wiener schnitzel is a featured entrée, of course. Munich Chicken is rotisserie roasted and served with rice, mixed vegetables, and sweet-and-sour red cabbage, which is very German. Steak and

Chicken Esterhazy pairs the meats with carrots, mushrooms, and onions in a cream sauce over a fried potato cake. Knockwurst and bratwurst are also represented.

If you're not in the mood for German, go American with vegetarian pasta of the day, prime rib, grilled sirloin, or sweet garlic chicken. Chef Richard creates interesting specials every day. Desserts include cobblers, German chocolate cake, and apple cake.

A wide selection of domestic and imported beer and wine is complemented with an equally impressive list of fine German wine and beer. Not being a wine connoisseur, I do not often comment on wine. However, the German whites such as Riesling and Piesporter are my favorites.

The bier garten has cafe-style dining outside and is open daily as weather permits, with live entertainment offered on Saturdays. Edelweiss Gift Shop has a neat selection of German gifts and collectibles, cuckoo clocks, wooden toys, German boy and girl dolls in traditional dress, ornaments, and lovely boxes from Poland.

The 200-seat dinner theatre is the highlight at Wohlfahrt Haus. The productions are all musicals, all fun, all enjoyable. Check the website for the production schedule. Reservations are necessary almost all the time. From I-81 or I-77, take Exit 73 and follow the signs.

Joey's Country Kitchen

100 SOUTH MAIN STREET
RURAL RETREAT, VA. 24368
(276) 686-4911

Style	Home-style
Meals	Breakfast and lunch, seven days a week; dinner, Thursday through Tuesday
Price Range	Inexpensive
Superlatives	Cheeseburgers, coconut pie

This town's name is a perfect match for the setting—a rural village one could easily retreat to for a meal, a weekend, or a lifetime. The people are friendly. The scenery is pastoral. And there are lots of church steeples, as small towns should have. At 2,640 miles above sea level, Rural Retreat is the highest point on the Norfolk-Southern Railroad that runs between Norfolk and New Orleans.

After crossing the railroad tracks less than two miles east of I-81's Exit 60, you'll find Joey's on the left. It's housed in a boxy, yellow building with huge letters on the roof, which say JOEY'S COUNTRY KITCHEN. The original restaurant on this site opened in the 1950s and sat closer to the road. This building went up in the late 1980s, and Joey Majors bought it a couple of years later.

If you sit on one of the half-dozen counter stools, you'll face the pies topped high with meringue in a glass-front pie cabinet. If you sit there, you might have to order pie. There are nine booths and a couple of tables with ladder-back chairs. Dark green swags on the windows accent wood-paneled walls.

Breakfast is served all day, and the 12 local favorites on the menu are called Billy, Kim, Donnie, Roger, Mr. Mitchell, Jack, Cleve, and so on after the customers who regularly order such combinations. The Roger is one homemade biscuit and sausage gravy with two tomato slices, while the Cleve pairs standard breakfast fare of two eggs and home fries with country ham and toast.

The ground beef is fresh, and the hot dogs are all beef. Sandwiches include grilled cheese, hot ham and cheese, bacon and egg, grilled chicken, and tenderloin on a bun, or you can opt for a burger and dress it up as you like with cheese, mushrooms, onions, or bacon. Cottage cheese and peaches fall under the salad category, and dinners all come with two vegetables and your choice of roll, cornbread, or biscuit.

They claim the rib-eye is grilled to perfection. Tenderloin is basted and grilled. Dinner selections also include chicken, country ham, flounder, and other meats. They are available with side orders such as fried squash or okra, pickled beets, yam sticks, fried mushrooms, as well as more common offerings such as macaroni and cheese, potato salad, and baked apples.

Just don't forget about the pie. The coconut pie is very good.

A la Carte Café

123 SOUTH CHESTNUT STREET, SUITE 110
MARION, VA. 24354
(276) 782-4495

Style	Casual nice
Meals	Lunch, Monday through Saturday; dinner, Tuesday through Saturday
Price Range	Moderate
Superlatives	Crab cakes, orange mandarin cake
Extras	Full bar

*I*n March 1981, Gary Hart (not the former Colorado senator) was living in Abingdon, Virginia, with a buddy. His roommate's girlfriend from New Jersey came to visit, bringing along her friend, Sharon. Gary and Sharon met, fell in love, and married three months later. They moved to Marion the next year.

Sharon started a salon, while Gary went to work for the state's Department of Corrections. In 2000, they renovated part of a 1922 brick building for her salon and their new restaurant, A la Carte Café. Look for a green-and-white awning in the front of 123 South Chestnut. Then go to the right side of the building where you'll find A Cut Above Salon & Spa toward the front and A la Carte Café at the back. *A la carte* means "on the side" in French, so that's appropriate.

There are four umbrella tables on the deck outside. Lots of rattan and bamboo, contemporary art by Marion artist Denise Hoots, warm reddish brown colors, and a variety of bamboo sconces and paper shades, all create a cozy, Caribbean atmosphere.

Slate, rattan, wood, and metal tables—some bar height, some regular height—are available to seat around 40 people. Linen napkins and a jar candle adorn each table. The menu is cleverly tied to the top of a wood board with a leather lace. It's interesting.

There are six bread choices for sandwiches. You can order half of most of the sandwiches for 60% of the price or substitute a fruit cut for the chips for a small fee. Herb-seasoned tuna salad, fruited chicken salad, chicken cordon bleu, roast beef, egg salad, ham and Swiss, all beef hot dogs, and hamburgers are some of the sandwich options.

Salads are made fresh twice a day, for lunch and dinner, and they make their own salsas and tortilla chips. The house soups, which may not always be available in the summer, are tomato herb and cheesy potato, and they offer white chicken chili.

Dinner may begin with an appetizer of surf & turf skewer, black bean cake with two distinctive salsas, Jamaican bread, or chef's salad. Entrées include Monterey chicken, blackened tuna, marinated beef filet, black bean cakes, scallop or shrimp scampi, and daily specials. The crab cakes get my vote. The orange cake is luscious and homemade, like the other desserts, and you can order from the espresso and cappuccino bar.

A la Carte delivers lunch and dinner on real dishes to other locations in Marion, and they even come back and pick up the dishes. They also have all sorts of salon packages, with lunch and dinner catered to the spa.

This charming, Caribbean-theme restaurant has four generations working here now—Sharon, her grandmother, her mother, and a daughter. And it's less than a mile off I-81 at Exit 45.

MARION

Dip Dog
U.S. 11 WEST
MARION, VA. 24354
(276) 783-2698

Style	Drive-in
Meals	Lunch and dinner, seven days a week
Price Range	Inexpensive
Superlatives	Dip dogs, homemade onion rings, frozen custard

*M*arion is named for Francis Marion, the "Swamp Fox" of Revolutionary War fame. It's a pleasant small town with some good antique shops on Main Street.

The Dip Dog is a very small place with an old sign and enough cars in the middle of a weekday afternoon to pique one's curiosity. The building looks much newer than the sign and isn't much bigger than a two-car garage. Inside, there's a standing area a few feet deep and two order windows. All the food is listed on signs behind the person at the windows.

According to James Brown, a retired government worker who loafs at the Dip Dog and volunteers

Dip Dog

as maintenance man on occasion, "everyone knew about this place" when he was covering his territory from Dublin south to the Tennessee line.

There are four picnic tables outside, but it was a cold day when I visited, so most people were eating in their cars or standing and talking to occupants eating in other cars.

Started in 1957 by Lester Brown, the Dip Dog was acquired by Grant Hall, Sr., in 1965. Hall's son Grant, Jr., bought it in 1980 and constructed a new building five years later. The old sign was on the roof of the original building and had neon lights on it. Grant plans to renovate the sign with neon again.

Dip dogs—what the restaurant is famous for, at least locally—are 95 cents. It's a hot dog on a stick dipped in a special batter, then quickly deep-fried to a golden brown and served with mustard. "It looks like a corn dog, but it's not," stated Hall emphatically.

If a dip dog isn't your style, you have plenty of options—hamburgers, plain hot dogs, fresh onion rings, and sandwiches such as steak, pork barbecue, ham and egg, grilled cheese, and chicken breast. If you're really hungry, you can order a complete dinner of shrimp, oysters, flounder, or chicken and follow that with frozen custard, a banana split, or an ice cream sundae.

Grant and his wife, Pam, have a new enterprise, Spunk and Pam's Backyard Batch Barbeque Sauce (www.backyardbatch.com). Ask which items at the Dip Dog have some of their new sauces. The bottled barbecue sauce began as a family Christmas gift and just mushroomed after the holidays.

Despite working in such a small place, my order taker didn't seem to understand the concept of "not too big." I ordered a small frozen custard—"not too big, please." What I got measured nearly a foot from top to bottom, and less than a third of it was cone.

From what I heard when I mentioned this place to anyone within 30 miles, this was where you either had your first job or took your first date. Or both.

It's a good thing I pulled in when I did. By the time I left, the number of cars and pick-up trucks outside had about doubled, and the parking area was close to full—in the middle of a weekday afternoon.

The Old Mill

118 MILL STREET / LEBANON, VA. 24266
(276) 889-4310

Style	Family-style
Meals	Dinner, Monday through Saturday
Price Range	Moderate
Superlatives	Prime rib, pork barbecue sandwich, meat loaf
Extras	Wine and beer

*S*olomon's temple in ancient Jerusalem was built from the cedars of Lebanon. When this Virginia town was settled, it was named for the biblical event brought to mind by the wild cedar trees growing here. Lebanon is the county seat of Russell County. When the courthouse burned in 1872, thrifty local residents salvaged much of the rubble and used it to build a new one.

One of the town's old mills, constructed around 1918, was a ramshackle building with a rickety porch and a tin roof at the time it was purchased and turned into a restaurant. Touches from the old days remain. Some of the beams in the upstairs dining room continue right through the walls and across the whole building. Inside the front door is a staircase that starts into the air, then goes nowhere. Bands once played on the platform at the top of the steps. When the owners stopped having live music and remodeled the downstairs, they removed the bottom steps but saw no reason to take away the middle. Anyway, it's a conversation piece.

The Old Mill's steaks are a big draw. New York strip, rib-eye, and filet mignon are char-broiled to your liking, with or without Cajun spices. Prime rib is offered on Friday and Saturday evenings. And there's always a wide range of seafood entrées, as well as pork tenderloin and ground steak.

You can finish your meal with a hot fudge brownie or with strawberry shortcake in the summer.

Château Morrisette

MILEPOST 171.5, BLUE RIDGE PARKWAY
MEADOWS OF DAN, VA. 24120
(540) 593-2865
WWW.THEDOGS.COM

Style	Casual nice
Meals	Lunch, Wednesday through Sunday; dinner, Friday and Saturday. The restaurant is open year-round, but call ahead if the weather is questionable. Reservations are suggested for dinner.
Price Range	Moderate
Superlatives	Wine, setting, view, creative cuisine
Extras	A winery tour and tasting is offered for $2.00 per person.

*S*et against the backdrop of the Blue Ridge Mountains, this is one of only three full-service restaurants at wineries in Virginia. The state boasts more than 40 wineries, and Château Morrisette is one of the largest in terms of production.

The business was started in 1978 as Woolwine

Château Morrisette

Winery by William Morrisette. Four years later, his son David, then just 22, became company president. David took the small vineyard to a full-scale winery with a 120-seat restaurant and retail and wholesale operations.

Château Morrisette's wines are distributed in Virginia and North Carolina. Wine Club members number 3,000, and the mailing list for the newsletter tops 56,000. The winery attributes its popularity to "good wines, increased awareness of our product, repeat and word-of-mouth business."

Keep a sharp eye for Milepost 171.5, as the turn-off is easy to miss; it's 7.5 miles past the junction with Va. 8 to the north. Turn off the parkway, then immediately left on Winery Road.

Winery tours take about 30 minutes and are followed by a tasting. Château Morrisette produces more than 60,000 cases of wine annually.

The owners have long had a love affair with the black Labrador. Nicholas, the current mascot, will probably meet you near the front. There are Black Dog Jazz Concerts in summer. There's also a Black Dog red wine and a Black Dog Blanc. Our Dog

Blue, a semisweet wine with floral aromas, was introduced in 1996.

The food is innovatively prepared and presented, and the menu is changed to capitalize on seasonal game and produce. For lunch, you might find a Brush Creek buffalo burger, a grilled balsamic-marinated portobello sandwich, chicken pot pie in a light velvet sauce, or broiled catfish with rémoulade sauce.

Two of the more interesting appetizers on the dinner menu are alligator Françoise on garlic toasted points with lemon-butter sauce, and a shrimp and crayfish cake on a crispy stone-ground grit cake in smoked tomato vinaigrette.

Entrées include a variety of game, such as Carolina quail stuffed with wild mushrooms, and blackberry-cured duck breast served with three potato au gratin, carrots, zucchini, and apples. More common things such as free-range chicken and beef tenderloin are dressed up—the former with a creamy country ham gravy and speckled heart grit triangle, and the beef with roasted mushrooms, asparagus, three potato au gratin, and sauce Châteaubriand.

Before leaving, check out the gift shop. In addition to wines by the bottle and case, you'll find Château Morrisette glasses and clothing, books, unique items, and Virginia gifts.

Blue Ridge Restaurant

113 EAST MAIN STREET / FLOYD, VA. 24091
(540) 745-2147

Style	Home-style
Meals	Breakfast and lunch, seven days a week; dinner, Monday through Saturday
Price Range	Inexpensive
Superlatives	Chicken and dumplings, meat loaf

*L*ove at first sight. It can happen with a person, a puppy, or even a region so beautiful that one is motivated to find an opportunity to live, work, and raise a family there. That's how it happened for Lee and Gail Hook in 1986.

On their first visit to the New River Valley, the Hooks were enamored with the mountains, valleys, and simple country life. The same year, they bought the Blue Ridge Restaurant, an established little eating spot in a circa 1880 bank building in downtown Floyd. In the Great Depression, the bank collapsed, the building sold, and purportedly a bar that served food and housed the local bus stop opened in 1931.

"It's been a roller coaster ride," Lee said of having a small restaurant in a small town. Like most entrepreneurial ventures, it has been the center of the Hooks' lives. When their first grandchild was born, they looked for ways to work "smarter instead of harder" in order to carve out a little more family time.

They saved for five years to renovate and expand, increasing the number of tables and seats, adding new restrooms that comply with the Americans with Disabilities Act, and installing double doors to keep in the heat or keep out the cold, depending on the season. The old oak counter, so warped from age that a coffee mug could slowly slide off, serves as the new cashier counter.

The two cream-and-blue dining rooms sport ceiling fans and a variety of photographs and prints, which feature local scenes and birds. Saloon-style, swinging doors to the kitchen permit servers to push through when their arms are laden with plates of home-style food.

Breakfast comes hot and fast—homemade gravy and biscuits, eggs any way you like, hot cakes, omelets, combo egg sandwiches, country ham, baked ham, sausage, bacon—all the expected morning offerings. You can get breakfast, some piping hot coffee, and most of the local news—through newspapers or conversation—in one stop here.

The restaurant doesn't close all day. Breakfast is phased out around 11 A.M., and lunches of salads, sandwiches, burgers, and barbecue take center stage. Chicken salad is homemade. Sandwiches include grilled provolone and bacon on pumpernickel with grilled onions and peppers, a deluxe club, beef 'n' Swiss, and a few others.

There's a variety of home-style meals offered in the middle of the day, too. Beef, pork, chicken, seafood, and vegetarian entrées come with two sides such as fried squash, mashed potatoes, cottage cheese, applesauce, fruit gelatin, or potato salad.

Daily specials such as lasagna on Wednesdays and baked chicken on Sundays are very popular with the locals. Vegetables change daily, and you can order a plate with just vegetables.

When you finish your meal with a piece of homemade pie, you'll be well satisfied—with the food and the price. You can even buy a whole pie to go or advertise a little for them by springing for a Blue Ridge Restaurant T-shirt.

Pine Tavern

U.S. 221
FLOYD, VA. 24091
(540) 745-4482

Style	Family-style
Meals	Dinner, Wednesday through Sunday; Thursday through Sunday in winter
Price Range	Moderate
Superlatives	Seafood, "Chef's Choice"
Extras	Full bar

There's a lot of pine in this neck of the woods, so that's probably how Pine Tavern came by its name in 1927. It later became a lodge with a mess hall. In the mid-1930s, the taproom was added. The restaurant followed a few years later. It's all located a few miles north of Floyd on the west side of the highway.

The pine walls are original. There's also a pine floor and beam ceilings. Add to this some locally handcrafted ash, walnut, and cherry furniture and a solitary candle flame on each table and you have that wonderful, rustic warmth that wood evokes.

Michael Gucciardo, a native of Brooklyn, has been the chef here for more than a decade. He's part-owner, too. He's a creative kind of guy, and his "Chef's Choices" are popular—although guests may not know what they'll be eating until it's served. It's the ultimate compliment to have customers display such confidence—sort of like going to your hairdresser and saying, "Cut it any way you want," and trusting that the outcome will be satisfying.

The Pine Tavern's appetizers might include shrimp and smoked salmon in a special sauce, roasted peppers with artichoke hearts, or a creamy seafood chowder. The chowder is great.

The entrées range from plain, all-American cuisine to innovative dishes—sea scallops over fettuccine, chicken Madeira, Rigatoni Madechiara, Szechuan-style tofu, spicy red beans over polenta, and rib-eye steak. The Sunday menu is all-Italian. At 8:30, it's open mike for the evening.

The homemade desserts vary according to availability of fresh local produce. Michael tries to have one fruit, one nut, and one cheesecake dessert. The peach shortcake features peaches that Michael picks on the way to work. The dark chocolate torte with raspberry sauce uses fresh berries, as does the blackberry spice cake.

The Pine Tavern has a large outdoor pavilion and

hosts special events, usually of the musical variety. It is a neat spot perhaps 20 minutes off the Blue Ridge Parkway, less than an hour from Roanoke, and just a couple miles outside the quiet, little town of Floyd.

Tuggles Gap

VA. 8 / FLOYD, VA. 24091
(540) 745-3402

Style	Home-style
Meals	Breakfast, lunch and dinner, seven days a week
Price Range	Inexpensive
Superlatives	Tuggles Gap pie, Southwestern food
Extras	Beer and wine

Walking through the door is like taking a step back in time, but not too far back—the 1940s perhaps. Pine paneling, small wall lamps, a couple of ceiling fans turnin' slow, framed nature photos, and a paper place mat showing the map of Virginia at each seat.

You just know you're in the country mountains, and there won't be any fancy airs put on here. They're not fussy about whether you are ordering breakfast or lunch at 11 A.M. They'll make what you order and serve it with a smile.

A convenience store and gas station opened on this site in the 1930s; the little restaurant was added in the 1940s. It's been in continuous operation ever since. Cherie Baker and her mother, Neil, bought it in 1992. They were from Montana and had spent time in New Mexico and California, which explains the Southwestern cuisine on the menu. They had to upgrade the infrastructure and do a little cosmetic work, but not enough to change the character.

Tuggles Gap boasts all-American cuisine featuring down-home and Southwestern cooking. Your first evidence of this statement is right in the breakfast menu where you see pancakes, French toast, homemade biscuits and gravy, cheddar cheese omelets, or breakfast burritos.

The burrito is stuffed with scrambled eggs, cheese, tomato, and onion, all topped with red or green chili. There's also country ham and eggs, ribeye steak, oatmeal, and grits.

Lunch and dinner showcase the Southwestern specialties such as tacos, burritos, and enchiladas. You'll have to know tacos, or you can learn, to determine if you want soft tacos or crispy tacos. The burrito section of the menu features a flour tortilla filled with pintos and ground beef, smothered with red or green chili, rice, lettuce, and tomatoes.

You can get a plain burger or cheeseburger, Texas chili, a BLT, a fish sandwich, a chicken sandwich, a grilled sandwich, and a soup of the day.

A garden salad, fries, onion rings, a chef salad, or pinto beans come as side dishes. Tuggles' own chili and beans are sure to warm your tummy.

They prepare and bake all the pies. The Tuggles Gap Pie is scrumptious, even after breakfast!

Brush Creek Buffalo Store

4041 RINER ROAD
RINER, VA. 24149
(540) 381-9764
WWW.BCBUFFALOSTORE.COM

Style	Home-style
Meals	Lunch, Monday through Saturday; open until 6 P.M. Monday and Tuesday; until 7:30 P.M. Wednesday through Friday; until 5 P.M. on Satuday
Price Range	Inexpensive
Superlatives	Buffalo meat, homemade fries
Extras	Buffalo meat is for sale by the pound

*T*he village of Riner formed between 1827 and 1853, most likely because there was a sawmill nearby. After the Civil War, growth ensued when necessities such as a schoolhouse, tanyard, hotel, blacksmith shop, meeting house, barrel factory, and other enterprises were built. Though Riner never became an incorporated town, it now has its own post office and a population that loves the rural environment.

Jim and Jan Politis left Tennessee and their distributing business in the early 1990s to return to Jan's roots in Virginia. They looked at a few agriculture businesses such as ostrich farming before a neighbor shared an article about buffalo from a Farm Bureau magazine. The more Jim and Jan learned, the more they embraced the idea of raising buffalo.

Technically, the American buffalo is really not a buffalo. It's a bison, which belongs to the family of bovines, same as cows. However, the terms buffalo and bison are used interchangeably in casual speech.

In 1993, the Politises acquired their first buffalo in the herd of 50 they have today, and they opened this store in 1995. As news of the nutritional value of bison meat has spread, the demand has increased. In every 100 grams of cooked lean meat, buffalo meat is significantly lower in fat, calories, and cholesterol than beef or pork.

The store and restaurant are housed in a low, rustic building next to a convenience store and gas station. They are located on Va. 8, about five miles south of Exit 114 off I-81. It's a simple place, with flour sacks for curtains and an eclectic assortment of greeting cards, Western merchandise, mugs, T-shirts, key chains, and copies of *The Great American Bison Cookbook* for sale in the store.

They open daily, except Sundays, at 11 A.M., and the menu pretty much revolves around buffalo meat, though you could order chicken or a grilled cheese sandwich.

The hand-pattied buffalo burgers, with or without cheese and trimmings, are the most popular. The barbecue sandwich is a house recipe of slow-cooked buffalo stew meat with a honey barbecue sauce. Burritos feature buffalo stew meat, and quesadillas have specially seasoned buffalo taco meat.

French fries come skinny with the skins on 'em, and one look will tell you that they're hand cut and fried right behind the counter. They cut the onions for the onion rings right there, too.

The buffalo burger has a slightly richer taste than hamburger, but not at all gamy like venison. It's a little more expensive than hamburger, but it's much better for you. Brush Creek Buffalo operates a booth at the Blacksburg Farmer's Market every Saturday morning, just a couple blocks from my home, so I keep a few bison burgers on hand all the time now.

They also sell a wide variety of buffalo steaks, as well as buffalo sausage, barbecue, tongue, liver, roasts, ribs, and jerky. You'll have to call and talk personally to them about buffalo by-products such as hides, hooves, head mounts, and other things.

DUBLIN

Graffiti's Café

793 BROAD STREET (U.S. 11)
DUBLIN, VA. 24084
(540) 674-4861

Style	Café
Meals	Lunch and dinner, seven days a week
Price Range	Inexpensive
Superlatives	Healthy food preparation, 1950s atmosphere

*I*f you like Chubby Checker, "Rock Around the Clock," and "The Monster Mash," you'll be right at home here. Painted aqua on one side and pink on the other, with black trim all around, Graffiti's doesn't have graffiti on the walls, contrary to what you might expect. It's got James Dean and Marilyn Monroe posters and scores of black-and-white high-school photos. It's bright and clean and reminiscent of the days when baby boomers were preteens.

The building was originally a convenience store, then a fabric store. Late in 1995, Graffiti's owners, brothers-in-law Ricky Morris and David Mauck, signed a lease and renovated the building in order to move their three-year-old ice cream shop here. According to Morris, the bankers wanted more than ice cream to go along with the financing, so the brothers-in-law were forced to expand their repertoire.

"We wanted to serve hamburgers, and tater tots, and french fries, all that stuff, but we also wanted to be health-conscious," stated Morris. So they looked into an "instant burger" machine that uses fresh meat, takes 50 percent of the fat out of it, and retains the juices and flavor. Graffiti's can make six quarter-pound hamburgers at once. The machine is used for tater tots and french fries, too. "The health department loves it," Morris continued. "It's a whole lot easier to keep the place clean when you have no grease."

Morris is a Dublin native and a member of the class of 1974, the last class to graduate from the now nonexistent Dublin High School. His sister Connie married David Mauck. The whole operation has become a family affair. Connie finally left her teaching job to work full-time at the restaurant. Morris's wife, Regina, does whatever needs to be done. And all of their kids have worked at the restaurant at one time or another.

Besides hamburgers, tater tots, and french fries, Graffiti's serves buffalo burgers, foot-long hot dogs, grilled chicken, barbecue sandwiches, and a variety of subs, salads, and side orders. Some of the daily specials are spaghetti, meat loaf, pot roast, and salmon cakes.

Graffiti's offers lots of flavors of Hershey's ice cream, available in a dish, a float, a malt, a milk shake, a banana split, or with hot fudge cake.

It's the kind of place where people sit and talk awhile and nod to one another—a place where you can get a healthy burger and groove to 1950s tunes.

BLUEFIELD

The Last Fountain

566 VIRGINIA AVENUE
BLUEFIELD, VA. 24605
(276) 326-1166
WWW.NEWGRAHAM.COM

Style	Home-style
Meals	Breakfast and lunch, Monday through Saturday
Price Range	Inexpensive
Superlatives	Chocolate ice cream soda, hot dogs, homemade chili

*T*he day was sunny, but I was feeling listless. It was a long drive from Covington, Virginia, to Beckley, West Virginia, and down to Bluefield. I cruised into the Virginia side of this two-state town and popped into the bank for suggestions for lunch.

The Last Fountain is about the only place right downtown, so I headed across the street.

For someone who needed her day brightened, this was the place to come. I entered on the gift shop side of the store—and stayed there for the better part of half an hour. I bought a gift book, a battery-operated computer keyboard vacuum about the diameter of a pencil, some cards, some bookmarks. There were also gifts for men, for the kitchen, for brides, for babies—for every occasion, and in all price ranges.

The Fountain opened in 1935, and Michael Dye took it over in 1999, after having been a part-owner for 20 years. Michael grew up in town, and he's also known for selling knives via a website.

The Last Fountain, located on the other side of the store, made the day doubly bright. It's an old soda fountain with about 10 stools and about 40 seats. There was one vacant table—a round oak table nestled in the corner by the windows on the far side. It proved to be best spot in the place. Lively conversations, happy waitresses, and a nostalgic atmosphere obliterated the morning's woes.

A Western omelet, various egg sandwiches, French toast, and eggs with bacon, sausage, or country ham are offered at breakfast.

There are 18 sandwiches, along with about a dozen hamburger and hot dog variations. Side orders include peaches with cottage cheese, onion rings, and a scoop of salad on lettuce with tomato and crackers.

At the next table, the waitress delivered two

fountain items that looked like something right out of a magazine. I had to ask. "Chocolate ice cream soda" was the answer from my fellow diners, who then proceeded to offer accolades about their choice. This wasn't their first visit—and it certainly wasn't their first chocolate ice cream soda. The restaurant also has homemade pies, cakes, and cobblers if it's too cold for ice cream.

This whole place was very refreshing. I'd go out of my way to stop in again for gifts and one of those old-fashioned fountain delights.

BT's

RADFORD

BT's Restaurant

218 TYLER AVENUE / RADFORD, VA. 24141
(540) 639-1282
WWW.BTSRADFORD.COM

Style	Pub
Meals	Lunch and dinner, seven days a week
Price Range	Inexpensive/Moderate
Superlatives	Friendly atmosphere, sirloin steak
Extras	Full bar

As a college hangout, this ranks pretty high—a bar, pool tables, dartboards, televisions, booths, and tables on two levels. As a place to eat a meal, it holds its own very nicely.

Wooden booths line the walls of the small dining area downstairs. There are a couple of tables in the middle of the room. Around a corner from the dining area are the bar, more booths, and a dartboard area. Behind the bar is the game room. More tables are located on the second level. There are big windows upstairs, and it's always fun to watch what's happening outside on the streets below.

The surprise was a mid-afternoon snack of steamed shrimp and an apple. A healthy portion of shrimp came on a large plate, garnished with red and green peppers artfully arranged around the edge. And just a few minutes after it was ordered, the apple arrived in the shape of a bird. It was photo-worthy.

The service, typical in college towns, was very friendly. Manager Ken Day was cooking that day, and he stopped at my table to see if everything was okay. Perhaps at 2:30 in the afternoon, there's time for that.

The restaurant's name comes from the two men who started the business in 1983. The *B* has since bowed out, but the *T*—Tom Whitehead—still oversees every facet of the business.

The menu is pretty common young-people stuff—

"appeteasers," sandwiches, burgers. There's a special every day of the week. On Friday, it's seafood; on Tuesday, it's "South of the Border"; on Sunday, it's all-you-can-eat spaghetti.

A popular entrée is the 12-ounce rib-eye steak. It's called the "Governor's Choice," and the governor has been here. Governor Mark Warner ate at BT's when he was in town in May 2002 to deliver the commencement address at Radford University. I don't know what he had, but since this has been on the menu for years, it must have been named for someone else.

The "Governor's Choice" and its half-pound cousin, the "Dalton Hall," come with a baked potato, salad, and bread. Other house favorites are lasagna, St. Louis–style ribs, jambalaya, and the "Radford Rio"—a spicy taco salad. And there's a vegetarian section on the menu.

Dozens of drinks are printed on the back of the menu, along with one of my favorite sayings. It's been modified, the word *food* replaced by *libations*: "If you have enjoyed our libations, tell a friend. If not, tell us."

Beamer's

THE MARKETPLACE
CHRISTIANSBURG, VA. 24073
(540) 381-5000
WWW.BEAMERBALL.COM

Style	Casual nice
Meals	Lunch and dinner, seven days a week; Sunday brunch
Price Range	Moderate
Superlatives	Chicken Milanese, coconut shrimp, desserts
Extras	Full bar

*F*rank Beamer has made quite a name for himself since coming to Virginia Tech in 1987 as head coach of the football team. He's also enhanced Virginia Tech's reputation in the football arena.

A country boy from southwestern Virginia, Beamer played football while attending Virginia Tech in the 1960s. He graduated with a degree in marketing education and followed that with a master's degree in guidance from Radford University. He began his athletic career in earnest at The Citadel before returning to his beloved Virginia Tech.

In almost two decades, he has educated and guided the football program into the national spotlight and garnered numerous "coach of the year" awards from the media and colleagues. When Frank was approached about lending his name to a restaurant, he was flattered and thought, "It better be good."

While he is not involved in day-to-day restaurant operations, he offered his input on menu development. Meat loaf had to be there, along with prime rib, rib-eye steaks, and mashed potatoes. Here's a comfort food guy for you.

The restaurant is next to OfficeMax in an unassuming strip mall where lots of restaurants have come and gone. The name is a draw, but like any draw, there must be substance to keep it going. It's a little dark, quite classy, and very sports-oriented inside. The VT logo is everywhere—on the football helmets under glass, the jerseys on the walls, the framed memorabilia, and the trophies in glass cases.

Large television screens show, well, duh, Virginia Tech football games. But only some screens; others have outdoor and wildlife programs or the news.

Beamer's is a good place to come for lunch salads. They offer an avocado and jicama salad as well as mixed fruit, chef, spinach, mushroom, and Mediterranean salads. If Frank comes for lunch, he's most likely to order a crab cake sandwich or wings. Me, I always get Chicken Milanese with the Gorgonzola sauce.

There are other lunch items, and you also can get crab cakes and Chicken Milanese at dinner. Alaskan king crab legs, a Louisiana sampler, Maine lobster with crab and rice stuffing, and a shrimp and scallop pasta accompany a fresh fish of the day on the seafood list.

Pork chops, pasta primavera, slow-roasted pork, and Havana chicken are some of the entrées offered at lunch and dinner. Sunday brunch features some of the salads and items typically found on a brunch menu such as eggs Benedict and seafood omelet.

Frank and I agree on one favorite: homemade dessert. We like them all, so just order whatever tickles your palate. They rotate seasonally, like football. Go Hokies!

The Farmhouse Restaurant

CAMBRIA STREET
CHRISTIANSBURG, VA. 24073
(540) 382-4253

Style	Casual nice
Meals	Dinner, seven days a week
Price Range	Moderate
Superlatives	Prime rib, steaks, onion rings
Extras	Full bar

*N*amed for Indian fighter William Christian, the town of Christiansburgh was incorporated three years after George Washington took office. Somewhere along the way, the last letter of the town's name fell off. On May 9, 1808, the first rifle duel known to have occurred in Virginia took place here, on a hill near Sunset Cemetery. The site proved prophetic, as both participants died. Today, Christiansburg is the site of the Wilderness Trail Festival. On the third Saturday in September, Main Street—the former Wilderness Road—is closed to automobiles during this celebration of local history.

The Farmhouse Restaurant opened in 1963.

Fourteen years later, 26-year-old David Leinwand bought it. Although he had no restaurant experience, Leinwand had business acumen. Once a 100-seat restaurant with 11 employees, The Farmhouse now has 625 dining seats, 110 lounge seats, and 100 employees. The banquet facility added in the early 1990s accounts for much of the growth.

A few years back, the *Roanoke Times* conducted a survey in the New River Valley, southwest of Roanoke. The word respondents most often associated with The Farmhouse was *consistent*. According to one Blacksburg resident, The Farmhouse serves "the best prime rib and homemade onion rings in the valley." Another local fan said it was one of the few places where grilled pork chops are available.

The house is part of a farm built in the 1800s. In the early 1970s, a train caboose was incorporated into the dining area; you'll note some narrow passageways with wooden, crate-like booths on each side. An eclectic collection of art, antique tools, and old photos hangs on the walls.

Among the appetizers served here are oysters Rockefeller and scallops wrapped in bacon.

The Farmhouse is well known for its steaks. Just about every cut is on the menu, including specialties such as Châteaubriand. Other house specialties are dill salmon and seafood Newburg. Ribs, chops, chicken, seafood, and pasta dishes are also served.

For those who enjoy wine but aren't sure what's what, there are helpful descriptions of some of the wines sold by the glass.

In 1996, Kevin Murphy, a restaurant consultant who was teaching at Virginia Tech, came to The Farmhouse as full-time general manager with a five-year lease and an option to buy the place. When that arrangement did not work out, a northern Virginia man bought the restaurant and turned over the management function to someone who really understands the details of running The Farmhouse — Barbara Wade.

She started working here as a waitress in 1963, and if anyone knows what's been happening over the years, what works and what does not, it's Barbara. She figures she's got a lot in common with those antiques hanging on the wall.

CHRISTIANSBURG

The Summit
95 COLLEGE STREET
CHRISTIANSBURG, VA. 24073
(540) 382-7218
WWW.SUMMITRESTAURANT.US

Style	Fine dining
Meals	Dinner, Tuesday through Sunday
Price Range	Moderate
Superlatives	Seafood, vegetarian dishes
Extras	Wine and beer

*P*ort Said is located where Egypt meets the Sinai Peninsula, on the southeastern coast of the Mediterranean Sea and the northern end of the Suez Canal. Traffic passes through Port Said from all over the world.

It was in this multicultural environment that The

The Summit

Summit's owner and chef, Abdul Hameed Hassan, was raised. Trained as a lawyer and judge in his native land, Abdul is just as comfortable in a kitchen as he is in a courtroom.

In 1994, he purchased Sal's Pizza in Christiansburg, sight unseen, and took over what he understood was more of a fine restaurant than it turned out to be. Abdul began the tedious process of renovating not only a building but also a reputation.

The language barrier was a challenge he tackled by connecting with Literacy Volunteers of America. There, he met Robin Laing, who helped him learn English while increasing her knowledge of Arabic. In June 1995, they were married. Today, both of them devote their full-time energy to The Summit.

Originally named Giovanni's Gourmet and housed in a simple brick building, Abdul and Robin persevered with their vision of an upscale restaurant in lovely surroundings. To that end, they bought a stately, 1888 Victorian mansion in January 1999. It would be more than three years before their dream materialized, but every hurdle, every obstacle was met with determination and tenacity.

The Summit seats around 50 in intimate dining rooms, with double linens on the tables and period wallpaper and trim. The emphasis is on quality food in a refined atmosphere. As natural daylight gives way to evening, and the lighting dims romantically, your server will loan you a bright, pen light for perusing the menu. It's the only place I have encountered this, and it's a very thoughtful gesture.

The menu varies daily. The appetizers may include shrimp on the barbie, polenta with portobello mushrooms, or blue crab red. The latter is lumps of blue crab, topped with tangy white wine sauce and sweet red peppers.

The Summit makes its own salad dressings for the garden, the arbor, the Alps, or the Marrakesh salads. The soup du jour is always interesting and made fresh daily.

Abdul's vegetarian dishes are very popular, as are his seafood and veal entrées. Portobello crêpes, might be the vegetarian entrée; salmon la maison or Italian Angel could be the seafood options. Italian Angel is prepared with jumbo shrimp, large sea scallops, marinated artichoke hearts, sun-dried tomatoes, and mushrooms in a slightly spicy cream sauce, served over black pasta. Veal stroganoff, breast of duckling, the tipsy filet, and the nutty sheep are a few of the innovative presentations.

Desserts change often, too, although Italian cheesecake and the Italian Feather are stable menu items. The latter is mascarpone cheese with a touch of vanilla and amaretto served over homemade chocolate sponge cake.

From pizza parlor in a brick box to fine dining in an elegant, Victorian hilltop setting, The Summit has a story of perseverance and believing in something so strongly that each challenge is met, resolved, and overcome to accomplish a dream and fulfill a vision.

The setting is lovely. The food is excellent. The service is impeccable. Abdul and Robin have successfully created the fine dining restaurant they really always wanted. And the rest of us can enjoy a superior dining experience as a result of their commitment to quality and excellence.

Hale's Restaurant

U.S. 460 / SHAWSVILLE, VA. 24162
(540) 268-9809

Style	Home-style
Meals	Breakfast, lunch, and dinner, seven days a week
Price Range	Inexpensive
Superlatives	Homemade biscuits and gravy, country-style steak

Shawsville was named for Charles B. Shaw, chief engineer for the state of Virginia, in the mid-1850s, a few years after the southwestern turnpike was built, a route that possibly preceded what is now U.S. 460. There was also purportedly a rail stop for Alleghany Springs. An 1864 map shows a church and post office, but no train depot; however, Edward Pollard wrote about a hotel and railroad station in 1870. Today, Shawsville is bypassed by most people as they travel on Interstate 81.

Sandra Conner's parents, Herbert "Jim" and Marjorie Hale, opened Hale's Restaurant in 1967 with four tables and ten stools at the counter. Over the years, they expanded, and after it burned down once, they re-built. Sandra and her brother, Gary Hale, now own the business with Gary's wife, Cindy, managing daily operations.

What sets Hale's apart, Sandra believes, is the homemade factor. "We make as much as we can from scratch. It's time-consuming, but it's what our customers want."

There are now more than 130 seats in three dining areas and a few counter stools. While the locals pop in here on a regular basis, so do faithful patrons from Roanoke and the New River Valley. Some of the most frequent regulars have their food on the grill, in the toaster, or on the plate by the time they get from their car to their table.

It's very clean, simple, and friendly. If you don't know anyone when you walk in, you're sure to before you leave. It's that kind of friendly.

The homemade biscuits and gravy are a hit, along with eggs, omelets, country ham, pancakes, and French toast. In addition to bacon, ham, and sausage, they'll fry you up some bologna.

The hamburger meat is ground in the kitchen and hand-pattied. Hot dogs come with chili or chili and coleslaw. The vegetable beef soup and the cornbread are homemade. Sandwiches include egg, tuna, or chicken salad, ham, roast beef, fish filet, pork barbecue, home-style chuck-wagon steak, and others. Subs, platters, and side dishes provide several choices.

Dinners come with two vegetables and bread. The country-style steak and the Virginia country ham seem to be favorites, but there's always someone hankering for oysters, fried catfish, the shrimp basket, or grilled boneless chicken breast.

Hale's specialties are spaghetti with meat sauce, hot roast beef sandwich, and a vegetable plate. You can order a salad before dinner and a dessert afterward. Might I suggest the coconut cake? The cake is good, and the frosting is really good. Peach cobbler, pecan cobbler, and coconut pie are also favorite desserts.

IRONTO

Mountain View Italian Kitchen

3199 NORTH FORK ROAD
ELLISTON, VA. 24087
(540) 268-2512

Style	Italian
Meals	Lunch, Saturday and Sunday; dinner, Tuesday through Sunday. Reservations are recommended on the weekends.

Price Range	Moderate
Superlatives	Funky atmosphere, food quality and quantity
Extras	Wine and beer

*Y*ou can mail a letter to Ironto, but it won't go through the Ironto post office, because there isn't one. There isn't a town either, though there's an exit off I-81 named Ironto. Mail is handled by the Elliston post office on the other side of the interstate. According to the postmaster there, Ironto is just a nickname for the small area around the Mountain View Italian Kitchen.

This restaurant is the kind of place any marketing consultant would look at with skepticism. But the Mountain View defies conventional reasoning. It succeeds despite being in an old building, being off the beaten path, running no formal advertising, and having an odd atmosphere.

Atmosphere is an interesting concept. Though no place lacks it, some places definitely have more than others. The atmosphere is surely different here—funky might be the best description.

Late in 1996, the entrance was moved. Guests once stepped into the kitchen, then took a deep step to the left into the dining room. Now, you walk right into the linoleum-floored, concrete-block eating area. Inexpensive bright blue vinyl chairs; big, thick benches you're bound to trip over if you get up without paying attention; and functional tables make up the furnishings. Two large windows frame a field sliced by a railroad track backed by a hillside.

Not much has changed in this 1959 building, originally a convenience store and post office. Owner Richard Hamilton and his late wife, Linda, bought the place at auction in 1990. She ran a small deli, and he ran the convenience store. She had the brainstorm of selling pizza by the slice and putting in three tables. On the second day, the restaurant outgrew its space.

As Paul Harvey would say, now you know–or can figure out–the rest of the story. Richard retired in 2002, and a long-time employee named Darlene is managing things.

The Mountain View isn't spiffy or classy, but you don't come here for spiffy and classy. You come here for the food. It's tasty, fresh, generous, and delicious every time. And guess what? You'd better make a reservation. The last time I stopped without one, the wait was about three hours.

The restaurant offers both standard and gourmet pizzas: steak and cheese, sautéed spinach, primavera, veggie, and a stuffed one with ham, pepperoni, sausage, and salami inside. There are around five dinner variations for chicken, veal, and seafood. Pasta dishes are what the Mountain View is known for. The baked ziti is a fabulous, filling, and flavorful casserole.

For those who like variety, there are more than a half-dozen combination entrées. The one called "Little Bit of Everything" includes a broccoli-stuffed shell, Italian sausage, lasagna, and eggplant rollatini.

If you're going up or down I-81 and have an appetite, take Exit 128 and head west on County Road 603 for about four miles. Mountain View is the building on your left with old Coca-Cola signs on it. But the restaurant serves only Pepsi. That probably makes as much sense as anything here.

Gillie's

153 COLLEGE AVENUE
BLACKSBURG, VA. 24060
(540) 961-2703

Style	Family-style, vegetarian
Meals	Breakfast and lunch, Monday through Friday; dinner, Monday through Saturday; brunch, Saturday and Sunday
Price Range	Inexpensive, no credit cards
Superlatives	Oat pancakes, grilled tofu Reuben
Extras	Coffeehouse and bakery next door

*H*aving been an innkeeper for more than 10 years, it's hard to impress me with breakfast. But since breakfast remains my favorite meal, I trekked off to Gillie's for my morning repast. I have neither made, nor eaten, nor garnished such a wonderful pancake! I was very, very impressed and understand well why there's a wait outside the door most weekend and some weekday mornings.

Gillie's, with its red walls, wood floors and counters, and mismatched collection of wood tables and chairs, opened in 1974. The building was originally a mill, then an appliance store, and later a small jewelry shop. Owners Jan and Ranae Gillie are vegetarians and wanted a restaurant to suit their style.

The background music is usually jazz and blues or old rock 'n' roll—tunes Jan and Ranae grew up with. It's a very popular, upbeat, happy place, only a block from the Virginia Tech campus.

The breakfast plates are artfully arranged with pansies and assorted seasonal garnishes, a dollop of whipped cream, sprinkles of oats, or some other small touch. The oat pancakes were the special that first morning, and I have since gone back for the multi-grain pancakes. The heuvos rancheros are my husband John's favorite.

Lunches include green salads, side salads, soup and salad, or soup and sandwich options. The "burgers" are portobello burgers or bean-and-vegetable burgers. Sandwiches and wraps include seafood, tofu, woodland mushrooms, and sautéed garden vegetables. All the bread is homemade.

The vegetables, fruits, and eggs are organic. Much of the seafood is ordered from EcoFish, an innovative seafood company that promotes ecologically responsible seafood. Fish are treated as a gift from the sea, and the quality of the product rests with gentle harvesting and premium handling and care. Nothing is added, ever.

Barbecue tofu is a favorite dinner entrée, as well as smoked salmon with sautéed vegetables, penne pasta and feta cheese, or the bean burrito supreme. Foccacia pizza, quesadillas, wild mushroom béchamel, and veggie lasagna are also on the menu. Daily specials are posted on the chalkboard, and they all sound wonderful.

If you are not in the mood for a meal, but need a snack with tea, specialty coffee, or hot chocolate, slip in to Bollo's next door. It is an extension of Gillie's with great scones and baked items, and the best oat-and-fudge bar on the planet. If you are full, you can just get one in a bag "to go" and savor it later.

BLACKSBURG

Nerv

221 PROGRESS STREET
BLACKSBURG, VA. 24060
(540) 961-3004
WWW.NERVRESTAURANT.COM

Style	Casual nice
Meals	Lunch and dinner, seven days a week; Sunday brunch. Reservations are recommended on the weekends.
Price Range	Moderate
Superlatives	Cornbread, stuffed flounder with crabmeat
Extras	Full bar

The philosophy behind opening this restaurant was something like this: Someone, in this case Kendall Davies of Virginia Beach, had the nerve to open a restaurant in a building where a brief series of dining and entertainment establishments had not met with success or longevity. Davies was testing the waters in this, his first, restaurant venture, so he just named it "Nerv" to reflect what some said was his nerve.

Within weeks, Nerv became one of the most popular dining spots in town, known for generous portions, good service, and excellent food.

The tan, boxy, two-story building stands downtown in a parking lot behind the buildings on the north side of Main Street. There are large windows with blinds, handsome globe chandeliers over the center of the two dining rooms, and small hanging lamps over every booth along the edges. The walls are gold over wood with contemporary art and framed posters.

The booth seats are a bold, modern print, and a variety of music plays continuously. There is a bar in the back corner and an entertainment space with dance floor and another bar on the second floor.

I haven't eaten much cornbread in my life. I find it mildly boring and usually dry. Well, not so at Nerv. A small cast-iron skillet containing freshly baked cornbread with a knife across the skillet arrives right after you order. It's made from scratch, and you'll know as soon as you pull out a pie-shaped wedge that it's not dry. The texture is coarse, the look is moist, and the taste is impressive—for cornbread.

Lunch sandwiches include Smoky Mountain peppered turkey and applewood bacon, an Eastern Shore grilled jumbo lump crab cake, or blackened yellowfin tuna melt. There are others, but lots of people opt for a salad, especially the crispy goat cheese with field greens, cucumber, Roma tomatoes, and mango dressing. There's also a Nerv Caesar with herb croutons and a Santa Fe jerk chicken salad among others.

Soups of the day change, but Chesapeake she-crab soup is almost always available. House specialties at lunch are things such as Cajun bourbon

tiger shrimp with beef tenderloin; beer-braised baby back ribs; and baked lasagna.

The flounder stuffed with crabmeat and topped with lemon tarragon sauce is outstanding, as is the Smithfield pork tenderloin stuffed with chorizo sausage, Monterey Jack and smoked Gouda cheeses in roasted garlic-clove sauce. Grilled chicken Alfredo, pasta luigi, potato chip–encrusted crab cakes, Thai shrimp, and chicken stir-fry are some other options.

The desserts are all homemade. Key lime pie, cheesecake, skillet peach cobbler, and Grand Marnier bananas Foster are the Nerv signature sweets. It's good for the Blacksburg dining crowd and the myriad of visitors who come to town that Kendall Davies, who owns two bars in Virginia Beach, had the nerve to try his hand at a restaurant in this college town.

Poor Billy's Seafood Restaurant

201 NORTH MAIN STREET
BLACKSBURG, VA. 24060
(540) 951-2200
WWW.BIGALSSPORTSBAR.COM

Style	Pub
Meals	Dinner, seven days a week
Price Range	Moderate
Superlatives	Fresh seafood, filet mignon, Key lime pie
Extras	Full bar

Poor Billy's

*B*ig Al's was a hair salon on the corner of Main and Jackson streets in downtown Blacksburg for twenty years. Big Al is Al Edwards, a local man who bought the building in the 1960s and started his hairdressing business in 1977. His daughter, Julie, followed in his footsteps as a hairdresser.

Julie left Big Al's and moved away, never to return, so she thought. Her brother Billy also left town for greener pastures. Somewhere along the way, Al got tired of cutting hair, and started selling hot dogs out the back door of the establishment. Billy convinced Al and his mother, Shirley, to start a sports bar upstairs and a restaurant downstairs.

Julie moved back to get involved, and Big Al's Sports Bar opened in February of 1998, and Poor Billy's the following summer. The four of them run both enterprises successfully. The food and service are great, and dad, mom, sister, and brother get along well. They all agree that their success can be attributed to their friend and mentor, Jimmy Dobbins.

The restaurant is narrow and deep. There's a bar in the front, a crescent-shaped bar along one side with a crescent-shaped second floor for restaurant dining above, and a small 4-stool bar at the back. Narrow balconies of tables run along each side at second floor level. The décor is black, and gray, and white, with Virginia Tech prints and photos, a large American flag with a 9/11 poster and tribute, and little rope lights lining some of the railings.

The grilled scallops appetizer is a favorite of mine, along with lobster bisque and Key lime pie. For the middle of my meal, I'm most apt to order broiled flounder, or shrimp and scallops with penne pasta in a Parmesan cheese sauce, or one of the fish specials. Julie says the filet mignon is wonderful, so by the time this book is in your hands, I will have tried that also.

There are daily specials on the chalkboard outside, and if you can't remember or didn't read them, your server will know what they are.

The music can be loud, no doubt about it. There are television screens in every corner, and it's generally a very lively place. The staff is young and energetic, and everyone seems to be enjoying themselves immensely. Remember, you are in the middle of a college town—small town, big university. Go Hokies!

Mountain Lake Hotel

VA. 700 / MOUNTAIN LAKE, VA. 24136
(800) 346-3334 OR (540) 626-7121
WWW.MOUNTAINLAKEHOTEL.COM

Style	Resort
Meals	Breakfast and lunch, Monday through Saturday; dinner, seven days a week; Sunday brunch. The resort is open from May to October.
Price Range	Moderate/Expensive
Superlatives	Setting, "Scallops Amaretto," "Lemon Berry Jazz"
Extras	Full bar

*P*atrick Swayze and Jennifer Grey danced here while filming *Dirty Dancing*. Rutherford B. Hayes, Reba McIntyre, and Sam Shepard have dined here.

Mountain Lake Hotel is a 2,600-acre resort with 101 guest rooms, a natural spring-fed lake, boats, swimming, table games, hiking trails, outdoor activities, and a few nice little shops. Built in 1936 from stones on the Mountain Lake property, it replaced a wooden structure that had housed overnight guests as far back as 1857. Many of the cottages date to the early 1900s. Individuals built and furnished them and held a 15-year lease. When the lease expired, ownership was transferred to the resort.

The 50-acre lake is one of only two natural freshwater lakes in Virginia, the other being Lake Drummond in the Dismal Swamp. It is fed from underground springs that keep the water at a temperature of less than 73 degrees.

The seven-mile drive up from U.S. 460 is pleasant, as long as you keep your eyes on the road. Actually, it's coming down that can test your nerves.

Breakfast and dinner are one price plus tax and tip. Breakfast consists of an appetizer, juice, a full breakfast platter, coffee, and tea. When more than 100 people are expected, a breakfast buffet is set up.

Sunday brunch is an extravaganza worth attending. Custom-ordered omelets, top-your-own waffles, freshly carved meat, and a plethora of brunch fare such as seafood, pasta, fresh fruit, breads, and fantastic desserts are offered. The focus at lunch is on salads, sandwiches, and burgers.

Dinner can be an enchanting experience. Candles and linens accent each table. Despite the large size of the dining room, there's an intimate ambiance. The menu lists five or six entrées that are changed nightly but always include one beef, one chicken, one fish, and one vegetarian dinner. You then have a choice of desserts—usually light ones that complement the meal perfectly. My personal favorite is the "Lemon Berry Jazz," a lemon chiffon pie with thin layers of berries in the middle and drizzled on top.

You don't have to be an overnight guest to dine here. And don't let the weather spoil your plans to go to Mountain Lake, as it's charming regardless of Mother Nature's mood.

Anna's Restaurant

100 NORTH MONROE STREET
NARROWS, VA. 24124
(540) 726-3545

Style	Home-style
Meals	Lunch and dinner, Tuesday through Sunday
Price Range	Inexpensive/Moderate
Superlatives	Country-fried steak, meat loaf, apple dumplings
Extras	Wine and beer

Anna's Restaurant

*T*his town's name comes from its location on a narrow section of the New River, which is really a very old river. Narrows—called "The Narrows" in its early days—was occupied by Confederate troops in 1864 when Union general George Crook was forced to evacuate Blacksburg.

After its days as a five-and-dime store in the early 1950s, the building that now houses Anna's went through stints as a sewing factory, a mini-mall, a co-op store, and a storage facility. The Fraziers—Jerry and Anna—started the restaurant in 1984. "I always said I'd put your name in lights," Jerry reportedly told Anna after naming the place for her.

The décor is country—old ice skates, ice tongs, antiques, two ladders suspended horizontally from the ceiling with assorted baskets and tinware hanging from them. One side of the restaurant is paneled. The opposite wall is painted white and decorated with hand-stenciling. The tables have blue-and-white-checked tablecloths under glass.

Everything that can be made from scratch is—pork barbecue, slaw, meat loaf, mashed potatoes, gravy, rolls, cream pies, apple dumplings, and bread pudding with butter rum sauce.

Anna's buffet is very popular on Friday and Saturday nights and Sundays. Four or five meats are offered—always fried chicken and fried fish, sometimes peel-and-eat shrimp or roast beef. Mashed potatoes with gravy and macaroni and cheese are two of the favorite sides.

There's a seafood buffet the first and third Fridays of the month, and another buffet Thursday nights when live bluegrass bands entertain.

This is a country kind of place with a country kind of cooking and all different kinds of folks coming in to eat and catch up on local news.

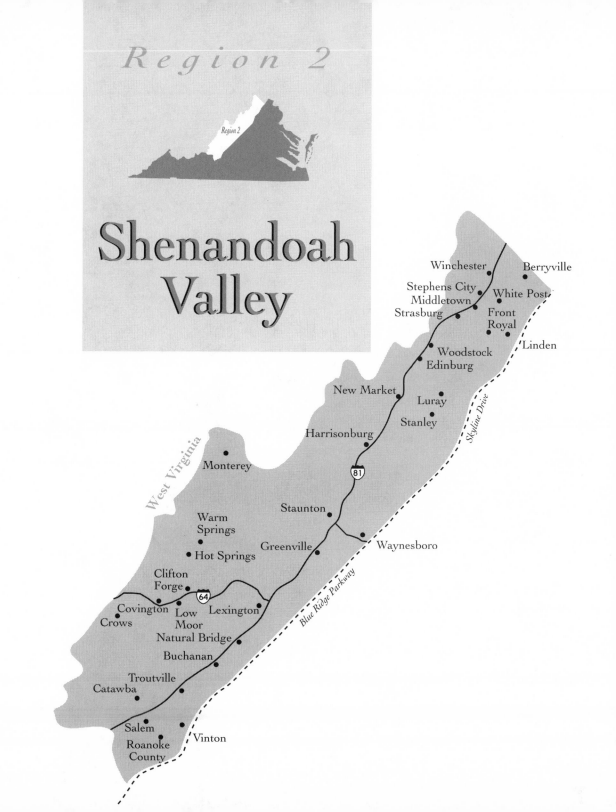

Region 2

Region 2

Shenandoah Valley

Winchester

Berryville

Stephens City

Middletown

White Post

Strasburg

Front
Royal

Woodstock
Edinburg

Linden

New Market

Luray

Stanley

Harrisonburg

Skyline Drive

West Virginia

Monterey

81

Staunton

Warm
Springs

Greenville

Waynesboro

Hot Springs

Clifton
Forge

64

Covington

Low
Moor

Lexington

Crows

Natural Bridge

Blue Ridge Parkway

Buchanan

Troutville

Catawba

Salem

Vinton

Roanoke
County

One of the prettiest words in the English language also happens
to be the name of one of the prettiest valleys anywhere—
Shenandoah. Some say the word means "daughter of the stars,"
while others claim it means "river of high mountains." But
there's no dispute that it connotes natural tranquility.

The valley is around 200 miles long and is bordered by the Blue
Ridge Mountains on the east and the Allegheny Mountains on
the west. You'll find a scenic panorama from the valley to the
mountains—and even inside the mountains. The limestone
caverns, underground streams, and unusual rock formations
here are world famous.

West of the valley are towns like Hot Springs, Warm Springs,
Healing Spring, and Falling Spring, all named for mineral
springs reputed to have therapeutic value for a variety of
ailments.

The natural beauty of the valley and the surrounding mountains
have made this region a popular tourist destination for travelers
from all over the world.

Claudia's Blues Café

300 EAST MAIN STREET / SALEM, VA. 24153
(540) 387-2523

Style	Café
Meals	Dinner, Tuesday through Saturday
Price Range	Moderate
Superlatives	"Bayou Dip," jambalaya
Extras	Full bar

Claudia's Blues Café

Some 230 miles south of Washington, D.C., and 60 miles north of the North Carolina line lies Salem, a city of close to 25,000 residents. Salem was settled in 1768 and was chartered as a city exactly two centuries later, in 1968.

An exciting attraction on Salem's pedestrian-friendly Main Street is Claudia's Blues Café. As far as restaurant sizes go, this is one of the smallest. But as far as restaurant popularity goes—well, let's just say it's a very popular spot, and for good reason.

Claudia Lambruscati, a bartender for many years and the wife of Steve Lambruscati, a fireman for the city of Roanoke, opened her tiny blues cafe in May 1996. Her husband, a former high-school industrial arts teacher, made all the tables and shelves and the bar.

The place can't be much more than 15 feet by 25 feet. It has eight barstools, one table for four, and three tables for two. The walls are decorated with prints, posters, and photos of blues artists. Many people stop in because of the blue neon light in the window, which Claudia had made for her café. Blues music plays continuously here. Some of Claudia's glasses are even blue. The plates don't match at all; it's an eclectic collection she's accumulated.

From a kitchen about the size of a walk-in closet comes some great Cajun food. Dinner can start with "Bayou Dip," shrimp cocktail, buffalo wings, or artichoke dip. Burgers and Cajun chicken sandwiches are a couple of the sandwich options. The entrées range from hearty salads, chicken pasta, and jambalaya to blackened chicken, blackened catfish, and blackened rib-eye steak. If blackened isn't your thing, that's okay, as items such as steamed shrimp, beans and rice, and a "Bayou Spud Platter" are also on the menu.

Claudia herself has an eclectic personality—charming and smart, with a homespun touch. She definitely knows her bar, her music, and her business. She doesn't have room to store Diet Coke, so I ordered "any light beer." She told me of a Mexican beer that goes well with spicy food, saying I was "guaranteed to like it." And indeed I did.

Fast Freddy's

816 WEST MAIN STREET / SALEM, VA. 24153
(540) 389-5409

Style	Family-style
Meals	Lunch and dinner, seven days a week
Price Range	Inexpensive
Superlatives	Gyros, Philly chicken, fresh fish
Extras	Wine and beer

*Y*ou'll find Fast Freddy's in a stone-and-aqua building with purple trim at a busy intersection in Salem. The restaurant opened in Roanoke in 1996 and moved to this spot in Salem a year later. The building was a gas station for a half-century or more, but there are no signs of that now.

A wood deck curls around the exterior on the intersection side. It looks nice. There are a dozen or so patio tables, with green Perrier umbrellas, nestled under branches of a mature shade tree. Inside are lots of oak booths.

You can go to your table with a menu and come back to the counter to order or just stand at the order counter and read it all on the wall. You can also drive up to the window and order for take-out.

Harry and Nancy Belcher bought Fast Freddy's in 2003, and when I asked them what set it apart, Harry answered, "Where can you get fresh mahi-mahi through a drive-in window?" Good point.

According to general manager, Shane Triplett, who has been here since 1997, ninety-eight percent of the food served here is handmade in the kitchen. "Someone is in the kitchen by 6:00 A.M. every day," he noted.

The fish is fresh, burgers are hand-pattied, the barbecue is cooked and pulled on the premises. Some of the daily specials include Freddy burgers, veggie burgers, or salmon burgers, each with soup and a drink. Blackened chicken Alfredo, grouper Montego Bay over dirty rice, vegetable baked ziti, Whiskey River salmon, and four cheese ravioli are other specials that come with salad and garlic bread. Black bean or gazpacho soups or chili will ward off a chill on cool days.

Freddy's favorites are wings, blackened yellowfin tuna, and blackened chicken, and there are pitas, Italian entrées, Greek gyros, and Cajun food. Cold subs and hot subs come with cheese, lettuce, tomatoes, onions, seasoning, and a special sauce.

Don't let the Styrofoam containers for the desserts throw you off. These are made in-house, and the chocolate mousse Grand Marnier is really tasty. There are plans in the works to upgrade from paper, plastic, and Styrofoam, to "add a little class," says Shane. And speaking of class, there's an Orvis outlet store behind Fast Freddy's.

The Homeplace

U.S. 311 / CATAWBA, VA. 24070
(540) 384-7252

Style	Family-style
Meals	Dinner, Thursday through Sunday
Price Range	Inexpensive
Superlatives	Fried chicken, homemade fruit cobbler

*T*he name Catawba comes from the Choctaw Indian word for "separated." Perhaps the town's name thus honors the nearby mountain of the same name, which separates it from the larger towns and the main roads on the other side. The Appalachian Trail goes along the ridge of Catawba Mountain. A popular summer resort called Roanoke Red Sulphur Springs was located near here in the 1850s. A sanatorium for the treatment of tuberculosis was established in 1909. Neither is still in operation.

Guests at The Homeplace can't make a reservation, but they'll find the wait—and there almost always is one—very pleasant nonetheless. You can wait outside under the shade of majestic maple and oak trees, on the old country porch, or in the gazebo. If you wait inside, you can sit in the Morgan Room, named for the previous owners.

The Homeplace is in a lovely white clapboard house with black shutters. Built in 1907, the home sits back from the road on 60 acres with a quintessential red barn and a pond. The restaurant opened in 1982, four years after the original dairy farm was divided into tracts and sold.

Harold Wingate bought two tracts—the one with the house and the one with the barn. He and his family renovated the interior by stripping varnish off the original oak trim and chestnut wainscoting, wiring new lights, and refurbishing the walls. The floors are all wood. Most of the furniture is oak. Tables and chairs are always being moved to accommodate family gatherings of various sizes.

But even a restaurant in the nicest of settings must have the best of food to maintain its reputation and attract repeat business. Harold's son Kevin attributes The Homeplace's phenomenal success to "good food mainly, good value for the money, as well as good atmosphere and good service."

Once seated, you may choose roast beef, fried chicken, or country ham. Then other dishes come—mashed potatoes, gravy, green beans, biscuits with great apple butter, pinto beans, slaw. All of this is hot and tasty—and it's all replenished until you ask the waitress to stop delivering.

Of course, then she comes along with cherry or peach cobbler to finish what you'll likely admit was a wonderful dinner.

Afterwards, ask yourself this question: For a reasonably priced, family-style restaurant, what could The Homeplace do better? You'll probably draw a blank.

Wildflour at Hollins

7770 WILLIAMSON ROAD / ROANOKE, VA. 24019
(540) 362-1812

Style	Family-style
Meals	Lunch and dinner, Monday through Saturday
Price Range	Moderate
Superlatives	White bean chicken chili, homemade bread
Extras	Wine and beer

Wildflour at Hollins in Roanoke County is less than two miles off I-81's Exit 146 and less than a half-mile from Hollins University, a small liberal arts school. It's a delightfully inviting place in a brick building with large pane windows in front. The interior is a compatible blend of wood, tile, brick, white paint, and stained wainscoting. Some of the artwork is for sale.

There are four booths, six counter stools, and seats for around 55 people, but it's laid out in an uncrowded fashion. Mark Henderson bought the restaurant in January 2002. He came with 22 years in the food-service industry and a business degree from Virginia Tech.

He started by cleaning the outside, painting the inside, slowly upgrading the menu, and insisting on consistency of food preparation. He pays close attention to what his customers want and uses the freshest ingredients he can find.

Homemade soups are incredibly popular and are served with homemade bread and butter. The soup of the moment might be tomato cheddar or Mexican corn chowder. White bean chicken chili used to be a Wednesday feature. When Mark noticed they were selling out by 12:30 on Wednesdays, he decided white bean chicken chili must be on the menu every day. Good call on his part. It's unusual and absolutely delicious.

Cobb salad, grilled salmon salad, surimi salad (snow crab with Alaskan pollack tossed in a tomato dill sauce), spinach garden salad, the Wildflour house salad, and others are there for a lunch complement or entrée, whatever you like.

Wildflour sandwich bread or the bread of the day is used for the sandwiches. The sandwich choices include barbecue, blackened chicken, tuna melt, club, Reuben, Italian, and more. There are half a dozen veggie sandwiches, along with burgers and veggie entrées.

Some of the most popular dinners are the fried oysters, Hollywood's famous crab cake, and spicy shrimp and andouille over Charleston-style grits. Gill & Grill pairs a rib-eye steak with coconut shrimp. The scallops and shrimp entrée is prepared with lightly roasted red pepper, broccoli florets, and Parmesan cream sauce in a puff pastry. All entrées come with a house salad and freshly baked bread.

The dessert menu is extensive and enticing. The blond brownie was our waitress's favorite, so that's what I ordered—the first time. It was as scrumptious as the chocolate raspberry brownie I had on my next visit. There are cookies and bars, as well as pie and cake by the slice. Cakes and dessert trays can be ordered in advance, and they do wedding and special occasion cakes, too.

If you're cruising up or down I-81, try planning your drive to stop for lunch or dinner at Wildflour. It's a neat place, and you could take some brownies or cookies to have in the front seat for the rest of your drive.

VINTON

Café Succotash

210 SOUTH POLLARD STREET
VINTON, VA. 24179
(540) 981-2100
WWW.CAFESUCCOTASH.COM

Style	Family-style
Meals	Lunch and dinner, Monday through Saturday; Sunday brunch
Price Range	Moderate
Superlatives	Lobster mashed potatoes, Chesapeake crab cakes
Extras	Full bar

Vinton was first called Gish's Mill for the family that established a grist mill here in 1797. It was incorporated in 1884 and re-named Vinton, perhaps a combination of two other prominent families: the Vinyards and Prestons. Someone else suggested it was an Indian name that sounded pretty. The annual Vinton Dogwood Festival is but one show of local community pride and friendly spirit.

When a small-town girl grows up and opens a small-town restaurant in a place that retains its small-town atmosphere, something good happens. Vinton may seem like it's been swallowed up in the environs of Roanoke, but just a few blocks off the main drag of Va. 24, the original downtown thrives in neat, tidy, brick buildings.

Fine clothing, antiques, flowers, country gifts, and books, along with great food, are clustered in a few friendly blocks. Becky Ingram grew up here. She remembers when the building her Café Succotash is in was built in 1959.

"It was what you'd call a beer joint," she recalls. "I never went in. My parents would have heard about it before I reached home. That's how small this town is."

In the back of her cute restaurant is the old door that went to the pharmacy next door—ummm, "a handy back route for those who didn't want to be seen going in and out of the drinking establishment," she said.

Her son, Drew, approached her in the late 1990s with the idea of having a restaurant. Becky knew he was serious about his food career. As a child, Drew wanted an E-Z bake oven for Christmas.

Drew, Becky, her husband Dick, another son Scott, and daughter Beth Byrd brainstormed for a name. Scott suggested "succotash," and everyone liked it. Becky says it represents a bunch of diverse things put together in a way that works. It's not a menu item, but a catchy name.

The place is cozy with an eclectic, contemporary appearance. Square, flat cushions covered with lime green, yellow, orange, or a bold, print

Small-Town Restaurants in Virginia 53

fabric, each sporting a small, black, tassel-like button, are randomly attached to the ceiling. The squares on the walls, among framed food prints, are lined up neatly. It seems the restaurant was too noisy, and architect friends suggested covering acoustic tiles. The sound was reduced dramatically, and the little restaurant was dressed up in an interesting way.

The lobster mashed potatoes are served in a large martini glass. Significant chunks of fresh lobster are submerged inside homemade mashed potatoes topped with a knob of lobster butter. Our waitress, Tabitha Taylor, has worked here for years, and she said people drive miles for this dish, and I just might become one of them.

If you're inclined to try something else equally unusual, that would be Southwestern-style black-eyed pea cakes. They've "won over many a black-eyed pea hater," and the cakes come cornmeal-crusted and pan-fried, plated with pit-cooked, pulled pork, fire-roasted tomato-jalapeño salsa, and smoky chipotle lime sour cream.

On the mainstream level, petite crab cakes, home-made soup, hot black bean nacho salad, Drew's Caesar salad, and enticing sandwiches, wraps, and quesadillas are offered for lunch. Dinner appetizers, homemade soup, and salads are followed by entrées such as chicken prepared a number of ways, beef tenderloin medallions Creole, marvelous lump crab cakes, Fire-and-Ice Mahi-Mahi, Roast Pork Latine, and other mouth-watering dishes. A green-plate special highlights a plethora of vegetarian

foods. Desserts are homemade and vary by the day, the season, or the whim of chef Drew.

TROUTVILLE
Greenwood Family Restaurant
U.S. 11 / TROUTVILLE, VA. 24175
(540) 992-3550

Style	Family-style
Meals	Breakfast, lunch, and dinner, seven days a week
Price Range	Inexpensive
Superlatives	Dreamsicle Shake, pan-fried chicken, meat loaf

I wasn't starving when I happened to drive by the Greenwood, but I knew I'd be hungry in another half-hour, and the number of cars in the parking lot convinced me to stop. Good thing, too, because there's some fine home-cooked food here.

The décor consists primarily of wood painted green, white trim, and wood paneling. There are large windows in both the front and back dining rooms. A model train runs around the back dining room near the ceiling. Overall, the place is attractive and very clean.

The Greenwood opened in 1952. It was purchased by Randy Marianetti in 1996. Randy wanted to be an electrician, but his father wanted him to go to college. He helped pay for his education at Virginia Tech by working in restaurants. He graduated in 1980 with a degree in communications.

Randy says there weren't many jobs in his field, so he went to work at something he knew, becoming district manager for a restaurant chain and getting involved in a number of restaurants in the Roanoke area. One lesson he learned is that you can take care of only one thing at a time if you want to do it right. So he now focuses all his attention on the Greenwood.

The place is very popular with truckers, whose main requirements are a large parking lot and good food. But don't let those 18-wheelers intimidate you. The Greenwood is just as popular with seniors, families, and young folks, too.

If you're over 40, treat yourself to a Dreamsicle Shake for old times' sake. If you're under 40, well, you're in for a treat without the memories.

The comprehensive breakfast includes eggs, country ham, pork brains, traditional salt fish, pancakes, omelets, and waffles with fruit and whipped topping. The bestseller is sausage gravy.

Sandwiches, sandwich platters, burgers, barbecue on a bun, chili, country-style steak, pot roast, soups, and salads are offered at lunch.

Dinners include a variety of seafood, rib-eye steak, baked ham, pork tenderloin, and the Greenwood's famous chicken, all served with two vegetables and bread. Meat loaf is also a local favorite.

The desserts are just what you'd expect—homemade and delicious. Among the choices are cobblers in season, Grandma's Carrot Cake, rice pudding, and an assortment of cakes and pies.

The waitresses are friendly and efficient, the food good and reasonably priced. And my car just might be in the parking lot when you stop.

To reach Greenwood Family Restaurant, take Exit 156 off I-81 and drive 1.2 miles south on U.S. 11.

BUCHANAN
La Tasse

19746 MAIN STREET / BUCHANAN, VA. 24066
(540) 254-2547
WWW.JAMESRIVERMERCANTILE.COM

Style	Bistro
Meals	Breakfast and lunch, seven days a week; dinner, Friday through Sunday.
Price Range	Inexpensive/Moderate
Superlatives	Chicken salad, black bean–base barbecue
Extras	Wine and beer

Of all his worldly travels, Dave Harlow likes French cafés the best. He owns the local pharmacy and mercantile store in this small town. He is investing more in the new La Tasse restaurant and an even newer, upscale, dining and entertainment center named Scarlett's, which opened in December 2003.

La Tasse is in a cozy, corner location with large, front windows and a green, white, and red thick-striped awning. The walls are rag-painted gold over coral. A variety of photos and prints hang on the walls, some with the Eiffel Tower in them. A neat mural features La Tasse on an imaginary street, perhaps in Buchanan, or maybe in an imaginary French town.

Hanging globe lamps; wood floors; a mix of bistro, wood, and fancy chairs; and print tablecloths under glass provide a small, bistro-style flair. Debbie Crouch manages both restaurants, and she just beams talking about either one.

Breakfast is limited with a pastry of the day; muffins and egg; cheese, ham, or sausage sandwiches. Substantial cups of coffee come in many flavors. Hot tea, mocha, and espresso are also available.

La Tasse flatbread is basil flatbread with artichoke hearts, carmelized onions, and roasted red peppers mixed with goat cheese. French bread is cut into dipping sticks and served with vinegar and oil, or you can try it with spinach-and-artichoke dip. Soups and salads are offered, with lobster bisque being a house special.

Sandwiches such as the sliced turkey with bacon, provolone, and raspberry vinaigrette dressing or the Parisian chicken salad come on a croissant. Roast beef sandwiches and the corned beef with smoked Gouda are made on the bread of the day. You can step away from the French influence with a sandwich of tender shreds of barbecued beef with Mexican flavors topped with salsa.

Dinner specials change each weekend and sometimes you'll find prime rib, chicken cordon bleu, lobster tails, and a variety of accompaniments in potatoes, wild rice, and vegetables.

The desserts are decadent and include cheese-cake, gourmet cookies, malted chocolate caramel pie, French silk pie, peanut butter bliss, and more.

Fanzarelli's

19857 MAIN STREET / BUCHANAN, VA. 24066
(540) 254-3070

Style	Italian family-style
Meals	Lunch, Thursday through Sunday; dinner, Tuesday through Sunday
Price Range	Inexpensive
Superlatives	Homemade sauces and breads, tiramisu

*F*anzarelli's is a clean, bright, Italian restaurant in one of two surviving, old Sunoco gas stations in the state. It was a large station in its day with four bays under the main floor accessed from the back of the building.

Marcello DiBenedetto has extensive experience in food and restaurants, starting with his childhood in Italy. He had a restaurant here in Buchanan for five years, then went over to Clifton Forge to help a cousin with his restaurant, Cucci's, also in this book.

The walls are white over green with a white chair rail, and there's a mural on one part of the wall in the main dining room that appears 3-D. It looks so real, you'll walk over just to see which twigs are real and which ones are not. It's all painted, but you'll have to get up close to believe that.

Sheers and print curtains tied back decorate the windows. Gray carpet and a few prints and posters on the walls contribute to an uncluttered, clean, and inviting dining area, which seats about 50. You can learn interesting information about Italian historic sites and buildings on the paper place mats on each table.

The aroma of garlic, tomato sauce, and fresh bread baking all vie for your senses when you walk in the door. The food quality and care of preparation is what makes it a popular family restaurant. A note on the menu says: "This restaurant is not a fast food restaurant. Please allow extra time for preparation."

Marcello is adamant about the sauces and breads being homemade on the premises, and he doesn't serve fried foods, either. There are more than a dozen toppings for pizza, which is sold in four sizes or by the slice. Spaghetti, manicotti, ravioli, eggplant parmigiana, and other Italian dishes are offered.

Fresh seafood includes tuna steak and mahi-mahi, along with a seafood combination platter. Hoagies, subs, and sandwiches are also available.

The tiramisu is fantastic—creamy, tasty, smooth, generous—yummy, yummy. And you can also order cheesecake, Chocolate Suicide, ice cream, or their homemade cannolis.

Peaks of Otter Lodge

MILEPOST 86 / BLUE RIDGE PARKWAY
BEDFORD, VA. 24523
(540) 586-1081
WWW.PEAKSOFOTTER.COM

Style	Family-style
Meals	Breakfast, lunch, and dinner, seven days a week
Price Range	Inexpensive/Moderate
Superlatives	Mountain scenery, country buffet
Extras	Full bar

The name Peaks of Otter refers to three mountains located in a small geographical area. While there are several stories about the unusual name, no one seems sure how it came about.

Peaks of Otter Lodge was built in 1964 and is privately owned. However, because the Blue Ridge Parkway is operated by the National Park Service, the restaurants are authorized concessions operated under contract with the park service.

The rustic building has lots of wood and stone and a gorgeous view over a small lake. There are 60 overnight rooms, some with two double beds or king beds, a private bath, and a private balcony or terrace.

The large dining room, open year-round, features spectacular buffets and regular menu entrées. The cozy coffee shop, located off the main lobby, offers light meals and snacks.

Breakfast is a hearty event featuring a variety of à la carte items and complete meals. French toast, ham biscuits, and country ham steaks are among the offerings. There's a morning buffet during busy times.

Soup, salads, sandwiches, burgers, fried chicken, quiche, trout, and roast turkey are some of the lunch options.

Dinner may feature a country buffet or seafood

buffet, both smorgasbords of meats or fish, vegetables, salads, and hush puppies. The entrées in the dining room may include prime rib, baked chicken, rainbow trout, roast turkey and dressing, and a selection of sandwiches. The coffee shop has a hot roast beef sandwich, filet of flounder, fried chicken, and hamburger steak.

Southern favorites such as bread pudding, cobbler, apple pie, and lemon chess pie are among the desserts.

If you're tooling along the parkway, you can plan your day around a meal here. Or you might take one of Peaks of Otter's hearty picnic lunches with you on a midday hike or drive.

Another option is stopping for some country-style cooking at The Otter Creek Restaurant at milepost 60.8. It has been open from April to November since 1958.

Fancy Hill

4832 SOUTH LEE HIGHWAY (EXIT 180 OFF I-81)
NATURAL BRIDGE, VA. 24578
(540) 291-2860

Style	Family-style
Meals	Breakfast, lunch, and dinner, Thursday through Tuesday
Price Range	Inexpensive/Moderate
Superlatives	Steak Diane, French onion soup
Extras	Beer and wine

According to legend, Natural Bridge was called "the Bridge of God" by the Monocan Indians, who worshiped it. Thomas Jefferson, the original American owner of the property, purchased Natural Bridge and 157 surrounding acres on July 5, 1774, "for 20 shillings of good and lawful money." "So beautiful an arch, so elevated, so light, and springing up as it were to heaven"—so goes Jefferson's description of the bridge.

Fancy Hill is an open, bright, clean family restaurant with a fantastic license plate collection in the pine-paneled dining room. Plates are posted from all 50 states. I also found Nova Scotia, Newfoundland, British Columbia, New Brunswick, Quebec, and the Yukon Territory. The oldest plate I could read was from 1922.

The photographs of sites in the Western United States filling one wall in the big dining room were taken by the owners during their travels. The interior is predominantly cream and mauve. Accordion blinds and lace café curtains soften the large front windows.

Fancy Hill's three "He-Man" breakfasts are steak and eggs, the "Big Boy," and country ham and eggs, each one as comprehensive a morning meal as you'll get anywhere. The extra large biscuits are just that.

Lunch features salads, flame-broiled burgers, and sandwiches. If the soup of the day is homemade potato, I recommend it.

Entrées come with a house salad, bread, and any two of several items—hush puppies, mashed potatoes and gravy, fried okra, french fries, fresh broccoli, and others. The flame-broiled steaks are handcut by the chef. The house specialty is steak

Diane—slices of tenderloin sautéed with mushrooms and onions and served with brown sauce. Chicken, pork, fish, and a half-dozen Italian meals such as manicotti and chicken breast parmigiana round out the menu.

The parking lot here is large, so it doesn't matter what you're driving or hauling. And if you happen to stop at the end of a weary day, you'll be glad to know that the Econo Inn is right next door. The place may have been built in the 1950s or 1960s, but it sure looks like it belongs in the 2000s—it's clean, inviting and well maintained.

CROWS
Eagle Nest
U.S. 311 / CROWS, VA. 24426
(540) 559-9738

Style	Family-style
Meals	Dinner, seven days a week
Price Range	Moderate/Expensive
Superlatives	Forest setting, seafood pasta, trout
Extras	Full bar

*L*ike so many towns, this one's name came from a man well known in the area. Actually, it's a variation, since his name was Crow—John Crow, the first colonel of the Alleghany Militia. He had 11 children, so everyone knew where Crow's place was. The community thus kept the *s* but dropped the apostrophe.

Since I arrived at the Eagle Nest on back roads, it

Eagle's Nest

seemed like I was in the middle of nowhere, but it's really less than five miles south of Exit 183 off I-64.

From the time you start your walk from the parking area, you'll be enchanted with the place. A fast-running stream spills over rocks into a deep pool right next to the wooden walkway. A tiny, one-room honeymoon cottage perches on a rocky outcrop on the other side of the water. Little cabins dot the hillside behind the main building.

This is an old hunting camp and looks every bit the part. The pitch of the floors gives testimony to its 75-odd years of history, and scores of initials carved in the log walls attest to the hundreds of folks who have passed through.

The hunting camp was built in 1929. The restaurant was originally next to the road. In 1970, it was moved up the hill and joined to a couple of other buildings to create the rambling log structure you see hugging the slope today.

Calling the Eagle Nest rustic would be an understatement. But the dining is, to quote the menu, "country gourmet." You'll note mauve tablecloths and napkins, little white lights around the windows on the porch, and cute little pierced tin wall lamps in one of the dining rooms.

Each dinner includes soup or salad, two vegetables, and homemade bread. The menu is comprehensive, from country-style entrées such as fried chicken, cured country ham, veal liver, and chicken livers to choice steaks and seafood. The steaks include New York strip, rib-eye, filet mignon, and porterhouse. Among the seafood options are rainbow trout, catfish, sea scallops, and frog legs. Daily specials such as fried oysters, beef burgundy, and trout stuffed with crabmeat are also offered.

The desserts include homemade brownies, bread pudding, and even éclairs.

There's nothing rustic about the service, the food, or the presentation here. Too bad the cabins aren't suited for overnight guests anymore. This would be a neat place to stay.

Cucci's

566 EAST MADISON STREET
COVINGTON, VA. 24426
(540) 962-3964

Style	Italian
Meals	Lunch and dinner, Monday through Saturday
Price Range	Inexpensive
Superlatives	Bread, sauces, turnover pizza
Extras	Full bar

Cucci's

Originally called Merry's Store or Merry's Stand, Covington was named for Peter Covington, the community's oldest resident at the time of the naming. The town was incorporated in 1833, but the incorporation was repealed six years later. Covington was incorporated again in 1849 and then again—perhaps for safe measure—in 1855. The Humpback Bridge, located just west of town, is the oldest covered bridge in Virginia. It spans 100 feet and is eight feet higher in the center than at the ends. The restored bridge is now part of a state wayside park.

Cucci's has been a Covington institution for nearly three decades now. Its story began at a pizza shop in New Jersey, where an impressionable teen named Janet met a young Italian named Victor Cucci. They got married and decided to open a restaurant. A brother of Victor's suggested they look around Covington.

They loved the town. The first Cucci's opened in

1977. Ten years later, Janet and Victor demolished their small building and constructed a new one on the same property. More than 10 years after that, Cucci's continues to enjoy a reputation for good food at a good price.

Everything still looks new inside. A huge central skylight allows abundant light into the dining rooms, which can seat around 100. Posters with Italian themes hang on the walls. You can learn a little about Italy from the place mats, which contain sketches of historic landmarks such as the Leaning Tower of Pisa and the Colosseum, a map noting Italy's major cities, and tidbits of information.

Of course, pizza is important here. There are a lot of sizes, toppings, and styles from which to choose. The "Cucci Special" has mushrooms, sausage, pepperoni, green peppers, onions, anchovies, and garlic. Turnover pizzas are popular. The dough is folded over the toppings—which I guess are no longer toppings, since they're in the middle. Pizza can also be purchased by the slice. Cucci's 18 sandwiches come on homemade rolls. You can buy a single trip to the salad bar or all-you-can-eat trips. The "Vittorio Salad" includes cottage cheese, tuna, peaches, pineapple, tomato, and lettuce.

Popular dinner entrées such as spaghetti, lasagna, manicotti, and ravioli come with bread and butter and one salad-bar trip. The bread is wonderful—it's yeasty, moist, and tasty and has a nice crust. Many customers like to dip it into one of Cucci's sauces.

The desserts number exactly two—cheesecake and chocolate cake.

James Burke House Eatery

232 WEST RIVERSIDE STREET
COVINGTON, VA. 24426
(540) 965-0040

Style	Café
Meals	Continental breakfast, Monday through Friday; lunch, Monday through Saturday
Price Range	Inexpensive
Superlatives	Historic building, chicken salad, crème de menthe brownies

*T*he property on which this restaurant stands was purchased at the original sale of town lots in 1818. Six years later, James Burke built a small, two-story brick home here—the second oldest in town. A one-room brick addition was constructed on one side of the house soon afterwards. A similar addition was built on the other side in the early 1900s, perhaps to balance the appearance. In the 1950s, the house was expanded in the back. And finally, the 1990s brought an interior renovation.

Today, local girl Diane Austin, Covington High School class of 1980, runs the business with her father and sister. Three tables are situated across from an old fireplace in the angled hall that connects the two dining rooms. The big windows in one of the dining rooms offer a view into a backyard of grass, maple trees, a sycamore, and well-kept brick buildings. The windows have custom-made, multicolored valances. A few little quilts adorn the walls.

Salad platters, homemade soup (usually available from September through April), and stuffed potatoes are among the popular choices at lunch. The potatoes come loaded with such hearty combinations as roast turkey, bacon, and muenster, or mixed vegetables, mushrooms, tomato, and cheese. There's quite a sandwich selection. The "Mad Ann" is corned beef layered with sauerkraut and melted Swiss on rye. The "Highlander" is pita bread filled with garden vegetables, lettuce, tomato, and fresh mushrooms, all of it topped with cheese. The really simple sandwiches are referred to as "Burke House Basics" on the menu. They include peanut butter and jelly, cheese, ham, tuna salad, and turkey.

Though you'll see some of the homemade desserts on display, be sure to ask what's in the refrigerator, because some of the Burke House's most delightful sweets need to stay cool. The crème de menthe brownie is always an excellent choice.

You can also get picnic baskets and box lunches here. Rest assured that if you're on the road and whatever take-out items you order need refrigeration, there's an easy solution—you'll probably eat them before you leave the parking lot.

The Cat & Owl

KARNES ROAD (EXIT 21 OFF I-64)
LOW MOOR, VA. 24457
(540) 862-5808
WWW.CATANDOWL.COM

Style	Casual nice
Meals	Dinner, Monday through Saturday; closed on holidays
Price Range	Moderate/Expensive
Superlatives	Shrimp, char-broiled seafood, banana fritters
Extras	Full bar

Who's to say it wasn't fate that brought Bruce Proffitt to this place to run a restaurant and full bar just a quarter-mile from where his great-great-grandfather Patrick Fox once ran a saloon? Proffitt was born in nearby Clifton Forge but grew up in Pearisburg and went to college in Blacksburg, graduating from Virginia Tech in 1969. So how did he get back here?

His father and uncle heeded a prediction that the Clifton Forge–Covington area would grow in the next couple of decades. They surmised that if that was the case, establishing a good restaurant would be a smart move.

Their vision included a railroad theme. In fact, the walkway to the front door was created to look like a railroad platform. They wanted to call the restaurant The C & O, after the railroad company of the same name, but when they found they couldn't use the name, they chose The Cat & Owl, figuring it would get shortened to The C & O. Well, a few glitches along the way twisted the theme to barnboard and Victorian, and the name—it was just unusual enough to stick.

Bruce helped his father and uncle tear down barns and move the weathered boards inside the renovated brick house. Whatever isn't barnboard in here is red. Bright red. The carpet, the lamps, the chairs. The wallpaper is not only red, but fuzzy as well. Eclectic accurately describes the collection of antiques, old sports equipment, framed photos of women and American presidents, and assorted odd pieces.

After an informal, two-week crash course at a friend's restaurant, Bruce began developing The Cat & Owl into a fine dining establishment with a great regional reputation. He eventually bought the place from his father. His cousin Scott is the chef.

The house appetizer is char-broiled shrimp. The unlimited salad bar is a hit because everything is so fresh. Bacon-wrapped scallops, fresh oysters, crab cakes, yellowfin tuna, and rainbow trout are some of the other seafood choices. The steaks are hand-cut in the kitchen each day. You can order one of four sizes of rib-eye or one of three sizes of filet mignon.

The "Best of Both Worlds" selections team rib-eye steak with shrimp, lobster tail, crab legs, or scallops. Chicken, pork loin, and beef kabobs are also available. The stuffed potatoes are wonderful, hand-stuffed in the kitchen here.

Heath Bar Crunch Pie, deep-dish apple pie, and lime sherbet are among the sweets, but banana fritters have become The Cat & Owl's signature dessert.

Club Car Shop & Deli

525 MAIN STREET / CLIFTON FORGE, VA. 24422
(540) 862-0777
WWW.CLUBCARVA.COM

Style	Café
Meals	Lunch, Monday through Saturday
Price Range	Inexpensive
Superlatives	Warm cashew chicken salad, sandwiches
Extras	Wine and beer

There aren't too many towns that can say there's no other place by the same name. But Clifton Forge can—it's the only one in the United States. It was named by W. L. Alexander, who had a forge here and an ancestral home called Clifton up in Rockbridge County.

The Club Car opened as a deli in 1995. Local resident Cindy Perry bought it in 2000 and moved it into an old pharmacy building on Main Street. Her husband, Glenn, had the pharmacy space for his medical supply business, Regional Home Care, and the Mountain Regional Hospice offices. He renovated another historic building and moved.

The Perry couple are local folks who believe in small town survival. They are doing their part by sprucing up a few old buildings and running small businesses in Clifton Forge.

With the move, Club Car became a nice gift shop and café with table service, instead of the former counter service. Most of the gift shop is on the right as you enter. They sell collegiate gifts (translate: University of Virginia and Virginia Tech stuff in the same space), nice kitchenware such as cutting boards and trays, Virginia-made items, and a nice selection of wines. Cindy also sells lots of custom assembled baskets for all occasions.

The café is outfitted in green-and-white-checked linens. One of the most popular salads is a warm cashew chicken salad with the homemade, poppyseed house dressing. There are more salads, as well as soups and freshly baked muffins.

Sandwiches keep the spirit of the railroad town with train names—all of them, that is, except "Chessie's Favorite," Chessie being the feline logo for the C & O Railroad. "Chessie's" is tuna salad on your choice of bread.

The "Allegheny" is a roast beef and provolone sandwich with roasted sweet red peppers, lettuce, and herbal vinaigrette on a French roll. The "Fast Flying Virginian" has turkey, cheese, lettuce, and tomato on marble rye.

Personally, I like the "Create Your Own" category and its three numbered instructions: (1) Choose a meat and a cheese; (2) Choose a bread; (3) Add the extras. This allows lots of combinations, as five meats, four cheeses, five breads, and nearly a dozen extras are available.

After your lunch, you can order a cookie, cheesecake, or a German chocolate brownie.

Cindy sees all the weight control and low-carb trends and has worked out calories, points, grams, and different details for those committed to some of the popular eating programs. Frankly, I'm surprised more restaurants don't do the same.

The Perrys are dedicated to their hometown, and they're certainly good for Clifton Forge.

CLIFTON FORGE

Michel Café
424 EAST RIDGEWAY STREET
CLIFTON FORGE, VA. 24422
(540) 862-4119
WWW.MICHELCAFE.COM

Style	Fine dining
Meals	Dinner, Tuesday through Saturday
Price Range	Moderate/Expensive
Superlatives	Steak au poivre, mountain trout, seafood
Extras	Full bar

Michel Galand grew up in France and trained under well-known chef Paul Bocuse before coming to the United States to work at The Homestead Resort in Hot Springs. He later opened a restaurant in Covington, then Michel Café in Clifton Forge in the early 1980s.

Two restaurants proved one too many, so when Clifton Forge passed a law allowing liquor by the glass, Michel closed his Covington restaurant and concentrated his energies on Michel Café. In fact, it was through the restaurant that he met his wife, Carmen, who was challenged by her boss at a local newspaper to sell Michel an ad. She did, and six months after the sale, they were married.

Michel Café is as pretty from the outside as it is

on the inside. Lace curtains, window boxes, and attractive awnings make a favorable first impression. Inside, white linens adorn oak tables, and black-and-white photos of France from Michel's personal collection are displayed on the walls. The second floor has more dining space and room for private parties. The third floor has a bar and is used for private functions.

The menu is changed frequently. You may find escargots or shrimp and basil in a puff pastry among the appetizers. The soup du jour could be shrimp bisque.

Steak au poivre is a house specialty, as is mountain trout, which may be prepared with almonds or stuffed with crabmeat and topped with champagne sauce. Filet mignon with Béarnaise sauce, quail, veal chops with mushroom cream sauce, duck breast, and lamb may be among the entrées, depending on the season.

Michel carries imported beers. The wine selection is subject to change, so the most convenient way to choose what you want is to make your way to the antique, solid oak, 12-foot-high walk-in cooler, which has been converted into a wine cellar and beer-storage unit.

Crème caramel or fresh fruit in a puff pastry with crème anglaise may prove a sweet ending to your fine meal.

Recommended well beyond the limits of Clifton Forge, Michel Café lives up to its grand reputation.

A Joyful Spirit Café

26 SOUTH MAIN STREET
LEXINGTON, VA. 24450
(540) 463-4191

Style	Café
Meals	Lunch and limited breakfast, seven days a week
Price Range	Inexpensive
Superlatives	Atmosphere, paninis

Louise Ward grew up in Canada and lived in North Carolina and Florida before opening her retail nature and gift shop in Harrisonburg in the 1980s. Encouraged by friends to expand, she renovated an orthodontist's office in downtown Lexington and opened A Joyful Spirit Café in August of 2002.

The name is often perceived to be a Christian reference, but it's really more general than specific. The interior is an ultra-clean, charming blend of tans, browns, and creams reminiscent of the desert and American Southwest. Textured walls, with a row of tile over an aqua chair rail, separate the top from the medium brown lower paint. The floor is beautiful terra-cotta tile.

Artwork by local artists hangs by wire from picture molding. The artwork is for sale and changes every three to four months. Blue vases on paper doilies hold fresh flowers on every table.

Louise settled on a downtown shop that contained a restaurant and a gift shop, but then decided to focus on the food. There are around a dozen tables in a long, narrow space, a small room with a few more tables in the back, and the sandwich assembly counter near the front.

"I like the idea of having the food prepared right in front of you," stated Louise.

The drink machine and a cooler are across from the counter, and after you place your order, you can find a seat and they'll deliver your food. I tried the breakfast egg and cheese bagel because I was a little uncertain about a microwave egg on a bagel. It's good. I'd eat another one. Nice surprise.

Besides the egg and cheese bagel, you can order a bagel with smoked salmon and cream cheese or a scramble, which puts cheese, tomatoes, red peppers, and/or mushrooms in with the egg.

Sandwiches come as paninis (grilled on ciabatta bread), melts on Texas toast, or wraps. The chicken fiesta panini is a zesty blend of cream cheese, salsa, grilled chicken, cheddar and pepper jack cheeses, roasted red peppers, avocado, and cilantro. Other paninis include a veggie and a smoked turkey.

You can order a wrap in a sun-dried tomato, garlic and herb, spinach, or plain tortilla shell with plain, pesto, or curry mayo or hummus spread. Melts include grilled chicken, smoked turkey or salmon, or regular turkey, all served with mozzarella cheese and avocado.

A Joyful Spirit Café bills itself as vegetarian friendly. Turkey, chicken, and smoked salmon are the only meats available—no red meat or pork. Conscious of trends and preferences, Louise offers periodic specials and menu additions, as well as low-carb fare. Just ask her friendly staff.

Maple Hall

3111 NORTH LEE HIGHWAY (EXIT 195 OFF I-81)
LEXINGTON, VA. 24450
(540) 463-2044 OR (540) 463-6693
WWW.LEXINGTONHISTORICINNS.COM

Style	Fine dining
Meals	Dinner, seven days a week
Price Range	Moderate
Superlatives	Historical warmth, lobster bisque
Extras	Full bar

Set on 56 acres and flanked by majestic maple trees, Maple Hall was built as a plantation house in 1850.

Dining is at garden level in three intimate rooms, where double linens, fresh flowers, candles, and fireplaces exude an elegant warmth.

The signature appetizer here is sausage pâté baked in pastry and served with sherry mushroom sauce. Other before-dinner treats may include smoked Virginia trout, a soup du jour, a special salad, or a chef's feature—crabmeat omelet the night I dined here. The lobster bisque stays on the appetizer menu all the time.

The menu is changed seasonally to take advantage of fresh produce and game, though the filet mignon is a stable item. The half-dozen or so entrées carefully selected by chef Robert Dytrych will please a variety of different palates. A vegetarian dish is usually listed—such as lasagna, layered with a medley of carrots, spinach, and broccoli in a cream sauce. The London broil comes from Virginia-raised Cervena deer and is marinated in bourbon and Worcestershire sauce and served with mushroom sauce. Sesame chicken marinated in teriyaki sauce comes with a sweet honey-and-pineapple glaze. A catch of the day is usually available. The pasta dish might be *Pasta alla Carbonara*, which is diced prosciutto sautéed with garlic, shallots, peas, and mushrooms. It comes in a cream sauce under crispy bacon and shredded imported cheese.

You'll have to have a ton of will power to resist Maple Hall's dessert tray. Like the appetizers and entrées, the desserts vary according to the chef's whim and the season, but be prepared for scrumptious carrot cake, pecan pie, Kentucky Derby pie, and cheesecake.

The service is the superior sort you expect in fine restaurants. Attentive but not intrusive. Friendly but not cozy. Professional but not stiff. Very nice.

There's no need to get on the road after dining here. Maple Hall has lovely, antique-furnished guest rooms in the main building and a few outbuildings. A pool, a tennis court, walking trails, and a stocked fishing pond are available, too.

Smokin' Jim's Firehouse Grill

107 NORTH MAIN STREET
LEXINGTON, VA. 24450
(540) 463-2283

Style	Home-style
Meals	Lunch and dinner, Monday through Saturday
Price Range	Inexpensive
Superlatives	Barbecue, fresh seafood

*I*n an old Pure Oil gas station, Jim Wade has turned his life around, bringing something really good—his barbecue restaurant—out of something not so good—a firefighting accident.

Jim served around 20 years as an EMT and firefighter with the Hampton (Virginia) Fire Department before falling through the roof of a burning building on a call in May 2000. Toward the end of a two-year rehab program, his firefighting buddies gave him a weekend in Lexington.

Jim noticed the old gas station with a Pete's BBQ sign. A little investigation and a few questions and answers later, and he was planning a restaurant he never dreamed of having, in a town he had never before visited.

There are large windows in the front, and Jim painted the inside of the garage door fire-engine red with gold-leaf hinges. The tables are covered with multicolor oilcloths, and firefighting memorabilia, including the bunker coat and boots Jim was wearing when he fell, can be found on shelves and hooks.

Barbecue plates—pork, beef, ribs, or chicken—come with coleslaw, bun, and your choice of baked beans, barbecued potatoes, fries, hush puppies, or the vegetable of the day. For a couple of dollars extra, you can mix the barbecue meats and try a couple of different ones. Fish and chips, a half-pound hamburger, a fresh crab cake sandwich, and all-beef hot dogs with homemade chili are also on the menu.

Brunswick stew is sometimes available, and there's usually a fresh soup of the day. Wings or beer-battered onion rings can serve as appetizers or accompaniments. Homemade cookies and brownies are for dessert.

For those with a hankering for barbecue and a shortage of time, Jim prepares take-out pints and quarts of beef or pork barbecue, with the sides such as baked beans and fries, or Brunswick stew and clam chowder, when available. I bet you can get some cookies and brownies to go also.

Catering for 50 to 1,000 is offered by Smokin' Jim's, and Jim's Hampton Fire Department buddies come over often under the auspices of helping him. Don't get me wrong, I'm sure they are helpful; firefighters are one helpful group of folks. But I just bet they dip into the barbecue pot quite a bit, too.

The restaurant was closed when I popped by, but he and those firefighting buddies were smokin' pig in the back for an event later in the day, so I got to tour the place and chat with Jim. On my way out the door, he thrust some shredded pork and two kinds of barbecue sauce in my hands for the road.

So, it is with experience and authority that I write that Jim Wade makes a fine barbecue product, even though I ate it at home the next day. Anything that's great the next day must be terrific on the first day!

Willson-Walker House

30 NORTH MAIN STREET
LEXINGTON, VA. 24450
(540) 463-3020

Style	Casual nice
Meals	Lunch and dinner, Tuesday through Saturday; lunch is not served on Saturday from January through March. Reservations are recommended.
Price Range	Moderate/Expensive
Superlatives	Historic house, local trout, veal
Extras	Full bar

William Willson's Classical Revival home was built in 1820. To lend some perspective, that was the same year Maine became the 23rd state, Daniel Boone died in Missouri, and native Virginian James Monroe swept the presidential election. A postmaster and merchant, Willson served as treasurer of Washington College, now Washington and Lee University.

The home was converted to a meat market and grocery store around 1911 by a fellow named Walker—thus the name Willson-Walker House. It is now owned by Josephine Griswald, who graduated from the New York Restaurant School and wrote her thesis on the creation of this restaurant. She opened it on June 25, 1985.

Stepping into the grand foyer, you can imagine the ladies and gentlemen of William Willson's generation descending the staircase in the fashions of the day. There's a formality to the Oriental rugs and the antique furniture upholstered in gold-striped fabric. The dining rooms have red walls, white trim, fireplaces, and wall sconces. Champagne-colored table linens are complemented with burgundy napkins. Jazz plays softly during lunch and classical music during dinner.

Lunch is a comprehensive affair starting with a very expensive house salad. Well, maybe the $195 on my menu was a typographical error, the decimal point omitted between the one and the nine. The daily lunch special includes a cup of soup or a house salad, an entrée, rolls, muffins, and a drink. Even familiar items such as burgers and open-faced chicken breast sandwiches are a little fancier than the norm here. For example, the burger comes on a multigrain roll with caramelized red onion, marmalade, and Béarnaise mayonnaise.

Dinners vary with the seasons. Crab cakes and teriyaki shrimp kabobs are a couple of the appetizers. You can almost always find trout and veal specials, as well as a pasta dish such as tortellini and a pork entrée such as pork loin with sausage stuffing, topped with spicy baked apples.

Cobblers and tarts are among the popular desserts, featuring fresh fruit in season, though chocaholics might prefer the "Chocolate Chocolate" dessert.

Sam Snead's Tavern
1 MAIN STREET / HOT SPRINGS, VA. 24445
(800) 838-1766
WWW.THEHOMESTEAD.COM

Style	Casual nice
Meals	Lunch, seasonal; dinner, Friday through Sunday from January to March and Wednesday through Monday from April to December. Reservations are required.
Price Range	Moderate/Expensive
Superlatives	Cozy setting, golf memorabilia, rainbow trout
Extras	Full bar

*I*n 1766, Thomas Bullitt built the first inn at Hot Springs because his house was being overrun by visitors to the 104-degree thermal springs. The inn changed hands in 1832 and soon began operating as The Homestead, which promoted the springs as a "cure for what ails you." Today, The Homestead is a world-class resort owned by Club Resorts, Inc.

Tucked in a former bank building, Sam Snead's Tavern was purchased by the legendary golfer in 1979 and was tastefully renovated by his son Jackie. The old vault is now a wine cellar. The Homestead owns and operates the restaurant.

If you love golf, as do many of the folks who

frequent The Homestead, Sam Snead's doubles as a mini-museum. Golf clubs, assorted golf memorabilia, and 35 of Snead's hole-in-one golf balls are on display.

The rich wood, the dark green and burgundy highlights, the gold picture frames containing golf-related prints and photographs—everything here evokes coziness. The stone fireplace crackles when the weather dictates, and the huge, triangular bar beckons.

In the fine tradition of The Homestead, the trout served at Sam Snead's is locally caught and the steaks cut from certified Angus beef®. Sam's personal favorite is a full-pound porterhouse steak. The "Hole in One" is a jumbo beef rib chop. The other half-dozen or so entrées include steaks, chicken, shrimp, and spareribs. Wonderful pies and cakes are served for dessert.

Although Sam Snead's is the focus here, I'd be remiss not to mention the other eating options at The Homestead Resort. The Dining Room is a jacket-and-tie place serving continental cuisine in elegant surroundings.

Slightly more casual is The 1766 Grille, which features tableside preparation of French and American entrées; jackets are required for evening dining. The Casino Restaurant and Bar isn't a casino, but a restaurant in an area where cards and games used to be played.

There's also a gourmet shop, a sports bar, a 19th-hole restaurant, a seasonal ski lodge restaurant, and clubhouses open to the public on three golf courses.

The Waterwheel

INN AT GRISTMILL SQUARE
VA. 645 / WARM SPRINGS, VA. 24484
(540) 839-2231

Style	Casual nice
Meals	Dinner, Tuesday through Saturday from November to April and seven days a week from May to October; Sunday brunch
Price Range	Moderate/Expensive
Superlatives	Historic mill décor, trout
Extras	Full bar

*I*f you're keeping track of the springs in this part of the state, you might remember that Hot Springs maintains a temperature of around 104. There's a larger variety of minerals in the water at Warm Springs, where the temperature is a toasty 98.

The first mill at Warm Springs was constructed the same year Thomas Jefferson built his first house at Monticello, three years before the Declaration of Independence was signed. The present mill was built in 1900. It operated for 70 years before being converted to this restaurant.

The big wooden wheel on the side of the building opposite the entrance once turned in Warm Springs Run. The creek still runs fast. If you look carefully, you may spot a turtle with a shell more than a foot in diameter. I've seen it.

The Waterwheel is part of the Inn at Gristmill Square, a unique assortment of 19th-century buildings renovated and opened in 1972 by the McWilliams family.

The pub at The Waterwheel is named for Simon Kenton, Indian fighter and friend to Daniel Boone, whose life Kenton once saved. During his seven weeks in Warm Springs in 1771, Kenton worked diligently at the mill. A fugitive from justice for having killed a man, he anxiously continued his journey west. He returned to Virginia one time, so the story goes, and ran into the man he was supposed to have killed.

The beams in the mill have stretched with age but retain their strength and character. White-washed wood, original mill hardware, white and light mauve linens, candlelight, and fresh flowers create an atmosphere of rustic elegance. In the wine cellar, the bottles are displayed among the gears of the old waterwheel.

Appetizers include bourbon shrimp and salmon mousse. Onion soup au gratin and a soup du jour are offered.

Trout is the specialty at The Waterwheel. You can order it pan-fried with black walnuts or baked and stuffed with shrimp, celery, and onions. The cordon bleu is not prefaced with the word chicken because it's made with cutlets of veal, topped with béchamel sauce, sugar-cured ham, and Swiss cheese. *Tournedos au Poivre, Tenderloin en Croûte*, and grilled rib-eye sound delicious, as do roast duckling with apricots and swordfish broiled with herb butter.

French toast with fruit filling, smoked chicken salad, eggs Benedict, and grilled trout are some of the Sunday brunch offerings.

The Inn at Gristmill Square has 17 cozy guest rooms. Continental breakfast is delivered to your room in a basket lined with a red-and-white-checked linen. Three tennis courts, a swimming pool, a sauna, and the historic springs all contribute to the quiet, relaxing mood that reigns in Warm Springs.

WAYNESBORO

The Purple Foot

1035 WEST BROAD STREET
WAYNESBORO, VA. 22980
(540) 942-WINE

Style	Café
Meals	Lunch and afternoon refreshments
Price Range	Inexpensive
Superlatives	Classy gourmet shop, "Lavender Lemonade"
Extras	Wine and beer

Founded in 1797, Waynesboro was originally known as Teesville, after the Tee brothers, local tavern keepers. It was eventually renamed for Revolutionary War general Anthony Wayne, better known as "Mad Anthony."

It's hard to imagine that the cute chalet that houses The Purple Foot was home to a dry cleaner before Erwin Bohmfalk opened the café in 1978.

The first decision you'll have to make when you get here is whether you'll browse the gift shop on your way to lunch or on your way out. This is the place to buy a cuckoo clock, Virginia wines, T-shirts, and some unusual stuff.

The Purple Foot

Assuming you'll wait until after lunch to browse, just walk straight through to the back room. There are seats for around 50 here and another 50 on the garden terrace. The interior features regional artwork and photographs. The charming terrace has rock gardens, hanging flower baskets, and a water fountain with a statue that looks like it's had a little too much grape juice, if you catch my drift.

Even after you've decided what you want to eat, read the entire menu. When you least expect it, it'll make you chuckle. The first item under "Very Special Sandwiches," for example, is a sub whose description is quite normal until the last sentence: "Hot, chopped peppers may be added for those of you with dead tongues." "Bush's Nightmare," one of the "Dream Potatoes," is a baked potato topped with—you guessed it—broccoli and melted cheddar. Other "Dream Potatoes" have Irish, French, German, or Mexican toppings.

Instead of using the word homemade, The Purple

Foot describes its French bread as "baked-ourselves," in case there's any doubt about where it's made. The café also offers "Pita Principals" and "Pita Puns." The crêpes are filled with either turkey and broccoli, snow crabmeat and whitefish, or knockwurst and sauerkraut, and they come with salad.

Desserts are delicious and change often. The regulars are cheesecake, baklava, coconut macaroons, and my personal favorite lunch dessert—cookies. Ask about the "Special Disgustingly Sinful Dessert" of the day.

Enjoy your lunch. Then go to the gift shop.

WAYNESBORO
Weasie's Kitchen
130 EAST BROAD STREET
WAYNESBORO, VA. 22980
(540) 943-0500

Style	Family-style
Meals	Breakfast, lunch, and dinner, seven days a week
Price Range	Inexpensive
Superlatives	Breakfast served anytime, pancakes

*F*ull parking lots at restaurants always get my attention. It was 5:30 or so on a Monday afternoon when I noticed all the cars here. There was no meeting going on inside, just lots of contented-looking local folks chatting and eating. Most of the 16 booths were occupied, so I sat at the counter.

The building was first a car dealership and then a Dairy Queen before Eloise "Weasie" Roberts opened her restaurant. Joyce Campbell started working at Weasie's in 1985 and bought the business a decade later.

Breakfast is served anytime. The pancakes are famous among Appalachian Trail hikers, who pass within five miles of Weasie's on the 2,144-mile trail. They are encouraged to sign a hikers' guest book, and records are kept of the most pancakes consumed in one sitting. Currently, a 1997 hiker called "Dieter" holds the title with 22 pancakes.

If you want something other than pancakes, try the "Breakfast Club," which is a toasted ham, cheese, and egg sandwich.

This is a casual place where appetizers are called "snacks" and the biscuits are made in the back. Dinners range from pepper steaks and spaghetti to fish platters, shrimp dinners, veal patties, pork chops, and grilled liver and onions. You get a roll and two vegetables, but the word *vegetables* carries a loose translation, since peaches, apples, and cottage cheese are on the list.

The sign outside looked a little worn, but you couldn't miss the message on it: "Where friends meet to eat." It sure seemed that way that Monday around 5:30 P.M.

GREENVILLE

Edelweiss

U.S. 340 AT U.S. 11 / GREENVILLE, VA. 24401
(540) 337-1203
WWW.EDELWEISSRESTAURANTVA.COM

Style	German
Meals	Lunch and dinner, Tuesday through Sunday
Price Range	Inexpensive/Moderate
Superlatives	"German Sampler," Black Forest cake
Extras	Wine and beer

Edelweiss the flower is the national flower of Austria, and one of the prettiest songs in *The Sound of Music* bears its name. Edelweiss the restaurant is an inviting log cabin perched on a hilltop. It's less than a mile from Exit 213A off I-81—just far enough off the highway to let you be enveloped in the aura of Europe.

Ingrid Moore and her former husband spent 16 years in New York City in the delicatessen business. For vacations, they went camping in Virginia, which reminded Ingrid of Germany, her homeland.

In 1981, they opened Edelweiss in a building constructed the year before. Wood enhances the inside and is complemented by beige and mauve linens. Four wagon-wheel lamps softly illuminate a dining area that seats 60.

If it's a popular German dish, it's on the menu—sauerbraten, Hungarian goulash, several entrées with the suffix *braten* or *schnitzel* or *wurst*. There's a vegetable plate for those who don't eat meat and a variety of pork and beef for those who do. Filet of flounder and chicken are also available.

For a comprehensive German dining experience, order the "German Sampler," which includes five favorite German dishes. "The German Sampler was introduced because so many repeat guests ordered the same thing over and over. I wanted them to try something different, but they resisted an entire meal of something they weren't sure of," explained Ingrid.

Fresh vegetables such as apple-flavored red cabbage, German fried noodles, green beans, Bavarian-style cabbage, sauerkraut, and mashed potatoes are served family-style with all meals. Children under 12 eat for half-price.

Most German meals are consumed with beer, so Edelweiss offers an interesting selection of light and dark beers, as well as wines.

Black Forest cake is a specialty, as are German-style tortes and rice pudding with meringue topping. The German-style cheesecake, made with cottage cheese, is not as heavy as New York-style cheesecake.

Ingrid's son Stephan Roscher helps out at the restaurant. He can verify that, in the best German tradition, recipes have been handed down through the generations, and that anything that can be made from scratch is.

The Depot Grille

42 MIDDLEBROOK AVENUE
STAUNTON, VA. 24401
(540) 885-7332
WWW.DEPOTGRILLE.COM

| *Style* | Family-style |
| *Meals* | Lunch and dinner, seven days a week; Sunday brunch |

Price Range	Moderate
Superlatives	Prime rib, crab cakes, fresh seafood
Extras	Full bar

*T*he Depot Grille was created next to railroad tracks where a dilapidated loading platform stood. It opened in 1990 with the kitchen in a boxcar. Inside, the restaurant has an awesome oak bar from a grand, old hotel in Albany, New York, with a most unusual, round marble rail attached to the front edge.

The adjacent, enclosed patio seats around 40. It has one wall of glass. The up-close view is of two retired cabooses on old tracks, and a few blocks beyond you can see part of the downtown area.

A separate dining area seats another 100 or so. Tables have white linens topped with brown paper. There's a cup of crayons on every table for amusement. The drawings on the menu are things customers have created on the brown paper. Some talented artists have been through The Depot Grille.

Hot crab dip, calamari, buffalo wings, and Cajun chicken quesadilla are some of the appetizers. Other appetizers include flat beds, which are potato skins with bacon and cheddar, and a seven-layer dip, with layers of refried beans, pico de gallo, olives, melted cheeses, guacamole, and sour cream.

Your entrée comes with a salad, but you may want a specialty salad such as Caesar, Cobb, pesto-grilled tuna, fresh spinach, Greek, mesquite-grilled chicken Caesar, or sesame-seared chicken. "Lite bites" include fried oysters, chicken tenders, smothered chicken, and a catch of the day.

Burgers, sandwiches, and wraps include a bison burger, which is almost fat-free, a crab cake sandwich, a garden grilled sandwich, or a veggie or smoked turkey wrap. Pasta dishes include shrimp and scallop scampi, Blackened Chicken Coal Car, fresh garden lasagna, and a Cajun veggie skillet melt.

Prime rib is slow-roasted and prepared au jus or seared with a special steak seasoning. It's available any evening and all day Sunday. Filet mignon, New York strip, rib-eye, and ground sirloin are fresh and hand-cut.

There are chicken dishes and an appealing mixed-grill sizzler of chicken, beef filet, and grilled shrimp all on a skewer with new potatoes. The seafood is fresh, and the Depot Grille makes its own crab cakes from a decade-old recipe. The Alaskan snow crab legs are steamed, and the serving is a full pound.

A seafood platter, shrimp and crab leg duo, and a seafood sizzler all let you indulge in a combination of fresh seafood. Salmon is often a healthy special.

The Depot Grille creates lots of its own sauces, such as barbecue and marinara, as well as its own salad dressings and desserts. Peanut Butter Heath Bar crunch, deep-dish apple, and chocolate enchantment mousse pies are some of the desserts.

Mill Street Grill

1 MILL STREET / STAUNTON, VA. 24401
(540) 886-0656
WWW.MILLSTREETGRILL.COM

Style	Casual nice
Meals	Dinner, seven days a week; Sunday brunch
Price Range	Inexpensive/Moderate
Superlatives	Beef ribs, seafood, daily specials
Extras	Full bar

*P*artnerships can be tricky business. Ron Bishop and Terry Holmes, however, seem to have figured out how to make things work by engaging themselves in different aspects of a successful restaurant they started in 1992.

They met while working at a fern bar–style restaurant. After five years as co-workers, they took their experiences and talents and opened Mill Street Grill. Ron, who hails from Page County in Virginia, does the cooking and manages the kitchen. Terry, who is a North Carolina native, handles the business side of operations. It works—for them and for those who dine at Mill Street Grill.

The interior of the old stone mill is a mix of stone, wainscoting, and delightful stained-glass scenes of kitchen work. Terra-cotta tile and carpet cover the floors. The tables are wood, and you'll find dark green linen napkins. Yes, cloth napkins in a place known for barbecue ribs.

There's crab dip, oysters Rockefeller, steamed spiced shrimp, pepper jack cheese sticks, and other appetizers. If you simply cannot decide, you can order an appetizer sampler. Grilled Cajun shrimp spinach salad is offered, along with chicken avocado bacon salad, Greek salad, grilled ahi tuna salad, and a few other green salads.

Entrées of chicken, seafood, pasta, and vegetarian run the gamut from artichoke chicken and crab cakes to chicken and shrimp marinara to vegetable primavera Alfredo. Someone with a lighter appetite might peruse the sandwich list. Each offering has a local name, so you'll have to read the descriptions of The New Street and The Greenville Wrap, though you can figure out The Mill Street Burger.

The New Street is thinly sliced prime rib; The Greenville Wrap combines zucchini, onion, mushrooms, yellow squash, peppers, broccoli, and other veggies inside a cheddar cheese flour tortilla.

But it's the ribs that get my attention, especially the beef ribs. They're wonderful, and it's hard to find beef ribs in Virginia. You could order a combination platter with beef ribs and back ribs to have some of both. All ribs come with coleslaw and your choice of fries, baked potato, garlic mashed potatoes, rice, or the vegetable of the day.

There are several other combinations if you don't want ribs for all your meal. You can order ribs and steamed shrimp, for example, or pass on the ribs and get steak and crab cake, pork tenderloin, prime rib, filet mignon, or another type of steak.

There are no ribs on the Sunday brunch menu, but the Mill Street Skillet sounds great—a skillet of home fries topped with bacon, cheddar and Monterey Jack cheeses, scallions and tomatoes, poached eggs or scrambled eggs, and cinnamon apples. Smoked trout and crab cake Benedict or fried green tomato and shrimp Benedict are listed along with French toast and steak and eggs.

There are as many as a dozen specials every day, and cakes and cheesecakes are homemade in-house with fresh ingredients from the local Mennonite farms.

Mrs. Rowe's Family Restaurant and Bakery

ROUTE 4, BOX 88 (EXIT 222 OFF I-81)
STAUNTON, VA. 24401
(540) 886-1833

Style	Family-style
Meals	Breakfast, lunch, and dinner, seven days a week
Price Range	Inexpensive/Moderate
Superlatives	Baked goods
Extras	Wine and beer

When Mrs. Rowe was traveling in Canada some years back, she met some Canadians who raved about a red restaurant they stopped at every year going back and forth to Florida. "When I found out it was my place, I started flying the Canadian flag," she recalled. That's why you'll see the distinctive maple leaf waving next to the Stars and Stripes at this one-of-a-kind restaurant.

Mrs. Rowe and her late husband opened the place in 1947. Since then, it has been featured in *Boston Globe Magazine, Restaurants & Institutions, Good Food*, and other publications.

Among all the rooms, 230 guests can be seated. Children's art and P. Buckley Moss prints are on the walls. The service is friendly and efficient.

Home cooking is the specialty. Bread, biscuits, and pies are prepared from Mrs. Rowe's own recipes, many of which are included in a cookbook for sale here, *Mrs. Rowe's Favorite Recipes.*

Breakfast is standard Southern, with a few variations. Pumpkin, blueberry, and plain pancakes are available. The creamed chipped beef is homemade, as is the bread for toast. The cinnamon rolls and sticky buns are divine.

At lunch, regular sandwiches are served with potato chips. Deluxe sandwiches—such as "Hot Minute Steak" and a hot turkey sandwich—are served with mashed potatoes and gravy.

Dinner specials come with two vegetables or one vegetable and a garden salad. The vegetable choices include cucumbers and onions (that's one dish), baked tomatoes, turnip greens, pickled beets, lima beans, green beans, mashed potatoes, and applesauce. T-bone steak, baked pork tenderloin, deviled crab cutlets, country ham steak, and Southern fried chicken are generally among the entrées.

The recommended dessert is warm apple pie with cinnamon ice cream. You can also have gelatin with whipped cream, pecan pie, or other baked goods.

Catherine Eckel of Blacksburg, a Virginia Tech professor who occasionally travels to Washington, D.C., said that Mrs. Rowe's has "the best mincemeat pie with rum raisin sauce—the kind made with real meat." Eckel probably doesn't stop for just one piece on her trips up and down I-81. If she's like many longtime fans of Mrs. Rowe's, she buys a whole pie.

STAUNTON

Wright's Dairy-Rite

346 GREENVILLE AVENUE
STAUNTON, VA. 24401
(540) 886-0435

Style	Drive-in
Meals	Breakfast, lunch, and dinner, seven days a week; opens daily at 9 A.M.
Price Range	Inexpensive
Superlatives	Nostalgic atmosphere, onion rings, foot-long hot dogs with homemade chili

*I*n the year 1952—and not necessarily in their order of importance—Queen Elizabeth II was crowned, Dwight Eisenhower won the presidential election, and the Wright family opened its drive-in. The current owner, James E. Cash, was married to a Wright. His son, James R. Cash, is the manager. Cash the elder is looking into the possibility that this may be the country's oldest drive-in restaurant under the continuous ownership of a single family.

Twice during the year, Wright's hosts a "Cruise-in," when people roll in with their beloved vehicles—old, new, truck, sedan, roadster. Votes are cast for the best vehicles, with dash plaques awarded to the ten favorites. Not to be left out, motorcyclists have started a midsummer "Cruise-through" at the drive-in.

Curbside service is always available, although trays are no longer perched on car windows. Now, orders come on a tray that is set on the speaker, which is then pulled over to the car window.

If you go inside to eat, you'll most likely sit in the addition built in 1991. The Statler Brothers, native sons who keep a low profile in the area, came for the ribbon-cutting ceremony when this, the Annie Small Room, opened. Annie Small was a longtime employee who died of cancer in 1991. No doubt, she served each of the brothers at one time or another. It's equally likely she served their kids, who also frequent the drive-in.

There are phones at the booths and tables for placing your order. Curb-service menus from 1958 and 1961 and a working Wurlitzer jukebox loaded with 1950s music provide nostalgic touches.

The menu is what you'd expect—hamburgers, hot dogs, chicken, or fish on a bun, and so on. A low-fat section includes a vegetarian sub, salad, and veggie wrap. The "Super Burger" is very popular.

My husband, John, was happy because Wright's has pineapple malted milk shakes. All the shakes, cones, floats, and splits contribute to the atmosphere of a 1950s drive-in.

The neon sign is the third one on the premises, the first two having rusted out. It's identical to the original sign. Just spotting it is a reminder of simpler times.

MONTEREY
Highland Inn
MAIN STREET / MONTEREY, VA. 24465
(540) 468-2143
WWW.HIGHLAND-INN.COM

Style	Casual nice
Meals	Lunch, Friday and Saturday; dinner, Wednesday through Saturday; Sunday brunch
Price Range	Inexpensive/Moderate
Superlatives	Old-fashioned atmosphere, rainbow trout
Extras	Beer and wine

*L*ocated 3,000 feet above sea level, Monterey is the county seat of, and the largest town in, Highland County. The county is often referred to as "Virginia's Switzerland" for its gorgeous rolling hills, pastoral views, and mountains as high as 4,500 feet. Monterey boasts more than a dozen historic buildings. The oldest of them is a cabin built around 1790, which was first used as a tavern. Several Victorian structures with classic gingerbread trim date from the 1800s.

The Highland Inn is one of them. Built in 1904, the inn is now listed on the National Register of Historic Places and is a Virginia Historic Landmark.

The building still has its original porches and

gingerbread trim. Its old-time charm has been retained while modern amenities have been added. Each of the 18 guest rooms now has a private bath, for example.

The inn is white with dark green trim and matching rockers along the porch, which spans the entire front of the building. Hanging baskets and flowers lend a country look.

The floors inside have the obligatory squeak of wood a century old. The Black Sheep Tavern features antiques, old quilts, old typewriters, and lace on the windows. A small piano room has books, games, and puzzles. In the Monterey Room—the main dining room—the linens are white, and single candles adorn each table in the room, which seats 50. A large potbelly stove adds warmth on winter evenings.

The dinner menu changes to maximize quality and freshness of ingredients, and there are several specials every day. Prime rib, rainbow trout, quail, and chicken are popular entrées. A country buffet is offered on Wednesday nights.

Sunday brunch may include chicken and dumplings, flank steak, and a bountiful soup and salad bar.

The complimentary continental breakfast is available only to overnight guests. So when you call here, you'll be wise to make two reservations—one for dinner, one for the night.

Blue Stone Inn
9107 NORTH VALLEY PIKE
HARRISONBURG, VA. 22802
(540) 434-0535

Style	Family-style
Meals	Dinner, Tuesday through Saturday
Price Range	Moderate/Expensive
Superlatives	Local baked stuffed trout, seafood
Extras	Wine and beer

Route 11 was the main north-south artery through Virginia more than half of the 20th century. As motor travel increased in the 1920s, lodging and food establishments sprang up all up and down this highway. The Blue Stone Inn is one of them, and while the lodging part has succumbed to the chain hotels, good food never goes out of favor, so the restaurant flourishes.

Ernest and Katharine Olschofka emigrated from Germany in 1919 and worked in the hospitality business in New York City. They tired of city life, so when their son, Karl, returned from World War II, they bought The Blue Stone Inn and moved to the quieter pace of the Shenandoah Valley. Karl's son, Mike, took over the business in 1976 and runs it today with his wife, Janet.

The building is stone, and the trim is bright blue. Inside is a warmly rustic interior with deer trophies, lamps at every booth, and green oilcloths on the tables. It's like dining in an oversized cabin.

Mushroom caps, shrimp cocktail, French onion soup, steamed shrimp, or garden salad are offered before your meal. Steak and roast duck dinners come with either soup or salad, vegetable of the day or potato, and dinner rolls.

Rib-eye steak options include just the steak—a nice, 12-ounce portion with sautéed mushrooms—or the steak with fried oysters, scallops, shrimp, or lobster tail. Prime rib and New York strip steak come in 14-ounce servings. The half roast duck is baked crispy and served with orange sauce and red cabbage.

Fresh seafood and trout stuffed with crabmeat are specials of the house. You can order baked rainbow trout unstuffed, if you prefer, or you can order fried oysters, scallops, shrimp, or a seafood platter. Shrimp also come steamed, and scallops can be baked in butter and wine sauce.

A whole baked captain's platter includes shrimp, scallops, oysters casino, a crab cake, and mahi-mahi or salmon. There's usually a fresh fish of the day, and broiled lobster tail is priced daily.

The children's menu lists hamburgers or cheeseburgers, hot dogs, chicken nuggets, popcorn shrimp, and grilled cheese and crab cake sandwiches—all served with fries.

Dining is a leisure activity at the Blue Stone Inn, so dessert is a no-brainer. Cheesecake, chocolate mousse, chocolate cake, apple pie, and a dessert of the day are among the selections for the sweet finish.

This is a neat place to go for dinner—as a twosome or with friends and family. Reservations are necessary for groups of 6 to 12 people.

Hawksbill Diner

1388 MAIN STREET (U.S. 340 BUSINESS)
STANLEY, VA. 22851
(540) 778-2006

Style	Home-style
Meals	Breakfast, lunch, and dinner, seven days a week
Price Range	Inexpensive
Superlatives	Prime rib, stuffed pepper, spicy steamed shrimp

*I*t was a Monday night in mid-November at 6:20 P.M., on a two-lane country road when this incredibly packed parking lot came into our headlights. A small building with an excess of holiday mini-lights could be seen over the myriad vehicles. The sign out front read "Hawksbill Diner." We agreed to stop on the way back.

Two hours hence, the parking lot was empty, the door was locked, and the weary workers inside were mopping up. I drove back out in the morning, and the parking lot was not empty.

Woody and Nancy Atkins bought the diner in 1990 because Nancy always wanted it. It was built in 1942, and her mother worked here when it was a beer joint and gas station. Nancy decided that she would buy it if the opportunity came along—and she did.

The walls are wood paneling, and the tables have floral oilcloths. It's a down-home kind of place—simple, relaxed, friendly. There are seven stools at the old, solid oak counter. Shelves behind the counter hold photos of the Atkins' grandchildren, baskets, nature prints, a little tray, a bottle of Dr. Pepper, a ceramic pot or two, a mousetrap, a bottle of maple syrup—an eclectic assortment.

The menus are printed on gray paper with color food graphics, such as eggs and bacon in a frying pan, coffee in an aqua cup, a BLT. Orange, grapefruit, and tomato juice go along with eggs, omelets, hot cakes, breakfast sandwiches, and morning specials such as rib-eye steak or pork chops.

Western ham, grilled cheese, chicken filet, club, tuna, and BLT are some of the lunch sandwiches, as well as burgers, subs, hot dogs, and wing ding or shrimp plates. Interestingly, Hawksbill Diner offers Coca-Cola and Pepsi.

Since the place was packed for dinner on a Monday night, I'm guessing it's the price and camaraderie that are the big draws. Liver with fried onions, veal cutlet, country-fried steak, more ham and pork chops, hot roast beef, hot turkey, and fish 'n' chips are some of the dinner plates. Steaks and seafood include rib-eyes and T-bones, shrimp, flounder, oysters, crab cakes, fish strips, and a seafood platter.

You can follow everything with coffee or tea and pie, ice cream, or rice pudding. Hawksbill Diner is a country spot with home-cooked meals—real good meals from the looks of the parking lot.

The Farmhouse Restaurant at Jordan Hollow Farm Inn

326 HAWKSBILL PARK ROAD
STANLEY, VA. 22851
(540) 778-2285
WWW.JORDANHOLLOW.COM

Style	Fine dining
Meals	Dinner, seven days a week; closed two weeks in January
Price Range	Moderate/Expensive
Superlatives	Buffalo, herbed pork tenderloin, fudge ripple cake
Extras	Full bar

Stanley is a little settlement about 1,000 feet above sea level a few miles outside Luray. The roads are the country, two-lane variety, some more narrow than others, and the small town is documented as being 1.1 square miles.

More than two centuries ago, a public record of the property noted a home and barn among several hundred acres. The home is the log cabin, which is now a small dining room at The Farmhouse Restaurant. You can see the ax marks on the logs, and it makes one wonder how long it took to fell the tree and then shape the logs by hand to assemble this small, one-room cabin.

The other dining rooms have original floors or fireplaces. The burgundy or green walls have chair rails and are decorated with art that is for sale. Fresh flowers and glass oil lamps sit on tables draped with white, double linen tablecloths. It all combines to make a charming atmosphere that is historical and rustically elegant

The menu changes seasonally to take advantage of fresh produce and game. Appetizers may be stuffed quail, veggie ravioli in vodka and herb cream, sausage stuffed portobello, and the Jordan Hollow crab dip, which you'll find on the menu all the time.

There's a homemade soup du jour and a couple of fresh salads such as the fantastic spinach and hearts of palm salad. Warm, fresh wheat bread comes with honey butter. The tenderloin of buffalo can usually be found on the menu year-round. Two generous filets of Georgetown dry-age buffalo are char-grilled as you like it and served with sautéed wild mushrooms.

Other main entrées, depending on the season, might be stuffed golden trout, almond-crusted rack of lamb, or breast of chicken stuffed with Virginia country ham and smoked Gouda in a shallot and Chardonnay sauce. The crab cakes are made with a special recipe, and a vegetable jalousie is baked in a puff pastry.

The "Casual Side" portion of the menu features smaller portions of enticing things such as herb-roasted chicken, southern catfish, tenderloin beef stew, and a beef rib-eye. Prime rib is served Friday and Saturday evenings with a tasty horserad-ish mousse, potato selection, and a veggie. Better yet, you can decide on a 12-ounce, 14-ounce, or 16-ounce portion.

The fudge ripple cake and pumpkin spice cake are homemade in the kitchen. The Napoleon of Custard under puff pastry is drizzled with choco-late sauce and is delightfully light after a full meal.

The setting is tranquility extraordinaire. The guest rooms are cozy with mountain views, an-tiques, and oddities collected in the local area. Each room has a telephone and television, but you are free to ignore them and relax on a patio, soaking in the quiet, the peace, the majesty of creation.

LURAY

The Brookside

2978 U.S. 211 EAST
LURAY, VA. 22835
(540) 743-5698
WWW.BROOKSIDECABINS.COM

Style	Family-style
Meals	Breakfast, lunch, and dinner, seven days a week
Price Range	Inexpensive/Moderate
Superlatives	Spaghetti, catfish, buffets
Extras	Wine and beer

*F*orty-seven carillon bells at the Luray Singing Tower bring musical beauty to the mountain air. Rolling hills, pastures, and valleys framed by the Blue Ridge and Massanutten mountains lend the area visual serenity. The Luray Caverns are a ma-jor tourist attraction here, but there are also other things to see in this gentle mountain region, such as the Historic Car and Carriage Caravan, which has more than 140 antique cars on display.

Bob and Cece Castle are the fourth owners of

The Brookside and The Cabins at Brookside, located on U.S. 211 four miles east of Skyline Drive. To the best of their knowledge, some little cabins were built here in 1924, and the restaurant opened 13 years later. The original logo was a peacock, and there's a peacock on the property even today. It's "sort of a kid's attraction," Bob says.

With 17 years in the restaurant business and more than a decade in construction, Bob was well prepared to buy The Brookside in the winter of 1989. The cabins have since been renovated and expanded or completely rebuilt.

The spotless restaurant has cream-and-green calico curtains, wooden tables, and chairs with green seats. Shelves with samples of gift-shop items separate the two main dining areas. The walls are decorated with dried-flower arrangements, prints, paintings, and photos.

Breakfast is traditional country fare. The buffet is especially popular.

At lunch, you'll find all the sandwiches you'd expect—burgers and hot roast beef, hot turkey, pork barbecue, grilled ham and cheese, BLTs, and club sandwiches. It's noted on the menu that the grilled Virginia ham sandwich is "salty"; it comes on a toasted bun. The pita sandwich is filled with shredded beef or chicken and stir-fried vegetables.

In the evening, there's beef liver, chopped sirloin, rib-eye steak, pork chops, chicken served several ways, lots of seafood selections, and spaghetti. Among the healthy choices is a platter in which skinless chicken is basted with a nonfat vinaigrette and served with fresh fruit and vegetables. The baked potatoes come with broccoli and cheese, chili and onions, or chili, onions, and cheese. For vegetarians, there's a garden burger, vegetarian chili, or a large salad bar. Among the salads are a Greek salad and a grilled chicken salad.

The desserts include homemade pies, cakes, and cobblers.

The Brookside art gallery and gift shop is worth a look. Private log cabins have all the amenities of a fine hotel plus a private deck beside a natural brook. You can eat, shop, and sleep right here.

LURAY

Dan's Steak House

U.S. 211
LURAY, VA. 22835
(540) 743-6285

Style	Family-style
Meals	Dinner, seven days a week from April through October and Wednesday through Sunday from November through March
Price Range	Moderate/Expensive
Superlatives	Sirloin for two, steaks
Extras	Full bar

Built in 1937, Dan's has been through the beer joint to restaurant conversion. Jerry and Christi Baker bought it on the courthouse steps in July 1999.

The original road ran right in front of the building. Now, the new road is a few feet away and the original one is the parking lot.

Dan's is white outside and has a red sign. The inside is knotty pine cut from trees right here in Page County. You'll see wagon-wheel hanging lamps and hear oldies playing in the background. From the front dining room, there's a nice view down the mountain and across Page Valley and the town of Luray.

The sirloin for two is billed as a "Valley Tradition." It includes more than two pounds of aged beef broiled the way you want and served with a salad, potato, and fresh bread. Other steak choices include T-bone, porterhouse, New York strip, filet mignon, and prime rib. You can get most anything cut extra thick, since the steaks are hand-cut daily.

A couple of sandwiches, chicken breast, and pork chops are offered. Seafood dinners include catch of the day, fresh scallops, and steamed spiced shrimp. The menu tops out with the surf-and-turf combination of steamed spiced shrimp and filet mignon.

Dan's is the kind of place—and the Bakers and their staff the kind of people—that will make you feel like you've stepped into a group of old friends.

The restaurant is on the northern side of U.S. 211 five miles east of Exit 264 off I-81 and 12 miles west of Luray Caverns.

The Victorian Inn

138 EAST MAIN STREET
LURAY, VA. 22835
(540) 743-1494
WWW.WOODRUFFINNS.COM

Style	Casual nice
Meals	Dinner, Wednesday through Sunday
Price Range	Moderate/Expensive
Superlatives	Filet mignon, chocolate torte
Extras	Full bar, private label wine

*T*he Victorian Inn is part of Woodruff Inns & Restaurant, a collection of historic houses with guest rooms owned by Lucas and Deborah Woodruff. Lucas is from Florida, where his parents owned a restaurant. The couple met in Florida, though Deborah grew up in Washington, D.C.

They moved to Virginia and started looking for a place to open a restaurant. The first house they looked at in Luray could be a bed-and-breakfast establishment, but not a restaurant. So they started there with the Woodruff House and opened it as a B&B.

When a large, 1885 Victorian house on Main Street, which was zoned for commercial use, went up for sale, they bought it. They converted the upstairs into elegant suites and created a restaurant using the first floor and the outside. When they first opened, they offered *prix fixe* dinners only, but opened à la carte dining in March 2002.

Aptly named The Victorian Inn, the large, yellow house has roof peaks and a big front porch characteristic of late 19th-century construction. The front walkway is slate. Warm-weather dining is permitted on a brick patio on the side. There's more outdoor dining in the back around a pond. A white picket fence encircles it all like a picture frame holds fine art.

The interior ceilings are blue; walls are red; trim is white. Oriental rugs, fine linens, lace, and oil candles on each table create a cozy, Victorian atmosphere. The chandeliers are opulent, and the chairs are a black wrought-iron with cushions covered in prints with whimsical musical notes.

A tiny bar in the back has gold dollar coins imbedded into it, and there are just two bar stools. Barboursville Winery produces private label wines for The Victorian Inn, which you are welcome to purchase by the glass, or you can buy a bottle or two to go.

Broiled crab and shrimp cakes served with a Cajun rémoulade sauce are one appetizer. Another is Brie with fresh berries, sauce, and a French roll. These are sure to whet your appetite, which after all, seems to be the point of an appetizer. There are others, along with fresh salads.

Entrées vary often with availability and seasons. Lucas, who is the chef, enjoys creating special sauces for pasta dishes and some meat selections. You'll find this on pasta topped with vegetables. Pork tenderloin, for example, might have a spicy rub and barbecue sauce. Salmon is available most of the time, and the preparation technique varies.

Rack of lamb, marinated grilled chicken, and prime rib are often on the menu, and the mashed potatoes change flavors, also.

Kahlua tiramisu, Bourbon Street pecan pie, crème brûlée cheesecake, caramel apple cake, and others are on the dessert list. But you might skip

The Victorian Inn

them all in favor of Lucas's chocolate torte if there's still a crumb to be ordered.

And if you think the dinner is exquisite, wait until you check into your guest room. Wow. (Note: You do not need to be a guest to dine here, but it's a sweet possibility.)

NEW MARKET
Southern Kitchen
9576 SOUTH CONGRESS STREET (U.S. 11)
NEW MARKET, VA. 22844
(540) 740-3514

Style	Family-style
Meals	Breakfast, lunch, and dinner, seven days a week, except Thanksgiving and December 25 and 26.
Price Range	Inexpensive
Superlatives	Chicken, ribs, meringue pies
Extras	Wine and beer

*Y*ou should stop here even if you're not hungry. If you're a baby boomer or older, you'll love it. If you're in one of those other generations—X, Y, yuppie, dink, etc.—you'll get a charge out of it anyway. And you'll find something you want to eat.

Southern Kitchen is just about the same as when it opened in 1955—green and yellow booths, counter stools, little working jukeboxes in the booths, deer trophies. Several Virginia historical sites are indicated on the paper place mats: Cumberland Gap Historic Park, Woodrow Wilson's birthplace, Stonewall Jackson headquarters, and Mount Vernon, for example. The peanut region is noted in the southeast corner.

The Newland family still owns the restaurant, and Juanita Durrett, who started working here in 1955, still makes the pies. The restaurant still serves eggs, hot cakes, and salty Virginia country ham for breakfast, too. The "rise & shine specials" are "Virginia man's breakfast" of ham, juice, two eggs, home fries, and toast; the "farm hand breakfast" with a 6-ounce sirloin steak, juice, two eggs, home fries, and toast; and country sausage gravy over biscuits.

Lunch is a casual event of sandwiches, burgers, salads, and deluxe sandwiches. The latter come with fries, potato wedges, or mashed potatoes. The hamburger peach plate comes with half a peach.

You can order steak for two, rib-eye steak for yourself, a mini-steak, or "the traveler's suggestion"—a New York sirloin strip steak, 8 or 12 ounces. Home-style dinners include ham, roast beef and brown gravy, beef liver, breaded veal cutlets, barbecue short ribs, pork chops, and hamburger steak.

The special here is Lloyd's Virginia fried chicken. He's the founder, along with his wife, Ruby Newland. Chicken can be ordered as breast, thigh, and leg or breast and wing ding, or thigh and leg. Or you can select chicken livers or chicken strips.

Seafood is a hit, too. Some seafood dishes, such as oysters, come fried, and some, such as the rainbow trout or flounder, come broiled. They offer crab cakes, jumbo shrimp, and a seafood platter, all with baked potato and garden salad or two vegetables.

The "small appetites" section of the menu says "for all ages," and that's mighty considerate, especially for travelers who don't want to sit in the car on a full meal. These choices come with a hot roll and one vegetable. Chicken strips, haddock, a shrimp basket, ham, crab cakes, short ribs, a pork chop, and fried chicken are some of the small appetites possibilities.

Cheesecake, Grape-nut pudding, and ice cream sundaes are available, but I think Juanita's pies are the best.

EDINBURG

Sal's Italian Bistro
125 SOUTH MAIN STREET
EDINBURG, VA. 22824
(540) 984-9300
WWW.SALSITALIANBISTRO.COM

Style	Casual nice
Meals	Lunch and dinner, seven days a week
Price Range	Inexpensive/Moderate
Superlatives	Fresh seafood, Italian cuisine
Extras	Beer and wine

*S*al Di Roberto was raised in a family of fishermen, so he knows fish. He grew up in Italy, so he knows Italian food. He's a bright, energetic man, so he knows opportunity. His restaurant was recommended several times by other restaurant owners and people who had eaten there, so he's developed a solid reputation in a few short years.

Sal came to the United States in 1987 and worked in Philadelphia and New Jersey. When a friend told him of an opportunity in Virginia, he responded. He opened Sal's Italian Bistro in September 2000 and has since bought the building.

It's easy to feel the appeal right away. The warm aroma of garlic, pasta, and everything Italian fills the air. The walls are gold with burgundy trim. Tables are draped with burgundy linens over teal oilcloths. A cork wreath, bundles of garlic, and prints and paintings of Italy tastefully decorate the dining rooms.

Appetizers are standard fare such as wings and calamari, and Sal also introduces a "bistro appetizer" of marinated eggplant, mushrooms, and Gaeta olives with fresh mozzarella and proscuitto. Black mussels with banana peppers or fried ravioli are good starters, too.

Garden, Caesar, antipasta, Greek, and bistro salads are offered, along with subs, pizza pockets, white pizzas, and Napolitan pizza New York-style. Chicken and veal dishes include Marsala, piccata, eppeino, cacciatore, parmigiana, valdostano, and others.

A plethora of pasta sauces is available. Funghetti is a mushroom tomato sauce; Russian is marinara sauce with sun-dried tomato and a touch of cream; primavera has seasonal vegetables with garlic oil sauce; and pomodoro is fresh tomato basil sauce. There are several more.

But Sal shines with the fresh seafood. He drives to Baltimore once a week to choose the freshest of the catches. The "Poseidon" entrée combines fresh shell clams and chopped clams in red or white sauce. Shrimp Bistro comes with fire-roasted peppers, mushrooms, and garlic oil. Shrimp comes with broccoli, chicken, vegetables, scallops, lobster, banana peppers, and olives.

Seafood lovers can order the "seafood lovers" entrée of lobster tail, shrimp, mussels, clams, and salmon. Another seafood combination melds clams, calamari, mussels, shrimp, and marinara with a touch of cream.

Classic Italian desserts of tiramisu and cannolis are available, as well as Black Forest Cake, Caramel Pecan Passion, and Tartufo, a chocolate cocoa ice cream.

The menu has Sal's philosophy right on it: "Cooking is our passion. Happy customers are our obsession."

Valley Restaurant

16235 OLD VALLEY PIKE
EDINBURG, VA. 22824
(540) 984-4466

Style	Home-style
Meals	Breakfast and lunch, seven days a week; dinner, Monday through Saturday
Price Range	Inexpensive
Superlatives	Pork barbecue, cream pies

One could guess that people needed something to lift their spirits toward the end of the Great Depression, and a drive in the country for a bite to eat just might have fit the bill. I have no way of knowing if that was the motivation for "Doc" and Ida Guess to open a little sandwich stand in 1931, but it has stood the test of time and remains open and run by the same family today.

The Guesses were ahead of their time with the burgers and soda, as the American obsession with these things didn't really materialize until McDonald's and other fast-food franchises began expanding in the 1960s.

Doc and Ida also sold hot dogs, roast pork barbecue, and country ham sandwiches, with soft drinks and coffee. In 1934, they began making ice cream. The cones sold for 10 cents each, and the business grew to selling 75 to 80 gallons per week — a practice that continued until 1942.

Originally just 12 by 24 feet, the little building had two open windows at one end through which customers purchased their orders. A small porch was added, where a few country gifts are for sale. In 1980, a 20-foot dining room was built on the other end, and they opened for three meals a day. It is still fairly small, seating less than 50 at yellow or brown booths.

Breakfast is the typical mix and match of eggs, ham, rib-eye steak, pancakes, bacon, sausage, scrapple, and omelets. Egg sandwiches; hot, home-baked biscuits with sausage gravy; or French toast are also available.

The sandwich options have expanded from the early days to include fish, grilled cheese, chicken or tuna salad, BLT, breaded chicken filet, ham, or ham and cheese, but the originals, dubbed "Valley Classics," still sell well. The sliced pork barbecue or pulled pork barbecue, ham sandwiches, and burgers are served on large sesame seed buns with fries.

There's a Yankee sub, steak and provolone cheese sub, and triple-decker sub, as well as homemade vegetable and chicken noodle soup and chili.

All the dinners come with fries or mashed potatoes and a vegetable. Beef dinners feature T-bone or rib-eye steaks, beef liver with onions, or hamburger steak. Wing dings, fried chicken, and breaded veal cutlets are also offered. The seafood section includes a shrimp basket, a jumbo clam basket, breaded perch, oysters, or shrimp.

You can get those real comfort foods, also, such as hot roast beef or pork sandwiches with gravy and mashed potatoes. Check out the specials for the day.

If you don't see them posted, your waitress will know. She'll also know what kinds of homemade pies are still available. And you can have a French vanilla cappuccino with dessert—or for dessert.

Café & Bistro at Court Square

117 SOUTH MAIN STREET
WOODSTOCK, VA. 22664
(540) 459-8888

Style	Café and bistro
Meals	Breakfast, lunch, and dinner, seven days a week; Saturday and Sunday brunch.
Price Range	Inexpensive/Moderate
Superlatives	Fusion cuisine, bakery
Extras	Wine and beer, wine and gift shop

Woodstock, which epitomizes small-town America, is the appropriate setting for this delightful, busy café and bistro. The Wine Shoppe behind the dining tables stocks more than 400 labels. The gift and antique spaces in the middle and back have lots of interesting gifts and knickknacks.

Breakfast offerings go from "the basic" to "the full works," and you can order Spanish, Cajun, Denver, and el hombre plates. Brunch entrées include eggs niçoise, eggs Oscar, eggs Smithfield, and eggs Cubano—all versions of poached eggs on English muffins with hollandaise sauce.

Turkey and bacon Monte Cristo, barbecue ba-

Café & Bistro at Court Square

con grilled chicken, a portobello Gorgonzola entrée, and others round out the brunch menu.

Lunch sandwiches come with potato or pasta salad. "The Cowboy" is grilled flank steak sliced thin and served with mushrooms and Swiss cheese on Greek flatbread with honey mustard dressing. There's pulled-pork barbecue, sliced turkey, pastrami, and Muenster cheese and other choices, including soup and quiche.

Appetizers are as creative as delicious. You might not find pumpkin tarragon cream on the menu all year round, but if you do, try it. It's velvet smooth bisque with tarragon and Madeira topped with crumbled Gorgonzola cheese. The pan-browned chèvre is French goat cheese lightly breaded and browned and served over balsamic-dressed greens.

The pan-braised breast of duck is finished with a raspberry cognac demi-glaze, and shellfish espontana blends lump crab, mussels, and shrimp with garlic and fresh herbs, then it is pan-seared and placed over angel hair pasta with Madeira beurre manié.

Imagine this: Light pasta pockets filled with ricotta and lobster, settled in a light cream sauce around rock lobster tail medallions with hearts of palm and green peppercorns. It's a contemporary menu with delightful blends of herbs and sauces.

And save room for dessert. Tiramisu, Key lime pie, a southern pecan walnut chocolate chip pie, hazelnut pumpkin soufflé with caramel sauce, and sweet potato rum pie are sometimes available. With a bakery on site, I just went with a blond brownie—rich and delicious—with wonderful, apricot mango tea.

This is a neat place. It's busy, modern, and inviting. Everyone is so friendly, and there's so much to browse and so many interesting things to eat!

WOODSTOCK

Spring House Tavern

325 SOUTH MAIN STREET
WOODSTOCK, VA. 22664
(540) 459-4755
WWW.JESARA.COM

Style	Pub
Meals	Lunch and dinner, seven days a week
Price Range	Inexpensive/Moderate
Superlatives	Ribs, chili, Kentucky Derby pie
Extras	Full bar

*T*he county seat of Shenandoah County,

Woodstock lays claim to having the oldest courthouse in continuous use east of the Blue Ridge. The steeple and porch of the structure were built of native limestone in 1795. The town and surrounding valley can perhaps best be seen from Woodstock Tower, a 40-foot tower built by the Civilian Conservation Corps in the 1930s. From it, one can also see the seven bends of the Shenandoah River.

Spring House Tavern was acquired in 2000 by the partnership that owns the Cork Street Tavern in Winchester, New Town Tavern in Stephens City (see New Town Tavern, page 102), and Royal Oak Tavern in Front Royal. Joel Smith and Anthony Andriola are the business partners, and they have developed a successful formula for these casual restaurants.

After more than 10 years at Cork Street Tavern, Joel was feeling a little unchallenged. In a bold move, he and Anthony set out to place their experiences, recipes, and style in a few other small towns. Joel isn't feeling so restless these days, and travelers and local folks can order their award-winning ribs and chili without going to Winchester.

The place has lots of old barn wood with a mix of tile, wood, and carpeted floors. The bar and dining room in front have a sports theme. One small dining room has dried flowers. Another dining room with a multicolor tile floor has a board-game theme with game boards on the walls. Country-western décor dominates the back dining room.

Appetizers, soups, salads, burgers, and sandwiches compose the lunch fare. The split pea soup

Spring House Tavern

is great. A tortilla club or a turkey Reuben offer something a little different.

If you like ribs and eating with your fingers, this is the place to order them. The ribs have garnered many an award, as has the chili. But you can eat with a fork by having chicken, broiled trout, catfish, crab cakes, shrimp, or steak. West Side pasta combines hot sausage, artichoke hearts, onions, peppers, and spices over pasta.

Kentucky Derby pie is excellent, and there are pecan and peanut butter pies, as well as cheesecake.

Spring House Tavern has a nice selection of microbrews, beers on tap, bottled domestic and imported beers. The Cork Street coffee is a flavorful mix of spiced rum, Bailey's, Frangelico, coffee, and whipped cream. They say this recipe is stolen often. I haven't had it or tried to steal it, but it sounds good.

The Apple House
VA. 55 (EXIT 13 OFF I-66)
LINDEN, VA. 22642
(540) 635-2118
WWW.APPLEHOUSEVA.COM

Style	Home-style
Meals	Breakfast, lunch, and dinner, seven days a week
Price Range	Inexpensive
Superlatives	Barbecue, donuts, Alpenglow

*I*f you like country gifts, barbecue, donuts, and sparkling cider, you don't want to miss The Apple House. The place opened in 1963 as a processing plant for apples, but little by little, the retail side of the business grew.

In 1980, partners Ben and Jean Lacy created Alpenglow, a non-alcoholic, sparkling apple cider. Daughter Betsy Quarles managed the bottling plant until relocating to Fredericksburg. Daughter Debbie Hunter stepped in as sales manager. Son George McIntyre runs the gift shop, catering business, and restaurant with his daughter, Katie Tewell. It's a real family affair.

Alpenglow, the line of cider products, is now distributed nationally and available for private labeling. It's a fabulous drink, but don't take my word for it. There's a tasting station in the gift shop, and any one of the friendly staff members can assist you. Gifts ranging from cassette tapes and candles to quilts, T-shirts, chimes, throws, toys, and country crafts are available here.

The little restaurant, located to the left, has room for around 42. It's cream with wood trim, lace valances, and red-and-white-checked curtains.

There's a lot of barbecue to be had in Virginia, but there's none like George McIntyre's. Cooked over hickory, apple, and oak and served on a bun, it has a wonderfully spicy flavor.

There are a lot of donuts to be had, too, but George's are special. These cake donuts made with apple butter and rolled in cinnamon and sugar are fabulous. You may have breakfast all day at The Apple House.

At lunch or dinner, you can choose from among hot dogs, hamburgers, Virginia buffalo burgers, or roast beef, turkey, BLT, grilled cheese, and other sandwiches, as well as daily specials.

This is a great place to stop for gift shopping and a sample—or a few bottles—of Alpenglow. But it's a must stop for barbecue and donuts.

The Apple House is a long, low, red building just off I-66 at Exit 13. If you're going east on I-66, bear right at the bottom of the ramp and right again at the stoplight onto Va. 55. The Apple House is on the right.

Fretwells

Style	Casual nice
Meals	Breakfast, Saturday and Sunday; lunch and dinner, Wednesday through Sunday.
Price Range	Inexpensive
Superlatives	Filet mignon, barbecue ribs
Extras	Full bar, wine store, gift shop

Stephanie Fretwell was an Army brat right from her birth in the Air Force Academy hospital. After moving around in her young years, she settled in Washington, D.C, working as a contractor with the Department of Defense When her parents, Bob and Connie Fretwell, retired to Front Royal in 1999, she came often for the weekend.

Like many small business owners who have changed lifestyles, Stephanie found it more difficult to return to life in the fast lane on Sunday evenings. She had always been interested in food, so a concept took shape in her head. In January 2001, she opened Fretwells of Front Royal, Café, Wine, and Gift Shoppe.

It's contemporary, clean, uncluttered, and very appealing. Sconces, recessed ceiling lights, and mini-lights along the chair rail keep the place bright enough to see, yet soft enough to relax. The walls are white, and the linens are burgundy.

The left side of the space is the gift shop, which

offers a wonderful assortment of books, CDs, throw pillows, greeting cards, and home decorative items. The wine shop is toward the back, and the restaurant is on the right side.

Fretwells was recommended to us for dessert by staff at another restaurant. Next time I'm going for breakfast and dinner. Where else can you get ten versions of eggs Benedict? Some of them are traditional, of course, along with Spanish, corned beef, portobello mushrooms, spinach, chicken, and turkey. They are all topped with hollandaise and served with home fries.

Other morning entrées are omelets, walnut-and-maple-topped pancakes, raspberry and cream cheese stuffed toast, breakfast potato skins with scrambled eggs and bacon, and breakfast sandwiches.

There are five types of Reubens, a three cheese sandwich on grilled sourdough, club sandwiches, homemade soup, and house special sandwiches such as "everything under the sun." The salads include a heart healthy one with or without grilled chicken or a burger patty. Dressings are homemade and sell by the half pint with advance notice.

The dinner menu changes often. You might find filet mignon with Béarnaise sauce; barbecue ribs with special, homemade sauce; chicken cordon bleu; shrimp scampi; or baked lemon pepper flounder. There's a vegetarian entrée, also.

And that dessert? It was a wonderful piece of homemade blackberry pie eaten along with a cup of vanilla chai. The desserts are all homemade, and there's a variety of fruit pies, cheesecakes, and home-made ice creams. Sometimes there's chocolate torte. Whatever the dessert, I think you'll love it, and you can order chai in several flavors to enjoy with it.

Holmes Style Bar-B-Que

117 MAIN STREET / FRONT ROYAL, VA. 22630
(540) 631-0045

Style	Home-style
Meals	Lunch and dinner, Tuesday through Saturday
Price Range	Inexpensive
Superlatives	North Carolina barbecue, beef brisket

Kenny Holmes grew up around Wilmington, North Carolina, and learned to cook as a kid. As a grown-up, he worked a couple of decades in the printing business. In 1999, he purchased a bus, painted it white, and retrofitted it as a mobile restaurant. Then he leased a spot of land and set up shop in the summer months.

Kenny and his wife, Ola, were so successful with their barbecue bus business that they opened a permanent restaurant in Front Royal, next to the movie theatre.

Now he, his wife, and their son, Faheem, have a second bus as well as the restaurant. When this book is released in the spring of 2004, one of the Holmes Style Bar-B-Que buses will be just off U.S. 28 on Route 606, heading toward Herndon.

Otherwise, come right downtown in Front Royal for some delicious barbecue in a spiffy, clean restaurant with six tables.

In the front of the little eatery, there's a mural of a country scene with one of Kenny's white buses on a country road. The rest of the walls are cream over black with a red chair rail. A couple of green shelves hold a little straw with a couple of pig and cow ceramics, a plate, and a little country décor.

These people care what you think. There's a full-size mailbox for suggestions on the condiment shelf. Everything is neat, tidy, and attractive.

The North Carolina barbecue on a bun comes large or small. You can order ribs, chicken (all dark or all white meat), beef on a bun, half or whole slabs of ribs, and half or whole chickens. The "que-dog" is a grilled hot dog with barbecue sauce, chili, and coleslaw. Tuesday through Friday, there are daily lunch specials, and a senior discount is offered.

Dinners are the same, plus fish, shrimp, and scallops. Sides include hush puppies, traditional baked beans, potato salad, Apple House baked beans (The Apple House in Linden is also in this book), green beans, collard greens, and macaroni salad.

The desserts are homemade. I saw the cakes and forced my will power into high gear. Ola makes an awesome bread pudding, banana pudding, and sweet potato pie.

You can wash all this down with Alpenglow, the sparkling cider also from Apple House, or a soda, or tea. If you call ahead, your order can be prepared for pick-up.

And don't forget their bus business on Route 606, or call them to cater an event and they might roll in with the other bus. Either way, you'll have the best barbecue at your party!

Stadt Kaffee

Style	Family-style
Meals	Lunch, Saturday; dinner, Monday through Saturday
Price Range	Inexpensive/Moderate
Superlatives	German cuisine, wurst platters
Extras	Full bar, small gift shop

There just might be more *Reader's Digest* condensed books on the shelves in Stadt Kaffee restaurant than in any library. High above the floor, closer to the ceiling, are suspended shelves laden with books, a couple of German figurines, a few beer steins, a jug, and a six-pack of beer—an eclectic assortment, most items reflecting a German flavor, except for the books.

Elke Carter, a native of Germany, opened her restaurant in 1993. It's European-looking, with lace curtains on the front windows, white textured walls, and wood beams. Pink linens are placed over white ones. Green oilcloth place mats rest on the tables, along with arrangements of fresh, white roses.

Lunch appetizers and salads, like everything, lean

the German way. Tagessuppe is a soup, made daily and served with hearth German bread. Potato pancakes, deviled eggs on potato salad topped with caviar, and baked Brie with walnuts and apple slices are also offered. Vegetarian dishes and sandwiches will satisfy the light appetite, and German specialties are for those who might be making lunch their main meal of the day.

Similar appetizers and salads are on the dinner menu, along with tomato or cucumber salad in season. Bratwurst, a wurst platter, sauerbraten, and a sampler for two might be familiar to most people.

Elke also prepares *ungarisches gulasch* (traditional cubed beef in paprika sauce served over noodles) and *Kassler Ripchen* (oven-roasted smoked pork-loin steak on a bed of sauerkraut served with potato dumplings). *Schnitzel Holstein*, which is often ordered and enjoyed, is a breaded pork tenderloin topped with Black Forest ham and Swiss cheese served with potatoes, salad, and vegetable. Several dishes include Spaetzle, a German homemade pasta; others come with red cabbage.

Sautéed trout and poached salmon are there for the fish lovers. Vegetarians might prefer spinach crêpes, cheese Spaetzle, or the increasingly popular vegetarian platter.

Apfelstrudel, German chocolate cake, Schweartzwaelder Kirsch torte, or Black Forest cake are my favorites. Chocolate-covered cream puffs, tiramisu, and raspberry mango cheesecake sound mighty appealing, too, especially with Vienna coffee, topped with whipped cream.

Cristina's

348 EAST KING STREET
STRASBURG, VA. 22657
(540) 465-5300

Style	Family-style, Mexican
Meals	Lunch and dinner, seven days a week
Price Range	Inexpensive
Superlatives	Lime soup, *mole*
Extras	Full bar

*I*n summer, Cristina's building is awash with vivid color provided by the lush assortment of flowers reaching for the sun and spilling over their containers. In other seasons, you'll have to go inside for the color. The aqua textured walls, which are bright and bold, are decorated with colorful plates and vases.

The floor is black-and-white-checkered, and the tabletops are wood or faux marble. It's a lively place, in the colorfulness and the cheerful staff.

Donna Willis is the owner, and her blond hair might lead you to think she's not Mexican, but she grew up in Mexico City and lived part of her life in Yucatan. The fair complexion comes from her Welsh father's side of the family.

Donna specializes in southern Mexican cooking learned from her mother and her aunt. She worked with her mother between 1981 and 1992 in her mother's restaurant, which was located across the street in Strasburg. Seventeen years later, Donna bought this building and opened her own place, naming it for her mother.

Cristina's

Mexican pizza has a crispy crust with mozzarella and cheddar cheeses, onions, tomatoes, and hot peppers on request. The deluxe version has ham, beef, or chicken, also. Nachos, guacamole dip, and flautas are on the appetizer list. The flautas are small deep-fried chicken tacos with guacamole, sour cream, and chipotle dip.

Taco salad and black bean soup are staples. Yucatecan lime soup is a specialty. It has a hearty chicken broth flavored with *achiote* (a light sweet-and-sour tasting herb). Tortilla strips, cilantro, onions, tomatoes, avocado, and lime are sprinkled on top.

Quesadillas, tacos, burritos, chimichangas, chile rellenos, and enchiladas appear on the menu. Two of the most interesting and popular house specialties are *chocinita pibil* and *mole de pollo*. The former is roasted pork in achiote sauce; the latter is based on *mole* (an elaborate, rich sauce invented by in-digenous people of Mexico). It's an exotic blend of ancho peppers, almonds, peanuts, and cacao (Mexican chocolate).

Combination dinners are a great way to try different items. They are referenced simply as C-1 through C-10. C-3, for example, consists of a soft beef taco, a chicken sour cream enchilada, and a beef burrito. "A Taste of Mexico" is C-7, a cup of Yucatecan lime soup, a mushroom and cheese enchilada, *cochinita pibil*, a chile relleno, and a banana roll.

Caramel flan and fried banana roll are two of the homemade desserts. Cristina's also offers *tres leches cake*, which is traditional wedding cake—white cake soaked in brandy with meringue topping.

There are specials on weekends, and Cristina's is across the street from The Great Strasburg Emporium Antiques. This calls for at least a half-day excursion, antiquing and discovering the flavors of the Yucatan.

STRASBURG
Hi Neighbor
192 WEST KING STREET / STRASBURG, VA. 22657
(540) 465-9987

Style	Home-style
Meals	Breakfast and lunch, seven days a week; dinner, Monday through Saturday
Price Range	Inexpensive/Moderate
Superlatives	Local color, scrapple
Extras	Wine and beer

The town of Strasburg is synonymous with antiques. It's noted not only for the Strasburg Emporium and its 100 or so dealers, but also for the small antique shops scattered around town. The Strasburg Museum, located in a train station built in 1891, and the Museum of American Presidents, opened in 1996, are popular among visitors as well.

Look for the one-word banner hanging outside Hi Neighbor above the sidewalk. Its message is simple and direct: *Food*.

At noon, you'll find just about every kind of person—blue-collar people, white-collar people, people in uniforms, people in blue jeans, children. Some dressed up, others dressed down. Lots of just plain chatty folks and the friendly waitresses who serve them.

The dining room dates to the Civil War. Union general Philip Sheridan stayed here for several weeks, paying the owners with sugar, coffee, and other scarce items. At the turn of the century, the building became the Massanutten Hotel. Now, there's just the restaurant on the site.

If you don't want to order a full breakfast, you can choose from among 17 side orders, including egg substitute for the cholesterol-conscious. The cholesterol-unconscious will probably lean more toward the biscuits and gravy or the corned beef hash. Among more than a dozen breakfasts is the "Sportsman's Breakfast," which features rainbow trout.

But the specialty here is scrapple. Originally a Pennsylvania Dutch dish, scrapple is finely chopped pork scraps with cornmeal and pork liver added. The concoction is cooked into a mush, pressed into a loaf pan, and cooled. A serving is then sliced, fried in butter, and served hot, most often on toast or pancakes. Puddin' meat, also available, is similar to scrapple but without the cornmeal and liver. It's a coarse, crumbly food.

The sandwiches range from peanut butter and jelly to crab cake. Both pork and beef barbecue are available. Platters are served with french fries and slaw.

Everyone seems to know everyone else here, but they're friendly enough to make you feel part of it all, too.

STRASBURG

Hotel Strasburg

213 SOUTH HOLLIDAY STREET
STRASBURG, VA. 22657
(800) 348-8327 OR (540) 465-9191
WWW.HOTELSTRASBURG.COM

Style	Fine dining
Meals	Breakfast, Saturday and Sunday; lunch, Monday through Saturday; dinner, seven days a week. The Depot Lounge serves lunch and dinner seven days a week.
Price Range	Moderate/Expensive
Superlatives	Victorian atmosphere, antiques, Mediterranean-style food
Extras	Full bar

The Hotel Strasburg combines Victorian style and friendly warmth. Constructed in the 1890s as a private hospital, the building was converted to a hotel in the early 1900s. The interior was completely restored to elegance in 1977.

On New Year's Day 1994, Gary and Carol Rutherford bought the hotel, after having leased it for three years. The small front door belies the grandeur inside. To the left is the large walnut front desk with a huge Belgian sideboard behind it. To the right is the Depot Lounge, a cozy little spot with a bar and tables for about 35 people. Soup, salads, focaccia, nachos, appetizers, burgers, sandwiches, and desserts are served here all afternoon and evening. Dinners are available during dinner hours.

The halls and the dining rooms are cream with green trim. Artwork, antique plates, and mirrors with ornate gold frames grace the walls.

Breakfast is open to the public on Saturday and Sunday mornings. Overnight guests receive a continental breakfast each morning.

Chef Frank Asaro has been here more than a decade. He specializes in Mediterranean-style cuisine, although his signature lunch entrée is chicken pot pie, a made-from-scratch little casserole under a puff pastry. Other choices include an Italian steak-and-cheese sandwich, "Sea and Garden Focaccia," and "Focaccia Rustica"—grilled portobello mushroom with pesto, roasted sweet red pepper, and melted provolone.

There are four sections to the dinner menu. The section called "From the Sauté Station" includes pan-seared lamb chops, butter pecan chicken, and "Veal Gremolata." The "From the Charcoal Grill" section includes grilled pork chops, surf and turf, and veal cutlets. The items in the "Pasta Entrées" section come with a garden salad. The "Seafood and Vegetarian Entrées" include trout, crab cakes, catch of the day, and a vegetarian dish.

The guest rooms at the Hotel Strasburg are exquisite. They feature lots of dark walnut, marble, and fabulous headboards, all complemented by modern amenities such as private baths, telephones, and televisions. With all the classic Victorian décor around here, you might expect an atmosphere of stiff formality, but it's just the opposite. Here as elsewhere, the owners set the tone for their business, and Gary Rutherford just happens to be a cheerful, friendly fellow. His easy manner is reflected in the entire staff.

STRASBURG
Hungry Dog Café
219 WEST KING STREET / STRASBURG, VA. 22657
(540) 465-5500

Style	Home-style
Meals	Lunch and dinner, Tuesday through Saturday
Price Range	Inexpensive/Moderate
Superlatives	Barbecue, hot dogs
Extras	Full bar

*I*n a building that has been a bagel place, a bar, and a medical supply store, Carol Bush and Rick Wilkins have created a boldly colorful restaurant, which offers live entertainment at least half the nights they are open. The walls are bright yellow or bright aqua. Whether by accident or by design, most of the chairs are primary colors, with a few black ones included.

There are two dining rooms, which hold nine booths and around 10 tables for four. Those newly popular rope lights and fluorescent lights above keep the place well illuminated.

There are seasonal touches on the tables, such as gourds and dried corn in November. You'll also find Melinda's sauces on each table, which include taco, jalapeno, XXXtra reserve, and XXXXtra reserve, along with homemade barbecue sauce.

After settling on the name Hungry Dog, friends insisted that hot dogs be on the menu. You can order a plain dog, slaw dog, chili dog, kraut dog, or death dog. The last one comes with chili, cheese, onions, and jalapeno peppers.

Garden salad comes plain or with barbecue chicken or pork, and a special chicken salad is sprinkled with nuts and raisins. The soup changes regularly, so just ask what's in the pot today or consider chili, pinto beans, or baked beans.

Homemade salsa accompanies the tortilla chips, and Route 11 potato chips come with all the sandwiches. There's the Hungry Dog original pork barbecue, a South Carolina barbecue, pulled chicken barbecue, and a chicken salad sandwich on 12-grain bread. Other sandwich possibilities are the turkey Reuben, Monte Cristo, and grilled ham and cheese.

Dinners are primarily barbecue meat with two sides and cornbread. You can also order the crab cake sandwich or platter, which is served only in the evening. Fruit pies, coconut cream pie, German chocolate cake, and chocolate layer cake are some of the homemade desserts.

Stick around some of the weekend nights for music by the house band. Tuesday evenings feature an acoustic guitar musician.

MIDDLETOWN
The Wayside Inn
7783 MAIN STREET / MIDDLETOWN, VA. 22645
(540) 869-1797
WWW.WAYSIDEOFVA.COM

Style	Fine dining
Meals	Breakfast, Saturday and Sunday; lunch and dinner, seven days a week; Sunday brunch
Price Range	Moderate/Expensive
Superlatives	Historical atmosphere, peanut soup, trout
Extras	Full bar

*M*iddletown is a pretty little town with historic houses and the second-oldest professional theater company in the state. Wayside Theatre presents more than half a dozen productions between June and December. One of the town's most interesting buildings is Grace United Methodist Church over on Main Street, which has a 75-foot tower with a carillon and unusual sliding stained-glass windows in the sanctuary.

The Wayside Inn bills itself as the "oldest motor inn" in the country, having opened in 1797. Of course, there weren't any automobiles then. It would be another 99 years before Henry Ford made his first car. But the place has indeed provided food and lodging to travelers for more than two centuries.

Though he was probably not the first guest to motor in, John D. Rockefeller was certainly among the most famous. The 1922 telegram in which he requested two rooms—one for himself and the other for his driver—is now framed and displayed on a wall.

In the early 1990s, a third floor and new wings were added and the name was changed from Larrick's Hotel to The Wayside Inn. The inn is owned by Leo Bernstein.

Eggs, meat, hot cakes, and French toast are offered at breakfast, and Sunday brunch is a buffet with omelet and carving stations.

The midday fare includes salads, sandwiches, and entrées. Colonial peanut soup is The Wayside's signature soup, and there's also French onion soup and another homemade soup. The salad dressings are homemade for the tossed, spinach, grilled chicken, shrimp, or Caesar salads. The chicken salad is homemade, too. This is a homemade kind of place.

There are at least a half dozen sandwiches and entrées. Grilled tuna melt, hot turkey, and crab cake come as sandwiches. Old-fashioned chicken pot pie, Miss Irene's meat loaf, and the inn's famous smothered chicken are some of the meals.

First course choices include the soups, salads, baked Brie, crab-stuffed mushrooms, and Half Moon stuffed oysters. Main course offerings of filet mignon, apple-smoked pork chops, rack of lamb, and shrimp with pasta sound tasty. Classics such as roasted turkey and Virginia country ham steaks are also available, along with the inn's famous, homemade spoon bread.

Desserts will be brought right to you on a dessert tray. The offerings are tough to turn down, and they're homemade, too.

The Wayside Inn is a pretty place with a friendly staff, nice accommodations, and fine food.

L'Auberge Provençale

U.S. 340 / WHITE POST, VA. 22663
(800) 638-1702 OR (540) 837-1375
WWW.LAUBERGEPROVENCALE.COM

Style	Fine dining
Meals	Dinner, Wednesday through Sunday; Sunday brunch. Reservations are strongly recommended.
Price Range	Expensive
Superlatives	Pastoral setting, food quality and presentation
Extras	Full bar

This town was named for a white post that marked the way to Greenway Court, the home of Thomas, Sixth Lord Fairfax. It is said that the post was whitewashed frequently to enhance its visibility

L'Auberge Provençale

and probably its appearance as well, as a chipped or peeling post would not have made a favorable first impression.

If you can't get over to the south of France, L'Auberge Provençale is a superb place to experience the food, drink, amenities, and loveliness of that region.

The manor house was built in 1753 from fieldstones found in the area's pastures and valleys. The building rambles down a small slope; additions were constructed in 1890 and 1990. Eleven upscale guest rooms and suites feature Victorian and European antiques.

Alain and Celeste Borel bought the property in 1981. On the grounds, you'll find hanging baskets, colorful flowers in Celeste's collection of antique olive jars, the chef's vegetable and herb gardens, and more than three dozen fruit trees. A fourth-generation gourmet chef from Avignon, Alain makes good use of his fresh produce.

Inside the front door are framed awards and articles. Magazines that portray the finest in food— *Bon Appétit, Gourmet, Food and Wine*—have not missed L'Auberge Provençale.

Celeste is responsible for the fabrics and décor. The intimate dining rooms have their own color schemes. A rich royal blue is prominent in the front room, which has a fireplace. The large solarium room, built in 1986, is done in soft peach, a perfect backdrop for the copper pots and pans that belonged to Alain's great-grandmother.

Dinner is a five-course event.

It all starts with an *Amouse Bouche*, translated as a little something "to amuse your mouth." Not considered a course in itself, this might be a small salmon crêpe—just a little nibble to enjoy while you scan the menu.

The first course is the Entrée. Here, however, the familiar term simply means the entry to the meal—an appetizer. One possibility is sautéed frog legs with raspberry cream in puff pastry.

The *Deuxième Suite*, or second course, is soup or salad.

The Intermezzo is the third course. It may be a sorbet, the most common palate cleanser.

The fourth course is the main course. It might be lamb with carrot ginger sauce or sea bass with fish mousse.

An optional cheese course is offered after the dinner.

Dessert completes the dining experience. Among the possibilities are crème brûlée or a "Chocolate

Tower," filled with raspberries and white chocolate mousse.

You don't wait for a special occasion to come to L'Auberge Provençale. Coming to L'Auberge Provençale creates a special occasion.

New Town Tavern

356 FAIRFAX PIKE / STEPHENS CITY, VA. 22655
(540) 868-0111
WWW.JESARA.COM

Style	Family-style
Meals	Lunch and dinner, seven days a week
Price Range	Inexpensive
Superlatives	Ribs, Jamaican pumpkin soup
Extras	Full bar

Like many small towns in the Shenandoah Valley, Stephens City was settled by Scots, Irish, and Germans. The town was first called Newtown, then changed to Stephens City when it was formally established in 1758. The main street and side streets comprise a historic district listed on the National Register of Historic Places.

Joel Smith opened Cork Street Tavern in Winchester's old section in 1985. Anthony Andriola was a kitchen employee at the time. The restaurant met with success, expanded 10 years later, and won lots of awards for its ribs. Along the way, Anthony became partners with Joel.

When Joel got to feeling restless in the late 1990s, the pair looked for new opportunities where they could establish their successful concept. They opened New Town Tavern in 1999.

It's about a mile east of Exit 307 off I-81. The restaurant shares a strip mall with Food Lion, so there's always plenty of parking. There are shamrocks on the front windows, coach lights on the interior walls, stained-glass hanging lamps, and tons of beer cans behind glass display boxes.

The left side is the bar side. Smoking is permitted here, but not on the right side. The whole place can accommodate about 60 people at wood tables covered with dark green oilcloth. The décor also features small oil lamps and spindle-back chairs made of light wood.

Cork Street Tavern is famous for its ribs, and the same rib recipes are prepared here. In recent years, the restaurants have won chili awards, so this might be your first stop on the menu. The appetizers are the norm: potato skins, nachos, fried mozzarella sticks, buffalo wings, and the like.

There are ten dressings for the salads. The salads range from basic house, spinach, chicken, and chef salads to stuffed tomatoes. Burgers come with and without the usual trimmings. Some of the interesting sandwiches are the salmon croissant, the crab cake sandwich, and the tortilla club.

Pasta specialties include shrimp, tequila chicken, hot West Side pasta, and seafood Alfredo. The award-winning, barbecued baby back ribs are my recommendation, but if you are not up for chewing off the bone, you might order New York strip steak, barbecue chicken, shrimp scampi, broiled trout or scallops, or lemon pepper catfish. There are more seafood, chicken, and beef options than just these.

For more variety in your meal, you have combo possibilities such as steak and lobster, ribs and chicken, steak and crab, ribs and steak, shrimp and sirloin, or another version of surf & turf that comes with three jumbo shrimp and a New York strip steak. All the entrées are served with two sides. You can choose a baked potato, fries, rice pilaf, or a vegetable, and salad or coleslaw to go with your meal.

Desserts are delicious with Kentucky Derby pie at the top of my list. They also offer cheesecake, pecan pie, peanut butter pie, and others.

STEPHENS CITY

Roma

120 FAIRFAX PIKE
STEPHENS CITY, VA. 22655
(540) 869-5200

Style	Family-style, Italian
Meals	Lunch and dinner, seven days a week
Price Range	Inexpensive/Moderate
Superlative	Italian and Greek cuisine, seafood
Extras	Full bar

Benjamin Ritenour is a local boy from a hard-working, farm family. His first job off the farm as a teenager was at a pizza and sub shop. A highly motivated, smart, sensible young man, Benjamin bought the pizza shop, expanded three times, and

created Roma, a classy Italian and Greek restaurant less than half a mile off I-81's Exit 307.

The walls are a roughly textured yellow gold, covered with family photos. The floor is carpeted, and tables are teal with oak edges. It is warm and inviting.

Appetizers of bruschetta, antipasto salad, Greek stuffed mushrooms, calamari fritti, Italian cheese bread, and other things can get you started on a casual dining experience. Pasta fagioli (the most famous of Italian soups) is offered, along with minestrone and a soup of the day.

Salads run the gamut from grilled chicken Caesar and Italian chef to traditional Greek, yellowfin tuna, and mozzarella alla caprese. Burgers, sandwiches, and subs include a crab cake sandwich and hot vegetarian sub. Spanakopita is Greek pastry filled with spinach, feta, and onions wrapped with phyllo dough. You can blend Greek and Italian dishes by combining one of the gyro sandwiches or platters with a side of Italian meatballs.

There are enough specialty pizzas for everyone to find a preference. Greek, Italian white, chicken barbecue, Alfredo, vegetarian, all meat, Roma special, and pollo rustica are on the pizza list. If you insist, you can create your own pizza. Strombolis and calzones are served with salad or soup.

Baked Tuscany includes penne pasta, shrimp, chicken, and pancetta in a cream sauce, which is baked with Parmesan cheese. Melanzana Parmesan is battered eggplant and tomato sauce with Italian cheeses, served over pasta. Manicotti, spaghetti, lasagna, and other pasta dishes and combinations are available.

House and seafood specials feature veal or chicken dishes, grilled steak, and surf and turf of rib-eye and lobster tail. Grilled Italian sausage, snow crab legs, crab cakes, orange roughy Italiano, scallops, and seafood platter combinations come with a choice of potato and salad or soup.

Benjamin thinks sometimes he should have gone to college, but this self-taught entrepreneur finds the restaurant business "never boring, always challenging." He has purchased land across the street, and my bet is that his determination, initiative, and common sense will take him a long way on the road of success.

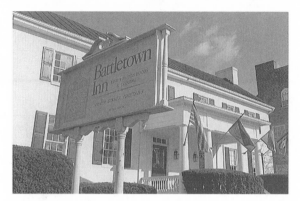

The Battletown Inn

BERRYVILLE

The Battletown Inn

102 WEST MAIN STREET
BERRYVILLE, VA. 22611
(800) 282-4106
WWW.BATTLETOWN.COM

Style	Casual nice
Meals	Lunch, Wednesday through Saturday; dinner, Tuesday through Saturday; Sunday brunch
Price Range	Moderate
Superlatives	Lovely atmosphere, peanut soup, "Rum Buns"
Extras	Full bar

*O*ne of the attractions around Berryville is Holy Cross Abbey, a Cistercian monastery that began in France in the year 1098. Another attraction—and an unusual one at that—is the Enders Mortuary Museum, which exhibits old caskets, embalming implements, and a horse-drawn hearse from 1889. Berryville was originally called Battletown because of its many tavern brawls. That may explain the museum, but what about the monastery?

It was in 1809 that a house was built in Berryville for Sara Stribling, daughter of the town's founder and namesake, Benjamin Berry. That house is now The Battletown Inn.

The inn looks important in its crisp white paint and dark green trim. The columns are elegant. Flags wave in the breeze. The American flag flies next to the navy-blue Virginia flag, adopted in 1861. A Clarke County flag and a hospitality banner are also displayed.

This place feels special the minute you walk in the door. It's light and bright, with fresh table linens and soft music. Windsor chairs are clustered around tables in intimate dining rooms on the first and second floors.

A smothered chicken dish is one of the popular items at lunch. Blackened prime rib sandwich and the "Chicken Blanquette"—creamed chicken and vegetables in a puff pastry shell—can be ordered with or without buttermilk-fried onion rings and what the menu bills as The Battletown Inn's "World-Famous Rum Buns." Soup, sandwiches, and burgers are also available.

Smoked salmon pâté and steamed mussels are among the appetizers. Dinners are served with a relish tray of apple butter, cottage cheese, watermelon pickles, and Jamaican relish, along with "Rum Buns," dinner rolls, and a sorbet intermezzo—often an apple cider sorbet made on the premises. The entrées include chicken and ham fettuccini, smoked pork loin, tournedos of beef, boneless duck breast, and vegetable stir-fry.

Desserts such as sweet potato flan, Shenandoah Mudslide, and blueberry apple crisp provide the perfect ending.

Prime rib Benedict might be worth the drive for Sunday brunch. Other entrées are quiche of the day, Chesapeake Bay Benedict, smoked salmon bagel, Huntsman's stew, and a crab cake sandwich.

The Gray Ghost Tavern, which opened upstairs in 1997, features fare such as pork barbecue, and black bean and sirloin chili, potato wedges, onion rings, Greek salad, chicken salad pita, and other simple stuff. It's open Tuesday through Friday evenings.

Bon Matin Bakery & Café

1 EAST MAIN STREET / BERRYVILLE, VA. 22611
(540) 955-1554

Style	Café
Meals	Breakfast and lunch, Tuesday through Saturday; light dinner, Friday; Sunday brunch
Price Range	Inexpensive
Superlatives	Baked goods

The name *Bon Matin*, French for "good morning," certainly fits this café. You're almost guaranteed to have a good morning if you start it here.

Jean-Francois Martin moved from France to Boston in the mid-1980s and found his way to Virginia. He opened Bon Matin in October of 1993.

The most prominent color inside is yellow. The entry is bordered by white lattice with real plants climbing up. Fluorescent lights on a wooden ceiling brighten an already well-lit space. Local artists bring their work in here to display and sell. It rotates every so often.

There's seating for a couple of dozen people at the round tables. You place your order at the bakery counter below the posted menu. It's then made fresh and delivered to you at your table or in a bag to go.

If you come for a morning repast, you can select a muffin or an éclair with juice, coffee—fancy or plain—or tea.

If you're here for lunch, it's a little more comprehensive. The house soup is tomato bisque, and there's a soup du jour, such as split pea or Maryland crab soup. The salad du jour might be navel orange on spinach with sliced red onions, strawberries, and strawberry vinaigrette. Regular salads include the "Mandarin Spinach Salad" and the "Savory Sampler."

There are three quiches each day. Among the sandwiches are turkey, chicken salad, tuna, ham and Swiss on sourdough, beef and herb cheese on French bread, and a seafood croissant.

And you can always get my favorite dessert—a cookie. If that's not enough, dive into some chocolate mousse cake or a fruit tart.

Sunday brunch consists of omelets, crêpes, quiche, French toast, a cheese plate, pastries, and assorted breads and muffins.

It's not a fancy place, but the food is handled with care, using fresh ingredients and healthy preparation. And they have cookies!

WINCHESTER

Café Sofia

2900 VALLEY AVENUE / WINCHESTER, VA. 22601
(540) 667-2950

Style	Casual nice
Meals	Lunch, Tuesday through Friday; dinner, Tuesday through Saturday
Price Range	Expensive
Superlatives	Bulgarian cuisine, fascinating place
Extras	full bar

*N*o matter how well traveled or well read you are, it's a safe bet that you'll know more about Bulgaria when you leave Café Sofia. The first lesson is that the restaurant is named Sofia for the capital city of Bulgaria.

Bozidar and Margarita Janakiev graduated in 1976 from Bulgaria's Institute of International Tourism and set out to introduce and increase awareness of Bulgaria, its culture, and cuisine. Instead of going to western Europe for a short time and returning home, the couple headed for the United States. They established their Winchester Restaurant at a time when lots of people couldn't put a pin on a world map to show where Bulgaria was even located.

Well, it's a country of 10 million, rich in tradition and beauty. It is bordered by Greece and Turkey on the south, Romania on the north, the Black Sea on the east, and Yugoslavia and Macedonia on the west. The famous Orient Express goes through Bulgaria.

The low building that houses Café Sofia is red, white, and green for the colors of the Bulgarian flag. On chilly days or evenings, a wood stove right inside the front door warms you immediately. The framed cross-stitch and embroidery on the walls and menu covers were done by Margarita, her mother, and her sister. Each one of these stunning detailed works of art showcases hours of tedious needlework. There's also a map of the country, etched in glass, and framed restaurant reviews, which have appeared in newspapers and magazines over the years, on the walls.

Your table will be draped in handmade linens with handmade plates. "Everything is touched by hand," Margarita points out. The personal touches are all around, and you will be filled with appreciation and warmed by the atmosphere before you taste a morsel.

Slavic cuisine with a Mediterranean influence is the focus of the food. Lunch is an à la carte adventure, while dinner is a three-course event.

There's a soup of the day, special Bulgarian salad with feta cheese, homemade breads, vegetables, and your choice of entrée. Appetizers and desserts are also offered.

Bulgaria is bordered on two sides by water—the Danube River on the north and the Black Sea on the east—so fish is abundant. Here at Café Sofia you may partake of salmon strudel, shrimp casserole, fresh flounder, crab cakes, or lobster tails broiled or stuffed with crabmeat.

Chicken pierogies, stuffed red bell peppers, shish kabob Spartacus, baked pasta with meat sauce, and stuffed cabbage rolls are among your choices. The vegetarian menu includes eggplant steak and stuffed grape leaves.

One of the house specials is Bulgarian mixed grill—*kebapcheta*, lamb chops, and pork tenderloin medallions, though you may order any one meat as a single dinner. *Kebapcheta*, the national dish of Bulgaria, is chopped beef and pork shaped into oblongs, mixed with spices, and grilled. The other house special is a Bulgarian trio of eggplant potato moussaka, beef goulash, and stuffed grape leaves.

Baklava, homemade yogurt (made daily) with raspberry sauce, and apple strudel are some of the sweet conclusions on the menu. This is a dining experience rich in culture and cuisine that shouldn't be missed by anyone.

Lynette's Triangle Diner

27 WEST GERRARD STREET
WINCHESTER, VA. 22601
(540) 667-7738

Style	Diner
Meals	Breakfast, lunch, and dinner, seven days a week
Price Range	Inexpensive. Credit cards and checks are not accepted.
Superlatives	Meat loaf, chipped beef gravy

*I*magine Patsy Cline serving up your breakfast, delivering a plate of honey-dipped chicken to your booth, or fillin' up your coffee cup. She worked in this diner as a teen, before her melodious voice captured the hearts of millions.

Lynette Booth also started working in the food business as a teen, rising to food and beverage director at a country club. Her dream was to have her own "mom and pop" place some day.

The Triangle Diner opened in 1948, and its slogan for decades has been "square meals since 1948." Lynette's dream came true when she bought the diner in October 2001.

The breakfast menu of eggs and meat, chipped beef or sausage gravy, hot cakes, French toast, omelets, breakfast sandwiches, grits and biscuits, and hot or cold cereal is served all day. Coffee is included in the prices, and Egg Beaters® are available for those watching cholesterol.

Two dozen sandwiches are available at lunch. Burgers, hot dogs, chili dogs, as well as grilled cheese, hot roast beef or turkey with mashed potatoes and gravy, tuna and chicken salad, BLTs, and club sandwiches—all that you expect from diner fare. There's also a crab cake sandwich, a grilled Philly steak and cheese sandwich with onions and fries, and beef barbecue on a bun. Chips and pickles are part of the sandwich deal.

The vegetable soup and the chili are homemade, and Lynette makes the meat loaf every day. Milk shakes are made the old-fashioned way with any flavor of the Hershey's ice cream at the diner. Sundaes and banana splits are offered.

For dinner entrées, you can find something fried, grilled, or baked. There's fried haddock or honey-dipped chicken, grilled chicken breast or pork chops, and, of course, meat loaf. The crab cakes, breaded veal steak with gravy, baby beef liver with onions, and shrimp in a basket come with two vegetables, a roll, and coffee or tea, like all the dinners.

Side orders include sweet potato sticks, beer-battered onion rings, applesauce, cottage cheese, macaroni salad, fruit salad, mashed potatoes, beets, and other things.

For dessert, you can order a piece of pie, which they will warm for you, or a slice of cake. And bring along a few quarters for the jukebox at your booth. They are some great artists' music from which to choose. I played all the Patsy Cline songs.

Tucano's Restaurant

12 SOUTH BRADDOCK STREET
WINCHESTER, VA. 22601
(540) 722-4557

Style	Casual nice
Meals	Lunch, Monday through Friday; dinner, Monday through Saturday. Reservations are recommended on weekends.
Price Range	Inexpensive/Moderate
Superlatives	Brazilian cuisine, shrimp Caesar
Extras	Full bar

*T*halma Ducarmo moved to Roanoke, Virginia, from Brazil in 1985 to live near her brother, Walner Pires, and his wife, Leila. They all worked in restaurants, and when they decided to have their own business, they looked for a small, historic town suitable for raising kids.

Winchester was chosen, and in November 1993, Tucano's opened. Tucano is the name of a bird native to Brazil, similar to the bird pictured on a box of Fruit Loops cereal, I'm told. The restaurant is in historic Winchester, and its old brick walls envelope an attractive white, black, and dark green interior.

At first glance, you might wonder if you'll understand the menu, but under the sections titled *carnes*, *peixes e mariscos*, and *aves*, after the Portuguese entrée name, you have a great description in English.

Entradas means "entry to dining" or appetizers. Hearts of palm in a cream sauce au gratin; sautéed shrimp in white wine with fresh tomatoes, onions, and garlic; and clams casino are three of the choices.

The seafood bisque has a tomato base, and Tucano's offer a unique potato soup, blended with collard greens and bits of sausage. The house dressing for salads is avocado vinaigrette.

Vegetarian entrées include *Prato Rico*, a delightful combination of rice, black beans, collard greens, fried bananas, and vegetable, or a dish with Shitake mushrooms and artichoke hearts. Pasta dishes with chicken, shrimp, or various vegetables are offered.

I've always enjoyed Brazilian cuisine for its fruit accompaniments and light sauces. The grilled pork loin, for example, comes with pineapple orange Calvado sauce, a fried banana, and vegetables. *Galinha tropicana* is chicken breast with pineapple and grapes in an orange brandy sauce.

Shrimp Caesar has shrimp rolled in veal, which is placed in a lemon-and-wine sauce, then served with pasta and vegetables. *Muqueca baiana* blends clams, scallops, shrimp, mussels, and white fish in a Brazilian sauce of palm oil and coconut. It is served with rice and Yuka sauce.

Veal medallions flounder, shrimp, scallops, clams, mussels, and several chicken entrées are offered,

in addition to chef suggestions for more house specials.

Brazilians don't rush through their food—in preparation or consumption, so you are asked to allow sufficient time for your fresh dinner to be cooked and served.

Homemade desserts such as crème brûlée and strawberry labomba are a perfect finish. The labomba is a torte similar to cheesecake, but better and lighter. Lighter is good, and Tucano's is great.

Violino

181 NORTH LOUDON STREET
WINCHESTER, VA. 22601
(540) 667-8006

Style	Fine dining
Meals	Lunch and dinner, Monday through Saturday
Price Range	Expensive. Reservations are recommended.
Superlatives	Homemade pasta, braised lamb shank
Extras	Full bar

*E*verything about Violino, including the owners, is a class act. On the outside, Violino is lettered on the building behind the American, Virginia, and Italian flags. A small outdoor dining area is neatly arranged for patio dining in nice weather.

Inside, the dominant color scheme is soft mint green with cream. The oil lamp on each table is like a small streetlamp with an etched globe. The chairs are light wood with green seats. The carpet is green. There are double linens and fresh flowers in tall vases on every table. Italian music is playing.

Many musical instruments are carefully mounted on the walls. There are violins, of course, trombones, a mandolin, guitars, a French horn, a saxophone, and others. Music students from the local Shenandoah Conservatory often stroll and sing in Violino during the weekend dinner hours.

Franco Stocco, who owns Violino with his wife, Marcella, and son, Riccardo, is a chef, an opera lover, and a former voice student. We don't know if he sings in the shower, but he might sing when he cooks, and he has been known to entertain with song in the dining room.

Franco and Marcella visited Washington, D.C., in 1985 and saw the opportunity to live and work in the United States. Franco worked for others and was in a restaurant partnership for five years before making his dream come true. Two dreams, actually. One to have his own restaurant, the other to become a United States citizen. He has accomplished both.

Father and son prepare traditional and contemporary Northern Italian dishes, using local, fresh produce and ingredients. Son Riccardo attended the highly respected Johnson & Wales culinary school, so he's a very well-educated sous chef to his dad.

All the pasta is homemade. Butternut squash tortellini and duck tortellini are a couple of their favorites. The braised lamb shank and braised rabbit are popular. Everything is prepared with great care. Vegetarian entrées are noted on the menu with a musical symbol. Veal, chicken, shrimp, salmon, as well as more fresh seafood and lasagna are offered in a variety of preparations.

The restaurant is entirely smoke-free, and they offer only Italian wines. Occasionally, they have limited quantities of unusual wines, which are offered by the glass or carafe. The family will assist you in any way with food explanations so your dining at Violino is a spectacular experience.

Espresso, cappuccino, coffees, and teas will accompany any of the homemade desserts, all of which are certain to be special treats. *Buon appetito*!

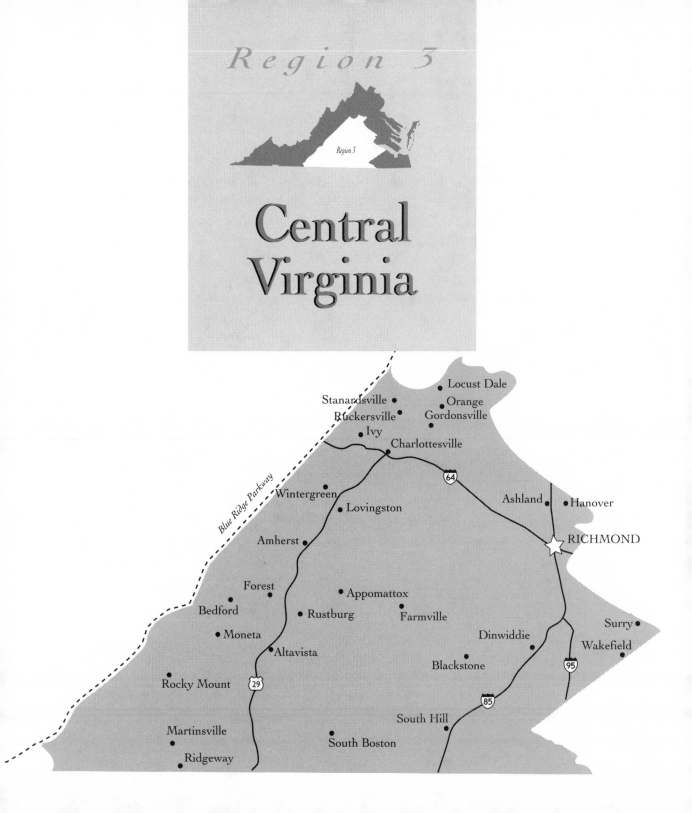

Region 3

Region 3

Central
Virginia

Locust Dale
Stanardsville
Orange
Ruckersville
Gordonsville
Ivy
Charlottesville
64
Wintergreen
Ashland
Hanover
Lovingston
Amherst
RICHMOND
Forest
Appomattox
Bedford
Rustburg
Farmville
Moneta
Surry
Dinwiddie
Altavista
Wakefield
Blackstone
Rocky Mount
29
95
85
South Hill
Martinsville
South Boston
Ridgeway

Blue Ridge Parkway

From the peanut farms and cotton fields in the southeast to the furniture and textile factories in the southwest to Thomas Jefferson's beloved homes in Poplar Forest and Charlottesville, this region is more diverse in geography and industry than any other in the state.

Buggs Island Lake, which straddles the North Carolina border, Smith Mountain Lake in the western part of the region, Lake Anna in the north, and the James River offer a plethora of water sports and some great fishing. Crabtree Falls in Nelson County is the highest waterfall in the eastern United States.

The land is gently rolling, the people are friendly, and the area is rich in history. Winery tours, horseback riding, antiquing, biking, golfing, and rock climbing are but a few of the activities to be enjoyed in the heart of the Commonwealth.

Clarence's

U.S. 220 / RIDGEWAY, VA. 24148
(276) 956-3400

Style	Family-style
Meals	Breakfast, lunch, and dinner, seven days a week
Price Range	Inexpensive/Moderate
Superlatives	Clean atmosphere, all-you-can-eat fish on Friday, "Pineapple Cheesecake"

*H*ere's a place with a good reputation far and wide—well, at least 50 miles to the north. All the way down U.S. 220, Clarence's was mentioned to me by regular folks and by restaurant owners as well.

This restaurant was opened by Clarence Pickurel in 1971. The big windows on the front and sides allow natural light into the cream and lavender dining areas. The vinyl chairs and booths are aqua. It's an unusual color scheme, but it's quite pleasant, especially with the prints of flowers and English-style cottages on the wall. Two private rooms with a single table in each are available for those who want to be away from the crowd. On the left in the back is a counter with five stools, a nice option for solo travelers.

Those who can't abide grits with their breakfast—that's us folks born north of the Mason-Dixon line—can get fried apples or hash browns with their eggs and breakfast meat. Brains and eggs, hot cakes, French toast, oatmeal, and all kinds of biscuits are also served.

Among the popular items at dinner are the "Chef's Specialties," which include a minced barbecue platter, chicken, chicken livers, and center-cut pork chops. The steaks are cut and prepared in the kitchen. Clarence's claims every bite to be tender, moist, and delicious, though the menu is clear on one thing: "Not responsible for well-done steaks." The fresh seafood comes with a baked potato or french fries, hush puppies, and slaw or a tossed salad. Golden oysters, frog legs, Gulf shrimp, catfish, and lobster are among the options.

The menu suggests that customers "ask about our delicious desserts," and indeed you should. The "Pineapple Cheesecake" is very popular. The other options include cherry pie and apple pie.

Don't give up if you're heading down U.S. 220 to eat here. It's an easy five miles past Martinsville in a stone building on the right.

Pigs R Us

1014 LIBERTY STREET
MARTINSVILLE, VA. 24112
(276) 632-1161
WWW.CHECKEREDPIG.COM

Style	Family-style
Meals	Lunch and dinner, Monday through Saturday
Price Range	Inexpensive
Superlatives	Barbecue

*T*ommy Houston volunteered as a fireman with

the Martinsville Volunteer Fire Company for years, then accepted one of the paid positions in the Martinsville Fire Department. When they needed someone to cook a pig, Tommy volunteered. "You're just babysitting a hog all night," he thought. "How hard can that be?"

Well, whatever it took, Tommy had the touch, and his barbecue career was born. He was asked to do cookouts for friends and cater some special events. The parties got bigger, and the requests continued to increase. In 1990, it was decision time for Tommy and his wife, Lisa. Is this going to be a hobby or a real business? Fortunately for barbecue lovers in the Martinsville region, they chose the business.

Firemen are a handy lot, and Tommy and his firefighter buddies built his brick building in the early 1990s. Pigs R Us officially opened, no joke, on April Fool's Day, 1994.

Of the many things that Tommy has learned along the way, one is that ham makes the best barbecue. You can make barbecue out of several parts of the pig, but Tommy insists on using only hams. They are leaner and make the best barbecue product.

On the menu, "Barbecue from the pit" lists dinners that come with two sides, french fries, and hush puppies. You can order pork, chicken, bones, pig out, or the chick-rib duo. "Between the buns" includes barbecue sandwiches, burgers if you must have one, hot dogs, and veggies on a bun.

There are salads, a kid's chow section, a couple of platters, and desserts headlined by a daily special and cobblers.

The good news is that you don't need to sit down and dine in to enjoy their barbecue. You can call or fax over an order for pick-up. They'll deliver in quantity. If you want more than five pounds, please give them 48 hours notice. Because they pit cook their hams every day, they occasionally run out. This may be inconvenient, but it certainly assures the freshest of pit-cooked barbecue.

Better yet, call together a bundle of friends, invite a few firemen perhaps, and let the catering arm of Pigs R Us handle your event. They have catered events all over the region and have participated in rib festivals as far away as Reno, Nevada.

Rania's Restaurant

147 EAST MAIN STREET
MARTINSVILLE, VA. 24112
(276) 638-4462

Style	Casual nice
Meals	Lunch and dinner, seven days a week. Reservations are recommended on weekends.
Price Range	Moderate
Superlatives	Seafood, rib-eye steak with Marsala or Bordelaise sauce
Extras	Full bar

Roberto Sanchez and Herber Albarado bought Rania's in downtown Martinsville in June 2001 and at once set about dressing it up inside and introducing more contemporary entrées.

Landscaped by low evergreen shrubs, Rania's is housed in a large white-brick building with a red sign. The interior is warm and inviting. Carefully refinished hardwood floors, wood trim, and a rustic wood ceiling are brightened with white walls and accented with red rope lights. Overhead recessed and track lighting is unobtrusive, and the dining areas are quieted and softened with red carpet.

Double linens in white and burgundy grace the tables, even at lunchtime, and fresh flowers and oil candles create a lovely environment for an enjoyable time. There is a variety of red chairs at tables, as well as semi-circle booths with chairs on one side of the tables. The booths have attractive, floral cushions on the wall benches on the other side of the tables.

Chicken and shrimp Alfredo, grilled salmon Caesar salad, flounder filet amandine, and fresh blackened tilapia are some of the lunch specials, and you can always order a club sandwich or turkey burger.

Pizza toppings run the gamut from pepperoni, ham, and ground beef to spinach, broccoli, eggplant, and garlic. To take your pizza to a higher level, you can choose to top with scallops, shrimp, and crabmeat or chicken, basil, and tomatoes.

There's a strong presence of pasta and Italian dishes such as baked ziti, manicotti, stuffed shells, lasagna, and eggplant parmigiana, but devote a fair amount of attention to the Rania's dinner specials.

Pork loin teriyaki, snapper Florentine, flounder with crab and capers, and filet mignon in a mushroom sauce are gaining in popularity as dinner favorites.

The desserts are homemade and vary often, with New York cheesecake, tiramisu, chocolate mousse cake, and crème brûlée with homemade vanilla ice cream appearing frequently.

On Friday and Saturday nights, light piano music is performed live on the baby grand, located right across the foyer from the entrance. The atmosphere is lovely; the staff is charming; the food is very good.

MARTINSVILLE

Runway Café

525 AIRPORT ROAD / MARTINSVILLE, VA. 24112
(276) 957-CAFE
WWW.RUNWAYCAFE.NET

Style	Casual nice
Meals	Lunch, Tuesday through Sunday; dinner, Friday and Saturday. Reservations are recommended for dinner.
Price Range	Moderate
Superlatives	Filet mignon, fresh seafood
Extras	Full bar

At the suggestion of someone in Woolwine, we followed the "Airport" sign off U.S. 58 about 15 miles west of Martinsville. In less than a mile, another sign took us left alongside a small runway to a one-story, tan, stucco structure. There was no sign here, so I popped inside to see where the Runway Café might be, only to discover the classy little restaurant right inside this unassuming terminal building.

There are well over 50 seats inside and four tables and a couple of benches outside. White walls with gray trim have a variety of flying-related prints and photos. Each table sports fresh bamboo shoots in water, and the whole place is clean and bright.

The brightness can be explained by the wall of glass that looks directly out on the runway. While mulling over the lunch menu of bombers (burgers served with seasoned fries), fighters (super sandwiches served with chips), and the kiddy cockpit choices for the young 'uns, it hit me. The sign.

Outside protruding slightly over the window wall was a bright blue awning. I walked outside and there it was. "Runway Café" printed neatly on the awning with their little logo of a plane towing the sign—for the pilots to read! You see, they're packed many weekend nights with people who fly in for dinner. It is logical, in retrospect, that the Runway Café sign should face the runway.

I passed on the B-52, B-24, and B-17 in favor of the B-25, a traditional cheeseburger grilled to perfection. The first-class Philly is served with caramelized onions and peppers, while the bi-plane consists of smoked turkey on marble bread with spicy Creole dressing, kraut, and Jack cheese—a Reuben sort of sandwich.

The ultra-lights are comprehensive salads such as grilled chicken with a bacon vinaigrette dressing, the chef salad, or mixed greens with plum tomatoes, radishes, cucumbers, and cheese. Torpedoes are franks with a flair.

The linens and small oil lamps come out for dinner. The appetizers include citrus Gulf shrimp and a Mediterranean appetizer for two of pita, feta, kalomata olives, cucumbers, shrimp, and special dressing. All dinners are accompanied by a house salad and warm bread and butter. The filet mignon is complemented with a white wine Dijon cream sauce and served with a blend of mashed seasoned potatoes, seasonal vegetables, and a blue cheese–stuffed plum tomato. Chicken, rib-eye steak, fresh fish, and daily specials round out the evening entrées.

White chocolate lemon cheesecake, espresso cheesecake, chocolate mousse layer cake, or the Snickers mountain specialty might be on the dessert menu.

Despite that lack of signage for us landlubbers, this restaurant is located at the Blue Ridge Regional Airport, which serves Martinsville. Maybe the sign is on the roof for the pilots. After all, this is an airport.

Style	Family-style
Meals	Dinner, Tuesday through Sunday
Price Range	Moderate
Superlatives	Old music, rib-eye steaks, homemade bread
Extras	Beer and wine

When Boston, Massachusetts, was closed by the British because of the Boston Tea Party, Virginians passed a resolution of support for the New Englanders and named two settlements Boston. When this city was chartered in 1796, it was called South Boston to avoid confusion with the Boston in Culpeper County. Located on the Dan River and incorporated in 1884, South Boston is one of the country's leading tobacco markets.

When the Thomas Long Steak House opened in a South Boston strip mall in 1976, there were three things on the menu: shrimp cocktails, rib-eye steaks, and cheesecake.

Soon thereafter, a high-school kid named Billy McGhee started working there. He bought it in 1988, and moved it to this freestanding log building on the edge of the parking lot.

Mary and Leonard Crabtree bought the restaurant in July 2002. She has worked as a waitress part-time over the years and retired from a CPA firm. Leonard retired from manufacturing. Some people just don't handle retirement well; they still have too much energy.

The wood interior with red-and-white-checkered fabric and soft ceiling lights sets a rustic tone in the two dining rooms, which can seat 160 people. You'll hear a musical mix of classical and local CDs.

Two of MC Crabtree's signature items are homemade, white or wheat, sourdough bread and zucchini banana bread. In addition to the soup and salad bar, diners may frequent the restaurant's cheese bar. Shrimp cocktails and rib-eye steaks still command center stage on the menu, but the entrées now include New York strip, filet mignon, scallops, pork, prime rib, seafood platters, hot or cold shrimp, and chicken. Baked potatoes, sweet potatoes, or steak fries come with the meals. Vegetables are steaming in the crockpot on weekends.

The desserts are homemade. Light, airy lemon pie, banana pudding, and chocolate éclair cake sound like great ways to end a dinner.

SOUTH HILL

Kahill's

1799 NORTH MECKLENBERG AVENUE
SOUTH HILL, VA. 23950
(804) 447-6941

Style	Pub
Meals	Breakfast, lunch, and dinner, seven days a week
Price Range	Moderate
Superlatives	Seafood and steak specials, 22-ounce prime rib
Extras	Full bar

In the days when South Hill was known by one of its early names—Ridgefork or Binford's

Tavern—financiers purchased 56 acres around the local railroad depot and laid out a circular town one and a quarter miles in diameter. It was incorporated as South Hill in 1901 and was one of only three circular municipalities in the United States as late as 1958. It has since been reconfigured. Today, fishing events are so popular in this area that South Hill has been referred to as "Tournament Town."

Located at Exit 15 off I-85, Kahill's is a former country store and rental house that has been transformed into an English-style pub and restaurant. Tom Flowers, the owner, opened the place in 1991.

The bar sports some old signs, a large Clint Eastwood poster, and banners from the University of Virginia and Virginia Tech. The neat, rustic dining room features an eclectic mix of antiques from Tom's father's collection, things Tom has picked up, and items brought in by patrons. Paintings by local artists adorn the walls and are for sale at reasonable prices. The wood-pegged floors and the log walls below the chair rail enhance the warmth of the place. In nice weather, the large outdoor patio is open.

Kahill's offers comprehensive meals three times a day.

You can select the "Cowboy Chili Breakfast," eggs Benedict, a breakfast burrito, or an omelet stuffed with your choice of cheese, crabmeat, chili, smoked salmon, salsa, or a number of other things. Cereal, grits, hash browns, and pancakes are also available.

Great sandwiches, burgers, and pasta selections

Kahill's

are offered at lunch. Reubens, steak sandwiches, big chili dawgs, knockwurst with pastrami, sauerkraut and Swiss, BBQ chicken, and smoked turkey croissant are among the favorites. There are also plenty of salads and quesadillas.

Pasta dishes are garnished with scallions and Parmesan and come with a garden salad or vegetable. Chicken, smoked sausage, and Cajun Alfredo is one possibility. Scallops with artichokes, feta, and sun-dried tomatoes is another, and there are several more.

Most of the dinner appetizers feature something from the sea. "Scallops Tova" and BBQ shrimp with bacon are among the choices. The entrées include a variety of meals such as pork tenderloin, cream cheese-and-herb-stuffed filet, baby back ribs, rack of lamb, teriyaki rib-eye, or blackened filet. Dinners come with roasted garlic mashed potatoes and a vegetable medley.

Business has been good here, as evidenced by the

addition of 75 seats in 1996. The place can now accommodate 150. Guests can join the crowd around the bar or take a quiet place in the dining room.

The Blue Moon
U.S. 220
ROCKY MOUNT, VA. 24151
(540) 483-2070

Style	Family-style
Meals	Lunch, Sunday through Friday; dinner, seven days a week
Price Range	Inexpensive/Moderate
Superlatives	Chicken kabobs, baby back ribs
Extras	Wine and beer

*I*n the year 1964, Beatlemania swept the nation, my brother Bobby and Bill Clinton graduated from high school (in different parts of the country) and 21-year-old Jerry Leonard began delivering bread to a Dairy Queen in Martinsville.

The DQ owner loved to complain about his partner, Jerry noticed. Soon after, the bread man became the new partner. That partnership, like the one before it, didn't last, but Jerry found he liked the restaurant business. In 1967, he opened the Redwood Steakhouse. Ten years later, he moved here, about a mile north of Rocky Mount and renamed the restaurant Jerry's.

In November 2002, Sam and Sandy Azzam purchased the place and a year later, re-named it The Blue Moon. The couple spent 20 years in the auto-repair business in Colorado. Sandy grew up in Charlotte, and while looking for a business in North Carolina, they found this one in Virginia.

The small eating area to the right can accommodate a couple dozen folks and the middle room where you enter the restaurant, another dozen; both rooms are wood paneled and have booths. At least 75 or 80 guests can sit in the comfortable wallpapered room to the left.

The inexpensive lunch specials are a great deal. Our waitress stressed that almost everything that can be made on the premises is. She recommended the liver and onions. My husband, John, eats anything, so he took her recommendation. I ordered broiled flounder, along with macaroni and cheese and peach cobbler for my "vegetables." Sandwiches, burgers, and salads are available, too.

Sirloin steak, chicken kabobs, baby back ribs, and surf and turf are among the house specialties. Fresh seafood such as deviled crabs, crab cakes, oysters, shrimp, and a seafood platter are offered. You can also order spaghetti, chicken, ham steak, and beef tips. All dinners come with a salad, a vegetable, and hot bread.

The brownie under hot fudge and ice cream is homemade. Considerately, they have sugar-free pies, along with coconut cream pie and gourmet desserts such as cheesecakes and specialty chocolate cakes.

The Blue Moon is a comfortable place where the waitresses are efficient and pleasant, and everyone is friendly.

Franklin Restaurant

20221 VIRGIL H. GOODE HIGHWAY
ROCKY MOUNT, VA. 24151
(540) 483-5601

Style	Family-style
Meals	Breakfast, lunch, and dinner, seven days a week
Price Range	Inexpensive
Superlatives	Chopped sirloin, Hawaiian chicken

*T*he Franklin Restaurant sits in an attractive brick building on the west side of U.S. 220 about half a mile south of the big furniture mart. The sign is large, and the outdoor window boxes are ablaze with color in summer. Two bay windows and two greenhouse dining areas in the front look inviting.

The building was constructed in the 1950s, and Kaye Perdue went to work part-time as a waitress in 1978. Just shy of 20 years later, she bought the business and continues to work here with her three sisters, Sandy, Jean, and Teresa.

The interior is a clean, cozy combination of striped wallpaper, teal colors, dark stained wood, and red brick. Breakfast starts every day at 6 A.M. Eggs, pancakes, French toast, country ham steak — the expected, the good breakfast foods.

The modestly priced, unlimited soup, salad, and vegetable bar attracts a fair amount of the lunch crowd. Others have chicken salad or tuna salad plates, burgers, subs, or club, grilled, or triple-decker sandwiches.

The hot open sandwiches are available for lunch or dinner. The chopped sirloin is incredibly popular, though sirloin, rib-eye, and New York strip steaks are also offered. Pasta dishes include chicken cutlet, and veal or eggplant Parmesan, all served with spaghetti. Lasagna and the spaghetti special include the soup and salad bar.

Country ham steak, sautéed chicken livers, pork chops, beef livers, and breaded chuck-wagon steak are served with two vegetables. Fresh catfish comes broiled or fried with your choice of potato and the soup and salad bar.

The pie and cake desserts change often. Other desserts, such as peach cobbler, are so good, they might run out before you order them. They also have ice cream such as cherry and pecan.

The Blackwater Café

4730 SCRUGGS ROAD / MONETA, VA. 24121
(540) 721-4333

Style	Family-style
Meals	Breakfast on weekends in summer; lunch is served occasionally; dinner, Tuesday through Saturday
Price Range	Moderate
Superlatives	Prosciutto-wrapped scallops, crab cakes, dessert tortes
Extras	Full bar

*T*he small town of Moneta is the main host town

The Blackwater Café

for Smith Mountain Lake, the second largest lake in Virginia with 500 miles of shoreline. Special water events such as a bass fishing tournament, wine festival, and antique and classic boat show go on all year.

While the rest of us were playing "house" or "school" or "dress-up" as children, Judy Johnson and her sister were playing "dining room"—setting tables, taking each other's orders, serving pretend meals and drinks. So, after years in the corporate world in Ohio and New Jersey, Judy decided to try her hand at the real thing.

She chose an Adirondack theme and a local river name. Bears, moose, canoes, outdoor themes, and rustic wood encircle you in the warm, inviting dining rooms.

Those who like to start at the beginning of the dinner experience will find appetizers from the sea, the meadow, and the garden. Fried calamari or escargot might be featured. Baked brie encrusted in puff pastry is highlighted with a raspberry pepper sauce, and Swiss chard wraps or spinach artichoke dip might whet your appetite.

House salad or Caesar salad is part of dinner though you can order a more elaborate blackened salmon Cobb salad or a Greek salad. Light fare items include an open-faced crab cake sandwich, a classic Reuben, and smoked chicken grilled with freshly roasted peppers and Fontina cheese on ciabatta bread. Soup of the day could be roasted red pepper and corn chowder.

The dinner menu has a wonderful variety of entrées. Their signature Porterhouse steak is a generous 16 ounces, and the slow-roasted, braised lamb shank brings a taste of the Piedmont region of Italy to your palate. Freshwater rainbow trout in a light butter sauce comes stuffed with crabmeat. One of the house specialties, prosciutto-wrapped scallops, is served in a smoked Gouda and basil cream sauce.

Pastas also come with salad or soup. Lobster ravioli, chicken and artichoke bowtie pasta, baked penne pasta and shrimp, and scallop linguini are some of the dishes.

It's not a big step from here into an Adirondack environment, and you can complete the outdoorsy feeling with campfire s'mores for dessert. You make them right at your table.

Should you prefer your dessert all made up for you, consider the hot fudge sundae cheesecake—New York-style cheesecake all dressed up like a sundae with hot fudge sauce, whipped cream, and a long-stem cherry on top. Bread pudding and little apple pies in maple-glazed crust—big enough for two—give you two more reasons to stick around for dessert. Or, you could start with dessert and work your way backward through dinner.

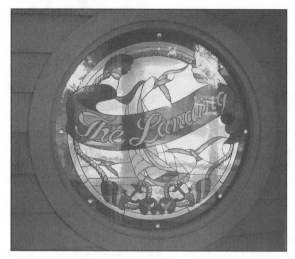

The Landing

The Landing

773 ASHMEADE ROAD / MONETA, VA. 24121
(540) 721-3028
WWW.THELANDING.NET

Style	Casual nice
Meals	Lunch, Wednesday through Saturday, during the summer only; dinner, Tuesday through Sunday, year-round; Reservations are recommended for dinner.
Price Range	Moderate
Superlatives	She-crab soup, homemade crab cakes, Polish pound cake
Extras	Full bar

*T*he intersection of Va. 122 and Va. 616 is called Westlake Corner. At this intersection, turn onto Va. 616, also known as Scruggs Road, and continue about 10 miles. Bear left at the Bernard's Landing Conference Center sign. The Landing Restaurant, which is not part of the conference center, is on the left less than a half-mile.

Peacefulness reigns at lakefront restaurants, and The Landing is no exception. The view from the dining room over the marina and across Smith Mountain Lake is lovely, and the soft gray and cream interior is soothing. Each table is covered with cream linens with a bottle of S. Pellegrino mineral water and a small oil lamp.

Howard and Janet Schlosser brought a wealth of restaurant experience to The Landing when they purchased it in 1997. A few years later, they started The Metro Restaurant in Roanoke, another casual nice, dining establishment, and their combined chef staff has taken numerous awards for culinary achievement.

Appetizers and lighter fare in dishes such as the quail salad and Bahamian-style conch fritters exemplify the chef's creativity. A seared yellowfin tuna is sliced thin and served over seaweed salad with kabiyaki and miso sauce. Specials on the salad list could be watermelon salad or heirloom tomato salad with Parmesan bruschetta toast.

Freshly seared grouper is a house specialty. Char-grilled swordfish, Peking duck, and prime rib also grace the menu. Plates are artfully arranged with potatoes and chef's choice of vegetable.

If it's not summer, call ahead for the lunch and brunch schedule. Lunch on the outdoor patio is pleasant. A canopy of oak leaves shades the entire area, and ducks quack and swim at the waterfront just a few feet away. Crab cake sandwiches, tuna melts, chicken clubs, salmon cakes, and prime-rib sandwiches are usually on the menu. Salads are generous, and casual fare includes fish 'n' chips, cornmeal fried oysters, hot wings, and a soup of the day.

Whether you boat over, drive in, or walk, The Landing will satisfy your appetite and provide a soothing dining experience.

Betty's Kitchen

534 MAIN STREET / ALTAVISTA, VA. 24517
(434) 369-5363

Style	Home-style
Meals	Breakfast, lunch and dinner, seven days a week
Price Range	Inexpensive
Superlatives	Cuban sandwich, hamburger steak

*M*eaning "high view" in Spanish, Altavista was the first town organized in Campbell County. It was chartered in 1907 by the Lane brothers, whose cedar chests are known around the world. Today, the Lane Company employs more than 1,000 people at its local plant.

What is now one of Altavista's favorite places to eat and catch up on town news started a little more than 15 years ago as a fancy establishment with linens, burnt-orange paint, and small brass chandeliers. After a couple of struggling years, the restaurant was taken over by Richard and Sandra Mattox, who immediately took off the linens and put in some booths.

In 1998, their niece, Debbie Lewis, bought the restaurant. She's decorated with old, black-and-white photos of the area, so you can get a history lesson and an idea of what things looked like a long time ago.

There's a feeling here that you've stepped back in time. And that's just fine when it comes to the food, which is simple, everyday fare.

Breakfast is a well-rounded meal of ham, bacon or sausage, eggs, home fries, apples, tomatoes, and homemade biscuits or toast. Of course, you can also order pancakes, waffles, French toast, cereal, omelets, breakfast sandwiches, and biscuits.

Lunch is equally simple: sandwiches, burgers, salads, homemade soup in winter. The Cuban sandwich is made with marinated pork, ham, Swiss cheese, pickles, and mustard on a grilled Hoagie bun. Debbie tested this one at a wine festival and found it was appealing to lots of folks, so it went on the menu.

The dinner plates number 25. They run the gamut from baked fish and salmon cakes to chicken livers,

Betty's Kitchen

pork chops, and country-style steak. Mashed potatoes and gravy come with some entrées; two vegetables come with most everything.

Debbie insists on serving homemade yeast rolls with dinners. The Saturday-night special is barbecued ribs, all you can eat, and fried catfish is one of the specials on Wednesday evenings.

If you're on the go, call in your order for pickup. If you're not in a hurry, you can sit back and enjoy yourself with cherry, apple, or peach cobbler.

Mitchell's

103 SOUTH MAIN STREET
BLACKSTONE, VA. 23824
(804) 292-4100

Style	Pub
Meals	Breakfast, lunch, and dinner, seven days a week
Price Range	Inexpensive/Moderate
Superlatives	Chicken, gyros
Extras	Full bar

There's an interesting contrast in decorating in this former five-and-dime.

The booths are old and high backed. There are two bars, located in the back on the left and right. The tables are topped with cedar wood. Tall plants—real ones—stand in the front windows. Variegated philodendrons weave their way across the front ledges.

Eggs, biscuits, and hot cakes are available at breakfast.

At lunch, you can order sandwiches and burgers. Fried chicken and rotisserie chicken are big sellers. There are lots of boxes and buckets to go.

Dinner is a more comprehensive event, with appetizers, salads, "Stella's Greek Menu," and house specialties. Stella is owner Gus Mitchell's mother. Her Greek salads, gyros, and steak sandwiches are very popular. The house specialties are surf and turf and "Fin-'n'-Feather." There are additional menu sections for beef, seafood, poultry, and pork. You can order such items as Delmonico steak, a seafood platter, a sliced turkey dinner, a country ham steak (which translates to salt cured), or a Virginia ham steak (which translates to sugar cured).

You shouldn't be surprised to see baklava on the dessert menu here. If that's a little rich, you can try rice pudding or pie. Or you can stick with something really simple, like soft-serve ice cream.

DINWIDDIE

The Home Place

14712 SPRING CREEK ROAD
DINWIDDIE, VA. 23841
(804) 469-9596

Style	Family-style
Meals	Breakfast, lunch and dinner, seven days a week; Sunday brunch
Price Range	Inexpensive/Moderate
Superlatives	Setting, apple pie, ribs, prime rib
Extras	Wine and beer

Formed in 1752, Dinwiddie County was named for Robert Dinwiddie, deputy to the royal governor and the earl of Albemarle. The county seat was at Dinwiddie Courthouse; the name was shortened to Dinwiddie somewhere along the line. Pamplin Park Civil War Site, located in Dinwiddie County, preserves the scene of the battle fought here on April 2, 1865. The site includes Tudor Hall, a plantation home built around 1812 that has been renovated to reflect its days as the headquarters of Confederate general Samuel McGowan.

The Home Place is one of those tucked-away

spots you might not find on your own, although it's just a few miles from Exit 53 off I-85 and a few hundred feet from U.S. 1. Your clue to turn off U.S. 1 is a little blue sign appropriately marked "Food." You'll be on a gravel road bounded by trees. The sign at the parking lot is a little more descriptive: "The Home Place Restaurant. Thanks for not giving up."

Owners William and Ethel Daniel live on the property. They've operated the restaurant since 1986 in a converted barn built by Ethel's parents in 1922.

The big, old wagon near the entrance overflows with colorful chrysanthemums and pumpkins in the fall. The brown-painted barnboard walls in the dining room feature old-fashioned wall lights akin to railroad lamps. Tables next to large picture windows opposite the front door overlook a small, peaceful, spring-fed lake you won't see until you're inside. Of course, you may have noticed the ducks and geese waddling about the grounds on your way in.

If you're here for breakfast, you can choose from among fresh eggs, Virginia country ham, sausage, bacon, homemade buttermilk biscuits, red-eye gravy, and pancakes.

For lunch, there's homemade soup, salads, onion rings, cheese sticks, and sandwiches.

You can order big-city stuff at dinnertime—shrimp cocktails, Delmonico steak, prime rib, beef or pork ribs, country-cured ham, and a number of seafood entrées, including homemade crab cakes.

The biscuits and pies are homemade from Mrs. Daniel's own recipes.

The restaurant's brochure says you'll find The Home Place "a refreshing change from the ordinary." And indeed you will.

The Virginia Diner

The Virginia Diner

U.S. 460 / WAKEFIELD, VA. 23888
(757) 899-3106
WWW.VADINER.COM

Style	Family-style
Meals	Breakfast, lunch, and dinner, seven days a week
Price Range	Inexpensive/Moderate
Superlatives	Peanut soup, peanut pie
Extras	Wine and beer

There's no traffic light in this town, so be alert. You'll see stores and gas stations on both sides of U.S. 460 for a short distance, then you'll be back in the peanut fields. This is the heart of peanut country. The town was named by Mrs. Billy Mahone for *The Vicar of Wakefield*, the classic Oliver Goldsmith novel. The wife of the president of the Norfolk and Western Railway, Mrs. Mahone was allowed to name some of the rail stops.

Started in a refurbished railroad car in 1929, The Virginia Diner has grown steadily thanks to its reputation for down-home cooking. Various dining rooms were added to the little train car for nearly 60 years, until it finally became necessary to replace the old with the new. At that point, the Galloway family, which has owned the restaurant since 1976, built a very large diner on the same land.

Big windows fill the place with natural light, and the red-and-white-checked tablecloths and bentwood chairs lend a country feeling. The aroma of peanuts from the gift and gourmet shop right inside the front door pervades the place. In fact, the diner is often referred to as the "Peanut Capital of the World" for once having served peanuts instead of after-dinner mints. The diner's flourishing mail-order business now ships peanuts around the world.

Breakfast is typical Southern fare: eggs, ham, bacon, sausage, grits, hash browns, homemade biscuits.

Ham sandwiches, crab cakes, and barbecue served with a special sauce are on the lunch menu. The entrées include ham, chicken and dumplings, country-fried steak, soft-shell crabs, and a crab cake dinner.

Southerners have a broad spectrum of what they consider vegetables. Here, spoon bread, macaroni and cheese, and applesauce are listed among the vegetable choices. But if you're serious about your vegetables and about being Southern, you can order black-eyed peas, turnip greens, candied yams, or green beans.

At The Virginia Diner, it's possible to begin and end your meal with the peanut theme, starting with peanut soup and finishing with peanut pie.

SURRY

Surrey House
VA. 31 / SURRY, VA. 23883
(800) 200-4977 OR (804) 294-3389

Style	Family-style
Meals	Breakfast, lunch, and dinner, seven days a week
Price Range	Inexpensive/Moderate
Superlatives	Ham, peanut soup, "Peanut Raisin Pie"
Extras	Wine and beer

After settling Jamestown on the northern side of the James River, some colonists decided they wanted to live on the southern side. They called their settlement Surrey, after the English county of the same name, which lies across the Thames River from London. At some point, a clerical error dropped the *e* from the names of the Virginia county and town, which have been written as Surry ever since.

The Surrey House, however, uses the original spelling. It's one of those places that takes you back in time not too far, just to the fifties.

Established in 1954, the Surrey House is a classic example of that era's roadside restaurants with motel units. It's white with black trim.

The restaurant has an unusual V-shaped counter and 10 stools right inside the front door. To the left and right are knotty-pine dining areas with royal blue linens. Between the booths and tables, 120 people can be seated.

The Surrey House serves Virginia cuisine under the watchful eye of Mike Stevens, who purchased the business in 1993. Early in 2000, he acquired the eleven motel units, so all the business is run under one hat.

Located just a quarter-mile down the road are the S. Wallace Edwards & Sons smokehouses, which have been curing award-winning hams for three generations. It's no surprise, then, that many of the menu items at the Surrey House feature ham. For example, you can order a Virginia ham dinner, a ham steak, ham croquettes, or ham with a quarter-chicken. There's a sandwich of Edwards ham and Swiss cheese stacked on rye. The chili is garnished with small slices of fresh ham laid neatly across the top under grated cheese.

Other entrées come from the water. The James River, located just a couple of miles away, opens into the Chesapeake Bay, from whence come the makings of crab cakes and various seafood dinners.

Among the desserts the Surrey House is most proud of are its world-famous "Peanut Raisin Pie," its freshly made cobblers, and lemon chess pie.

Charleys Waterfront Café

201B MILL STREET / FARMVILLE, VA. 23903
(434) 392-1566

Style	Casual nice
Meals	Lunch, Monday through Saturday; dinner, seven days a week; Sunday brunch
Price Range	Inexpensive/Moderate
Superlatives	Rustic atmosphere, "Peppercorn Filet Madeira"
Extras	Full bar

Though Farmville doesn't have the most exciting name in the world, most visitors are pleasantly surprised by this friendly, active, interesting town along the Appomattox River. Founded in 1798, Farmville has a nice blend of retirees, working folks, and students at Hampden-Sydney College and Longwood College.

Charleys Waterfront Café is located in a former tobacco warehouse more than a century and a quarter old. It was the first restaurant mentioned by everyone I surveyed in and out of the shops and offices along Main Street.

It's like a very large fern bar—lots of brass and cedar and plants with little white lights strung in them. Small copper hanging lamps illuminate the spacious dining areas. If the weather is agreeable, guests can dine at wrought-iron tables with dark green umbrellas on a patio overlooking the river. The whole place exudes a classy rustic atmosphere.

The sandwiches come with a dill spear and french fries. Charleys offers a chicken sandwich with chicken, sliced apple, cheddar cheese, and honey barbecue sauce on a sub roll. The burgers weigh in at half a pound, and you can order a po' boy of fried oysters on a baguette with lettuce and cocktail sauce.

Roasted red pepper and crab soup, beef and bean chili, and French onion soup are offered. The dinner menu is changed four times a year, so you may not always find the "Outer Banks Crab Cakes" and the grilled tuna. A quiche of the day and chicken fixed a number of ways are pretty constant on the menu.

With homemade desserts such as triple chocolate fantasy cake and flowerpot frozen mousse with marinated pound cake and Kahlua whipped cream, you might start with dessert and see if there's room left over for lunch.

There's another Charleys—called Charleys Stony Point Café—on Stony Point Road in Richmond. Once affiliated with the chain of the same name, these two restaurants are now independent. In fact, the name Charleys—with or without the apostrophe, and spelled *-eys* or *-ies* at the end—is supposedly the most popular restaurant name in the country.

Walker's Diner

307 NORTH MAIN STREET
FARMVILLE, VA. 23901
(434) 392-4230

Style	Diner
Meals	Breakfast and lunch, Monday through Saturday
Price Range	Inexpensive
Superlatives	Old-fashioned diner atmosphere, home-cooked vegetables

*H*ere's a tiny place you shouldn't miss if you have an affection for old diners. The entire restaurant measures around 24 feet long and eight feet wide. That's total width—customer walking space, stools, counter, worker walking space, grills, dishes. Almost everything behind the counter is stainless steel. At the far end—which of course isn't very far— are big windows and wallpaper with a blue flower print.

Eggs, omelets, hot cakes, bacon, sugar-cured ham, and a variety of other breakfast meats are offered. For the adventurous breakfast eater—or perhaps the person who needs to think hard during the day ahead—there are brains and eggs.

At lunch, sandwiches, burgers, beef stew, country ham, roast beef, breaded veal steak, salads, and a vegetable plate are among the choices. Daily specials are also offered. The barbecue special and the corn pudding and fried chicken special are particularly popular among the Hampden-Sydney College crowd who drop in here for a bite. Turnip greens are on the vegetable list. All the hot sandwiches are served with creamed potatoes—that's mashed potatoes made with cream—and gravy.

The dessert list is short: homemade cake. Depending on when you get here, there might still be some strawberry, pineapple upside down, or chocolate cake available.

Because this place is so small, you can expect any conversation to be overheard. The lady on the stool next to me passed along some information on restaurants she liked in other parts of the state. And she let me know that she often leaves her horse farm to drive to Farmville, her hometown, to stop in at Walker's.

Granny Bee's

MAIN STREET / APPOMATTOX, VA. 24522
(434) 352-2259

Style	Home-style
Meals	Breakfast and lunch, seven days a week; dinner, Monday through Saturday
Price Range	Inexpensive
Superlatives	USDA choice steaks, roast beef, homemade pies

*F*ormerly known as Appomattox Court House, this is one of the most famous towns in Virginia. It was here on Sunday, April 9, 1865, that Robert E. Lee surrendered the Army of Northern Virginia to Ulysses S. Grant at the home of Wilmer McLean.

That historic event is remembered today at Appomattox Court House National Historical Park. Appomattox is also the birthplace of country and bluegrass great Joel Sweeney, the man who invented the banjo.

Located on Main Street in Appomattox is the restaurant known as Granny Bee's. Granny Bee, whose real name is Betty Drinkard, got her nickname from her first granddaughter, Mary Elizabeth, who wanted to distinguish between her two grandmothers, both of whom went by Granny.

In the early 1980s, Granny Bee was looking for something to do, so she opened this restaurant. Lewis and Daphine Moore bought it in June 2000. Lewis retired from the transportation business, and Daphine retired from working at their dry cleaning businesses, which their son now operates. The Moores ate here all the time, so they just bought the place when it was available.

They expanded the restaurant into what used to be office space, so it seats about 90, and they brought in some antiques for decoration. Some of the antiques were given to them by customers. The most unusual one came from Jack Baker. It's a rope device designed to drop onto the head of a railroad fireman when his coal train was about to enter a tunnel, thereby warning him to duck.

The "Country Boy Special" is among the breakfast choices at Granny Bee's. It includes two eggs, home fries, two strips of bacon, a sausage, a pancake, and biscuits or toast. Waffles, eggs, steak, hot cakes, omelets, and biscuits are also available.

At lunch, sandwiches can be ordered on homemade rolls. The lunch plates come with a meat, two vegetables, a homemade roll, and coffee or tea.

USDA choice steaks, along with prime rib, rib-eye steak, and filet mignon are on the dinner menu, along with baked ham, country ham, grilled chicken, shrimp, and fish. Pork loin and chicken and beef livers have been added. All meals come with a choice of potato or vegetables or salad and homemade rolls.

Daphine makes lots of the desserts, such as cakes and lemon meringue pie, chocolate pie, and peanut butter pie.

RUSTBURG
Jack's Place
U.S. 501 AT VA. 24
RUSTBURG, VA. 24588
(434) 332-5491

Style	Family-style
Meals	Breakfast, lunch, and dinner, Monday through Saturday
Price Range	Inexpensive
Superlatives	Squeaky-clean setting, chili, peach cobbler

*T*he county seat of Campbell County, Rustburg was named for Jeremiah Rust, who donated land for the first local courthouse in 1780. The present courthouse was erected in 1848.

Opened in the late 1940s by Jack Puckett, Jack's Place has changed hands a few times. In the 1980s, it came into the possession of Maxine Morris. In the 1990s, it was taken over by her son, Matthew, and his wife, Stephanie.

The name has stayed the same through the changes in ownership. So has the collection of plates on the walls. There's a plate from Egypt, delivered by a friend of Matthew's. And there are plates representing at least half the 50 states, most of them brought in by customers. Unfortunately, some have been broken over the years.

Jack's is a small, uncrowded place with 59 seats. There are seven stools at a very wide counter, nine booths, and a few tables. The walls are light-toned wood paneling with blue trim.

A favorite at breakfast is the French toast sticks, which are bite-size pieces of battered, deep-fried French bread.

Sandwiches, burgers, salad, chili, and pinto beans are staples on the lunch menu. Jack's Place is one of few restaurants where you can still order a dish of corned beef hash.

Dinners include Delmonico steak, beef liver, breaded jumbo shrimp, and a seafood platter. Baked okra and creamed potatoes are among the vegetables.

According to Nan Foster, who has worked at Jack's for over 45 years—that's right, she started here at age 15—peach cobbler is the big dessert hit among customers. Jack's "just can't keep enough made," she said.

Matthew is a nut for cleanliness, and his restaurant routinely receives high marks from the health department. There's something reassuring about knowing that when you're visiting a restaurant for the first time.

Benjamin's

14900 FOREST ROAD
FOREST, VA. 24551
(434) 534-6077
WWW.COWSANDCRABS.COM

Style	Family-style
Meals	Lunch and dinner, Tuesday through Friday; dinner only on Saturday
Price Range	Inexpensive/Moderate
Superlatives	Steak, crab
Extras	Full bar

*B*enjamin's immediately became an exception to my rule that a restaurant be in business longer than a year to be included in this book. It was so crowded on a mid-week evening that there wasn't time to ask any questions. I didn't discover that it had been opened a short time until after I ate the best steak I've had in a long time. And, as a food writer and meat lover, I eat a lot of steak.

Benjamin McGehee is the youthful owner, well under 30 when his restaurant opened. He attended a local high school and graduated from Liberty University with a marketing degree. His restaurant experience started at a dishwasher station when he was 16. He worked through all the kitchen jobs, paying attention to everything along the way.

The brown, rectangular building was constructed

in 1932 and has been a gathering place and restaurant most of its days. Now it has a low, front porch and a back deck. The deck, which has its own bar and grill, overlooks open fields. The interior is casually rustic with old iron chandeliers, old tools, a couple of cowboy boots on a shelf, and nautical buoys on the restroom doors.

The traditional Caesar salad is made with shrimp or chicken, Cobb salad has grilled chicken, and the taco salad is served with black bean chicken chili. Or you can order the chili alone. The chowder or soup of the day is fresh and priced daily. Burgers, po' boys, and wraps comprise the lighter fare at lunch.

Some of the appetizers are calamari rings, crab legs, Freedom Chips-N-Salsa, miniature crab cakes, and potato skins. Entrées come with an assortment of breads, choice of baked potato or fries, half a salad, or the vegetable du jour. Cows-N-Crabs is a special entrée with two beef tenderloin medallions with crab legs.

I had the New York strip, which was luscious. South Carolina quail, 4-cheese chicken portobello, lemon thyme penne, and grilled pork chops are some of the other choices.

Benjamin's crab cakes are served in a tarragon cream sauce and boast "you can see crabmeat in every bite." Other seafood suggestions are the salmon, swordfish, seafood scampi, cornmeal pan-fried oysters, or a steamed seafood platter.

The food is really good, and you'll be challenged to save room for dessert of sweet potato pie with warm walnut sauce, apple cobbler, peanut butter pie with fresh peanut brittle, or one of the other delightful delicacies.

The restaurant should meet with great success. Benjamin has trained well in the field, so to speak, and he's bright, motivated, and surrounded with a wonderful family and staff.

FOREST

Bulls Steak House
1887 GRAVES MILL ROAD
FOREST, VA. 24551
(434) 385-7581

Style	Family-style
Meals	Lunch and dinner, Monday through Friday; dinner only on Saturday. Reservations are accepted.
Price Range	Inexpensive/Moderate
Superlatives	Prime rib, steaks, fajitas
Extras	Full bar

Sometimes it takes a few changes to find your niche, and so it was with Bulls. Started in 1989 as the Peppermill, the restaurant became Tex-Mex two years later. When that was misinterpreted as a strictly Mexican restaurant, owners Jim Lemon and Kevin Middleton went with Bulls. There's no easy way now to misinterpret the focus on beef.

Jim, a Lynchburg native, worked his way through the restaurant business the hard way—dishwasher to manager and everything in between. He earned a business degree from Lynchburg

College along the way. Kevin Middleton majored in hotel and restaurant management at Michigan State and stopped in Roanoke on his way to Florida in the late 1970s. He liked what he found, so he got a job and settled in Virginia. Their education and experience are evident in this efficient, friendly, comfortable restaurant.

Bulls is Western-themed, as you might expect. Black-and-white cowboy photos, Southwestern prints, and colorful blankets on dividers set the scene. Country music is subtle—not blaring—and vinyl, burgundy tablecloths cover the tables, which each sport a small oil lamp. There are wall sconces, lots of wood, recessed lighting, and a few strands of white lights on a couple of tall, artificial plants in corners.

Jim and Kevin take pride in all the food prepared from scratch on the premises. They make the ranch and bleu cheese dressings, for example, and fresh chickens are cooked daily for chicken salad. You can order the chicken salad in a crispy tortilla bowl or open-faced on a sub topped with bacon, tomato, and melted cheddar cheese.

A nice variety of burgers, a heated club sub, and prime rib cheddar melt are other lunch options, with the prime dip and au jus the most popular item. Each one comes with a house salad and choice of baked potato, fries, Tex-Mex rice, refried beans, or vegetables.

There are more than a dozen appetizers such as tacos, jalapeño poppers, guacamole, chips and chili, and shrimp scampi. Prime rib, filet, rib-eye, or the center-cut sirloin can all be ordered with sautéed mushrooms or blackened. While the Tex-Mex name didn't do well, the Tex-Mex entrées linger on the menu. Fajitas, burritos, tacos, or chimichangas are served with rice, refried beans, and fresh tortilla chips and salsa, but if you can't decide, then go for the fiesta sampler platter.

Jim's sister, Karen, contributed her homemade carrot cake recipe to the dessert menu, which also includes fried ice cream, Kentucky Derby pie, spiced apple cheesecake, and other delectable goodies. Bulls will fit the bill for a power lunch, family night out, or any other occasion. It's a happy place.

Bedford Restaurant

U.S. 460 / BEDFORD, VA. 24523
(540) 586-6575

Style	Family-style
Meals	Breakfast, lunch, and dinner, seven days a week
Price Range	Inexpensive
Superlatives	Beef and pork barbecue, homemade pies

Founded as the town of Liberty in 1728, Bedford has more than 200 structures in its historic district. Among the stately homes in the area is Thomas Jefferson's Poplar Forest. Jefferson's old home is appropriately named, as Bedford is the home of the largest yellow poplar tree in the world and the largest tree of any kind in Virginia.

The Bedford Restaurant is a small, tan building with dark brown trim on the northern side of U.S. 460 west of town. The parking lot is a gravel space whose size must have been planned for the 18-wheelers that pull in here. But don't let those big trucks intimidate you. There's some good barbecue to be had here. Not to mention the homemade pies.

Clay and Kathy Pope bought the restaurant in 1984 and have elevated it from a rough beer joint to a good family restaurant. Actually, the Bedford Restaurant was originally a two-story building across the road. When U.S. 460 was widened to four lanes, the building was moved to its present location. The second story was later destroyed in a fire, and the Popes put on the present roof. They expanded in the early 2000s to add a non-smoking dining room.

Breakfast items include eggs, sausage, bacon, grits, biscuits, toast, tenderloin, country ham, and pancakes. The restaurant makes fresh cinnamon rolls every morning.

The specialty here is pit-cooked barbecue, both pork and beef. It's available in sandwiches of two different sizes, with or without french fries and slaw. If you're on the go, you can buy barbecue by the pound.

Truckers are partial to the roast beef, mashed potatoes and gravy, and the specials, which include spaghetti, country-style steak, baked ham, whiting filet, and meat loaf. Meals come with two vegetables, which are defined as everything from applesauce, cottage cheese, rice pudding, and macaroni and cheese to pickled beets, okra, breaded squash, spinach, and broccoli.

Couples really need to work as a team in these mom-and-pop places. Kathy and Clay do this right down to the pie making—she makes the crusts, he makes the fillings. Of course, the earlier you stop in, the greater the selection. Pumpkin, apple, cherry, peach, and butterscotch are among the favorite pies.

According to Clay, their Bedford Restaurant fills a need. He says it can be hard for travelers to find a place with "food like you cook at home." That's what he and Kathy serve, and that's why they're popular with folks near and far.

BEDFORD

Olde Liberty Station

515 BEDFORD AVENUE / BEDFORD, VA. 24523
(540) 587-9377
WWW.OLDELIBERTYSTATION.COM

Style	Family-style
Meals	Lunch and dinner, Monday through Saturday
Price Range	Inexpensive
Superlatives	House-cut prime rib, catfish, cheesecake
Extras	Full bar

*T*he town of Bedford was once called Liberty, thus making Liberty Station the name of this rail stop. The building was constructed in 1905 and was moved here two years later. The trains ran through Bedford until 1971, and after that, the building was used for a variety of services. It is on the National Register of Historic Places.

Harry Leist was a company man—restaurant companies—that is. He'd spent 30 years in the chain-restaurant industry when the opportunity to buy the Olde Liberty Station arose in 2001. A combination of factors, including timing, made it seem right. Judging by the crowds here, it was the right move.

Harry and his wife, Marty, operate a top-notch, family restaurant, with assistance from daughter, Heather, and chefs, Michael Guess and Chris Miller. The hostess is inside a ticket booth right at the front door. To the left and right, you can see train murals on the end walls. Some of the seats are slatted benches, like the train station would have had.

The light fixtures are brass with three etched glass globes. From the wallpaper to the curtains and oak furnishings, everything is comfortable and very attractive. This is Marty's responsibility, and she certainly has a flair for decorating.

The lunch menu begins with "all aboard appetizers," then "Southern Line salads" and "side cars." The specials of the house, uh, I mean, railroad station, are the crab cake sandwich, Reuben, and the Atchison, a petit tenderloin of beef. There are also baby back ribs, chicken cordon bleu, quiche of the day, and other things.

Harry says one of the most popular entrées at lunch or dinner is the catfish. "It's our special salt-and-pepper breading," he insists.

The dinner prime rib is hand-cut and served au jus with horseradish cream sauce. Tenderloin, sirloin tips, chopped steak, and rib-eye are also here for the beef lovers. There are fireman's fajitas, raspberry chicken, liberty chicken, and some pasta plates, as well as a catch of the day in the seafood section and delicate Maryland crab cakes, another station house specialty.

The cheesecakes are dubbed "Harry's own cheesecake du jour," and they are delicious—well, at least the white chocolate raspberry cheesecake was. I didn't dare order each flavor and eat them all. Fried ice cream and apple pie are offered, along with Friazos—rich chocolate ice cream layered with chocolate mousse, chocolate fudge, and chewy bittersweet brownie pieces. Yum, yum.

AMHERST

The Briar Patch

U.S. 29 BUSINESS
AMHERST, VA. 24521
(804) 946-2249

Style	Pub
Meals	Breakfast, lunch, and dinner, Monday through Saturday
Price Range	Inexpensive/Moderate
Superlatives	Cozy atmosphere, great hamburgers
Extras	Full bar

*T*he town and county of Amherst were named for Jeffrey, Lord Amherst, a hero in the Battle of Ticonderoga during the French and Indian War.

Jeffrey was subsequently appointed royal governor of Virginia, but he never came to fill the post, instead sending deputies to conduct his business.

Set on the highway just south of town, The Briar Patch was purchased by Joanie Lingerfelt in the mid-1980s. It was built in 1948—the same year Joanie was born. She figures the name came from the college yearbook of the same title at Sweet Briar College, located just up the road.

The restaurant doubled in size in the late 1990s, then burned to the ground early in 2003. This book will be released in May 2004, the same month Joanie figures the new building for The Briar Patch will be finished and opened for business.

The words at the beginning of the old menu make you feel good about coming in: "Congratulations on your discerning taste, good looks, charming personality, and appreciation of the finer things in life. We make every effort to prepare each of our dishes to order; therefore, we are not a fast-food restaurant. During peak hours, it may take a little longer. So relax, have a drink, visit, and enjoy!"

Among the sandwiches served at lunch are burgers, a Reuben, a Monte Cristo, a French dip, and a Philly-style steak and cheese. The "Sweet Briar Special" is a warmed onion dill roll stuffed with chicken salad and served with steamed broccoli. (The warmed onion dill roll has another role on the appetizer list, where it's offered with homemade spinach dip on top and fresh veggies around it.) The "Veggie Cheese Melt" is sliced tomatoes, mushrooms, grilled peppers, onions, cheese, and a special sauce on rye bread. Salads, homemade soups, chili, and pizza are also offered.

The dinner choices include rib-eye steak, stuffed flounder, beef liver, chicken livers, and half a dozen seafood platters. Among the light entrées are nachos, seafood pasta, crab-stuffed mushrooms, quesadillas, and grilled chicken breast.

Almost all of The Briar Patch's business comes from repeat patrons—so I guess if you stop here once, you'll just have to stop again if you want to fit in.

What a Blessing Bakery & Deli

AMBRIAR SHOPPING CENTER
AMHERST, VA. 24521
(434) 946-0330

Style	Café
Meals	Breakfast and lunch, Monday through Saturday; Saturday brunch
Price Range	Inexpensive
Superlatives	Chicken salad, homemade bread

*I*n this little strip mall, Gilbert and Patricia Rose have created a neat little café. Inside the front door are the front counter and the glass cases filled with donuts, cookies, bars, fresh breads, and assorted bakery items.

Gilbert went to work as a teen at a major name bakery in Lynchburg. He and Patricia had a donut shop and bakery in the 1980s. There's an old non-

Biblical adage that goes "when the Lord closes a door, somewhere He opens a window." Well, not necessarily. Sometimes God asks us to wait. His ways are not our ways, and His timing is not our timing much of the time.

The Roses worked at other things until they felt led to open What A Blessing in 1998. The afternoon I came in—having hopped around much of central Virginia doing research for this book—the place seemed like a little slice of heaven. A cup of tea, a cookie, a little light Christian reading, and 20 minutes later, I felt immeasurably refreshed.

To the right of the entry and up a step is the café. It is enveloped in medium-orange walls, and throughout the café are several antique buffet pieces with trays of cups and saucers, teapots, and baskets of creamers, sugars, and the like. There are more than 40 seats at small tables with white, gray, or wood chairs. There's one large table for eight.

There are Christian books to pick up and flip through or read. Christian music plays all day in the background. All the tips go to buy more books or music.

The breakfast plate has eggs, potatoes, apples, and your choice of meat and toast. You can go à la carte with eggs, bacon, sausage, country ham, or a BLT. Toward lunch time, you might want some sort of salad such as spaghetti, chef, potato, spinach, chicken, or tossed. The grilled chicken salad comes with pineapple, mandarin orange, and almonds.

All the breads are homemade, so the sub rolls vary between 10 and 12 inches. There are eight subs on the list—American, tuna, chicken, roast beef, turkey, ham, veggie, and Italian. They are hearty; thus, the note: *We do not split subs. If our subs are too big for your appetite, please try our sandwiches.*

For your sandwich, you can choose from ham and Swiss, turkey, tuna salad, pastrami, chicken, or corned beef. Of course, since this is a bakery, it might be tough to do a lunch without a cookie, so save room.

If you don't feel like a sandwich or a sub, perhaps a smoothie with two cookies would make a nice snack! What a Blessing is a nice café, and, for me, it was a calming, mid-afternoon blessing for one weary writer.

Lovingston Café
165 FRONT STREET
LOVINGSTON, VA. 22980
(434) 263-8000

Style	Family-style
Meals	Breakfast, Friday through Monday; lunch and dinner, seven days a week
Price Range	Inexpensive
Superlatives	Reuben, crab cakes, fried oysters
Extras	Full bar

Jackie and Tom Brokamp met while working at the Wintergreen Resort here in Nelson County. His parents retired nearby in the 1970s, and after marrying and having a couple of kids, Jackie and Tom settled in to raise their family. In 1993, they opened the Lovingston Café and are very happy with their success.

It's an attractive mix of booths and blond-oak tables and chairs. Below the chair rail, the walls are light-stained wainscoting. The upper half is painted tan with dark green trim. Most of the artwork by local artists is for sale. The restaurant seats about 50, and the bar in the adjoining space accommodates 24. The inviting outdoor patio holds another 54 and is opened seasonally.

The four-day-a-week breakfast offers omelets and egg combos and an enticing selection of waffles, Belgian waffles, pecan waffles, and French toast. There's a breakfast buffet on Saturdays and Sundays. You can also get cheese strudel muffins, a bagel with cream cheese, a homemade biscuit, grits, or Cherrios and other à la carte items.

One of the luncheon plates is a three-cheese chicken quesadilla, and two of the specialty sandwich platters are blackened tuna aioli and their popular Reuben. Hearty hamburgers come with grilled onions on the side, and the café offers a Greek, a grilled chicken Caesar, or smoked trout salad. Eastern Shore crab cakes, smoked pork loin chops, and ruby red tuna are both lunch and dinner entrées.

On the creative side for appetizers, there's crispy crab wonton Napoleon (crispy wontons layered with fresh spinach and smoked crab mousse) or polenta basil cakes. The café offers two soups every day. Beyond the rib-eye, strip steak, and seared crab cakes, you might be tempted with chicken Morocco, polenta cakes, and sweet potato gnocchi or veggie Parmesan fettuccine. There are enough entrées to pacify the beefeater, fish lover, chicken personality, and vegetarian.

Jackie makes desserts such as maple walnut or pumpkin cheesecake and sour cream pie. For a small place, the Lovingston Café has an interesting, diversified menu in a comfortable, unassuming setting.

Houndstooth Café
U.S. 301
HANOVER, VA. 23069
(804) 537-5404

Style	Café
Meals	Lunch, Tuesday through Friday; dinner, Tuesday through Saturday
Price Range	Moderate
Superlatives	Fresh seafood, barbecue
Extras	Wine and beer

*H*anover County is noted for its native sons. Patrick Henry was born here in 1736 and Henry Clay in 1777.

Another local event took place in 1933. No, it wasn't on a par with the repeal of Prohibition or the launching of FDR's New Deal, which also took place that year. The event was the construction of a small country store with gas pumps on U.S. 301 at the intersection with Va. 54.

By the time the late Bob Cunningham and his wife, Connie, started Houndstooth Café in 1988, the old country store had been vacant for a decade. Now, it's bright, clean, and friendly. The burgundy valances on the windows, the hunt prints, the brass candelabra chandeliers, and the black-and-white floor tiles contribute to the casual atmosphere.

The appetizers are the same for lunch and dinner—seafood soup, a soup du jour, "Wing Dings," crab puffs, fried veggies, mozzarella sticks. The lunch entrées include barbecue—beef, chicken or pork—and char-broiled chopped steak. Among the hot sandwiches are burgers, a barbecue sandwich, a crab cake sandwich, a steak and cheese sub, and grilled cheese. The cold sandwiches are sliced turkey, chicken salad, and a variety of clubs. Spinach salad, chef salad, and a chicken salad plate are among the salad options.

Fresh seafood is the specialty here. In fact, it's so fresh that it's not even printed on the menu, as Connie is never positive what she's going to offer. A marker board lists seafood appetizers and entrées each day. It may include flounder, tuna, salmon, rockfish, scallops, oysters, or catfish. The flounder may be stuffed with crab, the catfish served with oyster stuffing—the options are countless. Stable dinner items include barbecue, surf and turf, crab cakes, and baby back ribs. All come with two vegetables and your choice of rolls or hush puppies. Among the vegetables are boiled potatoes, baked beans, applesauce, macaroni salad, and french fries. The "Houndstooth Feast for Four" is a whole barbecued pork butt with three vegetables, hush puppies, and iced tea or coffee.

For dessert, the homemade brownies are served with ice cream and hot fudge sauce. The "Houndstooth Derby Pie" is hard to resist, as are the homemade apple pie and homemade cheesecakes.

Connie has an attractive eatery noted for its great barbecue and fresh seafood. I want to return here for two reasons: the beef barbecue and the intriguing antique shop across the street called Two Frogs on a Bike, which was closed the day I visited.

The Ironhorse

100 SOUTH RAILROAD AVENUE
ASHLAND, VA. 23005
(804) 752-6410
WWW.IRONHORSERESTAURANT.COM

Style	Casual nice
Meals	Lunch, Monday through Friday; dinner, Tuesday through Saturday
Price Range	Moderate/Expensive
Superlatives	Tapas, Caesar salad
Extras	Full bar

You might think the name Ironhorse was chosen because of the railroad tracks and the daily trains running down the center of Railroad Avenue. But according to the owner, Texas native Mimi Siff, the name was actually taken from a 1960s television series called *Ironhorse*, a Western in which the star,

Dale Robertson, would hook up his railroad car to a train and travel around doing good.

Constructed in 1900, the building operated as the D. B. Cox Department Store for six decades. For three more decades, it was home to a variety of stores and offices. The restaurant opened its doors on April 4, 1991.

The building's status as a former department store explains the huge windows and the wide ledges inside, where many a mannequin must have stood. That space now holds a few plants and antiques and live entertainment on weekend evenings.

The overall color scheme is peach, cream, and teal. The place has high tin ceilings and lots of natural light. The bar, located to the right, has a piano, a mounted moose head, and several tables with captain's chairs. To the left is a large, comfortably uncrowded dining room that seats close to 100. The tabletops are dressed for dinner with vintage floral oilcloths. The photos and prints on the walls relate to the understated railroad theme.

Burgers and sandwiches such as roast beef, grilled chicken breast, Smithfield ham, tuna melt, and a Reuben are available at lunch. The Ironhorse's signature sandwiches are named for "Hall of Fame People," who are loosely defined as those who are "in a rut or [who have] provided some extraordinary service to the Ironhorse, or both." The certified Angus beef® burger with bacon, cheese, and pesto is called the "Ned Stiles" simply because he comes in a couple of times each week and orders one. The "Sheila Hunter" is named

for Mimi's good friend. The chicken and cheese quesadillas are named for the landlord, Art McKinney, who kept asking for something Mexican on the menu. Such items as noodles with spicy tomato sauce, chicken salad, and tuna salad are also offered. Side orders include coleslaw, grilled potatoes, and potato chips.

The dinner appetizers change monthly, and you might find seafood Mornay, risotto goat cheese, and rosemary fritters. Four salads are offered. Entrées such as duck confit, stuffed leg of lamb, and certified Angus beef® filet mignon can be expected.

All the desserts are made from scratch. Two of the most popular are vanilla bean crème brûlée and the chocolate truffle cake.

The Smokey Pig

212 SOUTH WASHINGTON HIGHWAY
ASHLAND, VA. 23005
(804) 798-4590

Style	Family-style
Meals	Lunch and dinner, Tuesday through Sunday
Price Range	Inexpensive/Moderate
Superlatives	Pig collection, barbecue, homemade pies
Extras	Beer and wine

*S*aying there are a few pigs here is like saying there are a few government offices in Northern Virginia.

The Smokey Pig

First, you'll see the restaurant sign with the pig on it. Then you'll turn into the parking lot at the "Pig In" sign. You'll see more pigs on shelves behind glass inside the front door. Porcelain pigs, plastic pigs, glass pigs, piggy-bank pigs. Depending on where you're seated, you'll view more pigs. Ceramic ones, metal ones, wooden ones, stuffed ones. Mobiles of pigs, photos of pigs, prints of pigs.

It's all nicely done, however, in three dining rooms with blue-and-white-checked tablecloths, sconces, and ceiling lights. The atmosphere is casual, warm, and friendly. The waitresses all seem to enjoy serving their customers, which was especially nice on the dark, rainy afternoon when I visited.

The building has housed a variety of stores and restaurants since opening in 1927 as a general store with overnight rooms upstairs. This Smokey Pig opened in the fall of 1978.

Of course, barbecue is the specialty here. Pork, chicken, or beef. Chopped or sliced. On a bun or not. As a sandwich or a meal.

Other lunch offerings include homemade soups, salads, sandwiches, and burgers. The lunch special for Tuesday is meat loaf. On Wednesday, it's chicken pot pie. On Thursday, it's "Chef's Choice." On Friday, it's a seafood potato—a baked potato smothered with a thick Mornay sauce to which seafood has been added.

Daily dinner specials are also offered.

The most popular dessert is the homemade brownie with ice cream and hot fudge.

The bar is inconspicuously located at the back of the center dining room. Its stained-glass hanging lamps flank a sign reading, appropriately enough, "Live well, laugh often, love much."

CHARLOTTESVILLE

Hamiltons' at First & Main

101 WEST MAIN STREET
CHARLOTTESVILLE, VA. 22902
(434) 295-6649
WWW.HAMILTONSRESTAURANT.COM

Style	Fine dining
Meals	Lunch and dinner, Monday through Saturday. Reservations are recommended.
Price Range	Moderate/Expensive
Superlatives	Crab cakes, vegetarian dishes
Extras	Full bar

*O*n Valentine's Day in 1996, Kate and Bill

Hamilton opened their restaurant in a former shoe store on the downtown mall. The interior is a contemporary study in bright yellow with a bold, blue angle painted in the front and lumpy-textured, terra-cotta walls sporting hanging globes and purple sconces.

It's cozy and appealing, with dining on the right side of the deep, narrow space, and seven bar stools at the bar on the left side. Claim your table early for lunch as the crowd presses in right around noon, and you may have to wait.

There's vegetarian soup, a featured fish, and a vegetarian special each day. Menus change often at fine restaurants, as they make the most of fresh produce and seasonal ingredients, so everything mentioned here may not always be available.

Salads are comprehensive, such as romaine hearts with house-made Caesar dressing, smoked salmon, grilled red onion, Parmesan crisps, fresh tomatoes, and herbed ricotta.

If this noontime festivity is your main meal, you're in luck. Hamiltons' offers pan-roasted, jumbo lump crab cake on jasmine rice with a Shiitake mushroom and Napa cabbage spring roll, cucumber noodles, watercress, a spicy Asian-style mustard, and a sweet-and-sour sauce. That's one entrée description.

Other entrées, shortened for space, include grilled petit beef tenderloin over whipped potatoes, or the spicy stir-fry of shrimp. On the light side of lunch desserts is the trio of sorbet, and one of the richer offerings is the chocolate hazelnut mascarpone brownie with vanilla-bean ice cream.

After the lights go down, more culinary creativity steps out. Smoked duck breast on an applewood bacon, thyme-crusted green pepper, and West Virginia Shiitake mushrooms on a goat cheese crostini with honeyed walnuts are two of the tempting appetizers.

Entrées may include pan-seared sea scallops with oven-roasted, baby red potatoes or jasmine rice stir-fry of roasted organic chicken, jumbo shrimp, and Asian vegetables. Rack of lamb, beef tenderloin, and a vegetarian "blue plate special" are prepared with innovative flavors and complementary accompaniments.

Fine dining restaurants create some of the finest desserts—no matter the cost in terms of calories or dollars. Lemon tart with raspberry coulis and a trio of fruit sorbets in a brandy snap cup appear on the light side. Chocolate, you may know already, has some redeeming nutritional value, so a dessert such as Chocolate Many Ways or a sampler of fine, handmade chocolates could be justified. There are other desserts, too, and they change often.

The Nook

415 EAST MAIN STREET
CHARLOTTESVILLE, VA. 22902
(434) 295-6665 (295-NOOK)

Style	Home-style
Meals	Breakfast and lunch, seven days a week
Price Range	Inexpensive
Superlatives	Nook burger, breakfast all day
Extras	Beer and wine

*T*he Nook is one of those old-time places where you feel comfortable whether you're eight or 80. It is more than half a century old and looks the part, though it's bright and clean. The marquee-style sign and glass blocks in the front are originals, as are the high-back wood booths and probably the clock.

Terry Shotwell bought the place in 1990 and ran it for a decade before enticing her daughter, Nancy, to leave the retail world and take over the popular, downtown dining spot.

Hidden fluorescent and track lighting reflect off cream walls and ceiling. One wall is painted blue, and all of them have old, black-and-white photographs of Charlottesville. With seven booths and around 16 wood tables, The Nook can seat 75 or more. There's a paper place mat at each place with The Nook ad in the center and a variety of local businesses advertised around the edge—the Whole Foods Market, Tuel Jewelers, a realtor, an insurance agent, professional movers. St. Nicholas Orthodox Church advertises: "Don't forget to feed your soul."

Near the entrance are photos of beautiful women, some Miss Virginia and Mrs. Virginia, and one Miss Maryland. Seems that Miss Virginia comes in every year before an annual parade. One of them dropped off a signed photo, and others followed suit. Not to be outdone, a Miss Maryland who saw the photos contributed hers.

Breakfast is served all day, and no doubt, that contributes greatly to The Nook's popularity. You order by the number here for the five most popular breakfast platters. Number two, for example, is sausage gravy over your choice of bread with hash browns. Number three, a.k.a. The Lumberjack, has two hotcakes or two slices of French toast or one waffle with two eggs any style and ham, bacon, sausage, or corn beef hash.

Egg dishes, breakfast sandwiches, cold cereal, grits, and oatmeal are also offered. Pancakes or waffles come as plain, blueberry, apple, pecan, banana nut, bacon, or chocolate chip. And you can get ice cream on your waffle!

The Nook burger takes top spot on the burger list. It's fresh, hand-pattied, topped with bacon and cheese and whatever else you want. The hickory burger has barbecue sauce on it, and the mushroom Swiss burger should be self-explanatory.

Other lunch options are pasta dishes, stir-fry things, sandwiches, different chicken preparations, a vegetarian plate, and traditional favorites such as a hot roast beef sandwich with grilled onions and gravy.

Salads, The Nook's special chili, appetizers, side

dishes such as chunky applesauce or southern-style coleslaw, and sandwiches can all be called in "to go" and picked up in a white bag.

The Nook is one of those places that will never go out of style. You don't come here to see or be seen or talk about having dined here. You come for the relaxing, clean setting, and the good, freshly prepared food. Whether you talk to anyone, come with a friend, or come alone and sit and read the newspaper, you'll find it a great place to get breakfast any time or lunch some of the time.

CHARLOTTESVILLE

Old Mill Dining Room

BOAR'S HEAD INN / U.S. 250
CHARLOTTESVILLE, VA. 22901
(434) 972-2230
WWW.BOARSHEADINN.COM

Style	Resort
Meals	Breakfast, lunch, and dinner, seven days a week
Price Range	Moderate/Expensive
Superlatives	Pork loin, stone-ground grits, trout
Extras	Full bar

A blue boar's head has symbolized good food and warm hospitality for centuries. The Boar's Head Inn, now owned by the University of Virginia real-estate foundation, delivers on both counts. It's a luxurious resort setting with sports facilities.

The Old Mill, the main dining room at the Boar's Head Inn, was built in 1834 and operated as a grist-mill for many years. Burned during the Civil War, it was spared major damage thanks to superior construction and a heavy rain. The building was disassembled in the early 1960s and reconstructed to take its place at the Boar's Head Inn. Fieldstones from the foundation were used to build the fireplace, and wood from the grain bins was used as paneling. The wrought-iron chandeliers, the beige linens, the fresh flowers, and the classy silverware all evoke a warm, rustic elegance.

Traditional fare—eggs, breakfast meats, salads, and sandwiches—are offered at breakfast and lunch.

Dinner is when you'll find innovative cuisine. The menu changes each season, and the staff uses local produce and meat as much as possible.

The soups may include black bean, French onion, and sweet corn and lobster chowder. Stilton and Brie tart, seafood ravioli, and smoked salmon with mushrooms, spinach, and mascarpone might be on the appetizer list. A classic Caesar and roasted quail with dried black figs on warm spinach are two of the salads that might be offered.

The Old Mill is best known for creative entrées such as cider-marinated pork loin with stone-ground grits. Or you can order the ever-popular rack of lamb, broiled salmon, or pan-seared tuna.

All the expectations one has when dining at a four-diamond resort are met in the Old Mill Dining Room—lovely atmosphere, excellent service, attractive presentation, and delicious food.

Oxo Restaurant

215 WEST WATER STREET
CHARLOTTESVILLE, VA. 22902
(434) 977-8111
WWW.OXORESTAURANT.COM

Style	Fine dining
Meals	Lunch, Monday through Friday; dinner, seven days a week. Reservations are recommended.
Price Range	Moderate/Expensive
Superlatives	Beef tenderloin, snapper, soufflés
Extras	Full bar

Alice Kim moved from northern Virginia to Charlottesville as a University of Virginia student. John Haywood came from Sheffield, England, to help a friend. They met working at Keswick Hall, and when decision time came for John—return to England or venture out on his own here—Alice and John joined forces for the venture.

Oxo, named for the British bouillon cubes, opened in February 1999 in a freestanding building next to the ice-skating rink. There's a nice front patio for outdoor dining as weather permits. The interior is painted white with just a few small prints on the walls. It's clean, contemporary, under-decorated even, except for the gigantic crystal chandelier from Belgium, given to John by a friend who couldn't use it. It looks as if it would be too big for almost anywhere, except here at Oxo.

There are open dining rooms on the right, left, and straight ahead when you enter. The bar on the left seems like the most interesting place to spend time. In front of each barstool are a small lamp, an 8-ball, and a stack of books such as *100 Games of Logic, The Conversation Piece: Creative Questions that Tickle the Mind,* and *Don't Try This at Home.*

Oxo boasts an extensive cocktail list, lovely tea service, and exquisite presentations. One of the lunch salads is smoked salmon with Brie and apple. One of the sandwiches is grilled chicken with goat cheese, pickled red onions, and pommes frites. Fish and chips, New York strip, marinated pork tenderloins, and salad niçoise with grilled tuna and accompaniments represent some of the lunch entrées.

The dinner menu is separated into "First," "Next," and "Then." You don't have to include one of the "First" appetizers, but it'll take lots of will power to resist lobster risotto with asparagus cream and tarragon mascarpone; oyster pot pie with fried rock shrimp; or other enticing Firsts.

"Next" is a refreshment of sorbet. "Then" presents more than half a dozen entrées. The beef tenderloin is very popular at dinner, and what sets the snapper apart is its arrival on the plate wrapped in a potato crêpe with roasted pearl onions, bacon, sautéed spinach, fennel salad, lemon mosto oil, and a 100-year-old balsamic vinegar. Broken Arrow Ranch venison, pan-seared salmon or scallops, oven-roasted duck breast, or roasted pork tenderloin are also offered.

The vegetarian dishes—carrot and Parmesan gâteau with butternut squash purée; wild mushroom spring roll; roasted garlic custard; braised radicchio;

and bleu cheese pear salad sound good enough even for a meat-lover to enjoy.

They offer dessert every night, of course, and I don't have much will power in this department. If you love chocolate, but have tired of the overdone, overly rich, double fudge stuff, order Oxo's dark chocolate marquis with Kahlua crème anglaise. It's delicious—not too rich, tasty enough, not too big, not too small. Just like Goldilocks said, "It's just right." I think she would say that about this entire restaurant.

Silver Thatch Inn

CHARLOTTESVILLE

Silver Thatch Inn

3001 NORTH HOLLYMEAD DRIVE
CHARLOTTESVILLE, VA. 22911
(434) 978-4686
WWW.SILVERTHATCH.COM

Style	Fine dining
Meals	Dinner, Tuesday through Saturday. Reservations are recommended.
Price Range	Expensive
Superlatives	Seafood, game in season
Extras	Full bar

During the Revolutionary War, Hessian soldiers captured at the Battle of Saratoga were marched from New York to Virginia. In 1780, they built a two-story log cabin here. That cabin is now known as the Hessian Room at the Silver Thatch Inn.

The middle of the inn was built in 1812 and the final wing in 1937. A small cottage with four of the seven overnight guest rooms was constructed in 1984. The inn has been featured in several magazines, newspapers, and books.

The Silver Thatch exudes an old-time warmth. The rich interior colors are called "Colony Red" and "Valley Forge Green." The dining rooms are predominately cream and green with white linens, candlelight, and a few sconces. There are seats for around 60. The tables are numbered for logistical purposes. Ironically, table 13 is unofficially referred to as "the Engagement Table." According to Jim and Terri Petrovits, the owners of the inn since 1997, more couples have gotten engaged while seated at this table than any other. It could be the window. Or possibly there's just some challenge in defying superstitious numbers.

Only lodging guests can partake of freshly baked muffins, cereals, fresh fruit, and hot coffee and tea at breakfast. Dinner is open to the public.

Evening appetizers might be gratin of scallops

Florentine, duck and foie gras sausage, or smoked trout ravioli. There's always a soup du jour.

Modern American cuisine—grilled meat and fish with healthy sauces—is the focus here. Venison, rabbit, antelope, and other game are offered in season. Vegetable strudel, pecan-encrusted rack of lamb, and certified Angus beef® filet mignon are also available. Braised veal shanks, sea bass, and roasted pancetta wrapped monkfish may be on the menu when you visit.

Innkeeper and long-time Silver Thatch employee Martin Dodge extends the kind of greeting that makes you feel as if you've entered a circle of old, familiar friends. And you can spend the night in one of the lovely guest rooms.

IVY

Duner's

U.S. 250 / IVY, VA. 22945
(434) 293-8352

Style	Casual nice
Meals	Dinner, seven days a week
Price Range	Moderate
Superlatives	Fish, sweetbreads, local game and poultry
Extras	Full bar

*T*his town is named for the native evergreen ground cover growing along the banks of Ivy Creek. The plant in question is really kalmia, but it looks a lot like ivy, so Ivy it is. Meriwether Lewis,

the explorer best known for his expedition with William Clark between 1804 and 1806, was born here in 1774.

Around Ivy, as on highways all over the state, you'll find 1950s motor courts in various states of disrepair. Duner's is the restaurant part of one of these now-defunct enterprises. The part that was once a motor court has been tastefully renovated into offices.

The restaurant is doing well under owner Bob Caldwell. He worked here as a cook in the mid-1980s, then bought the place in 1988.

The square, brick building has a row of newspaper boxes in front but is otherwise pretty basic. Inside, it's casually comfortable. A side room has deep red wallpaper, while the main dining room has cream walls and few decorations. Copper pot collections are displayed on two walls. There are 65 seats in the two dining rooms and several stools at the bar. Though the mural behind the bar seems a little out of place, it definitely adds an element of interest. It's an island scene with palms, a beach, and hula dancers. It was put here by the previous owner, a Turkish fellow whose nickname was Duner.

The menu changes every day. Lead chef Cathy Berry and her husband, Hayden, have been running the kitchen for a decade and a half now.

Soups such as lentil and cream of asparagus may be available. The appetizers might include crayfish in puff pastry, veal and green peppercorn pâté, and warm white bean and sausage salad.

Caldwell said he is especially picky about buying and preparing fish and about purchasing poultry, rabbit, or other game locally. Rockfish baked with oysters and served with champagne cream sauce might be an option, as might pan-fried mountain trout with caramelized onions, mushrooms, and tarragon. Most all the entrées come with a unique sauce or demi-glacé. A dried cherry and rosemary demi-glacé tops the grilled pork loin chops, and a ginger and onion cream sauce dresses up the marinated grilled flank steak.

The vegetarian choice might be eggplant and mushrooms in phyllo pastry. The pasta selections might include sautéed shrimp, tomatoes, olives, artichoke hearts, roasted red pepper, and spinach over linguine, topped with feta cheese.

A couple of sandwiches are also offered.

Desserts such as "Pumpkin Crunch Torte," "New Orleans Bread Pudding," and "Chocolate Soufflé Cake" are baked daily. Kudos to Bob, Cathy, and Hayden.

The Copper Mine

WINTERGREEN RESORT / VA. 664
WINTERGREEN, VA. 22958
(434) 325-2200
WWW.WINTERGREENRESORT.COM

Style	Fine dining
Meals	Breakfast and dinner, seven days a week
Price Range	Moderate/Expensive
Superlative	Steak au poivre, rack of lamb, "Bourbon Pecan Pie"
Extras	Full bar

*I*f you've never been to the Wintergreen Resort, you're in for a special surprise. The Mountain Inn, the main building here, is a rustic contemporary structure with great wooden beams and lots of native stone. Attached to it is the restaurant known as The Copper Mine. The whole place is friendly. In fact, one of the waitresses even invited me into the kitchen to try the daily specials with the staff.

The décor is teal, cream, and black. The dining areas ramble around corners and at angles to one another. Altogether, the restaurant seats around 140. Windows form one wall overlooking the Blue Ridge Mountains, and there's patio dining outside for around 28 guests. Each table has a small oil lamp and fresh flowers.

The breakfast menu offers an enticing list of fresh fruits, cereal, pastries, and entrées. French toast with Canadian bacon, toasted pecan hot cakes, Belgian waffles, omelets, and eggs Benedict are among the choices. The "Miner's Breakfast" consists of a layered dish of potatoes, Canadian bacon, and cheddar cheese topped with two eggs cooked your way.

The dinner appetizers include wild mushroom strudel and crabmeat and shrimp ravioli. French onion soup and seafood chowder are always available. Among the seafood entrées, you're likely to find swordfish with black bean and red pepper relish and rainbow trout accompanied by pecan pear salsa. The grilled entrées include filet mignon and tenderloin of pork. The Copper Mine's signature dishes are steak au poivre with a brandied cream sauce and Châteaubriand for two. According to chef Scott Estelle, a Culinary Institute of America graduate, the "Rack of Lamb Persille" is very popular.

My waitress recommended "Pineapple Bananas Foster" for dessert. "Bourbon Pecan Pie" is also a good choice.

You don't have to go hungry around here at lunch just because The Copper Mine isn't open. There are a couple of lunch spots—the Devil's Grill and The Edge—that offer their patrons lovely views down the fairway or out over the mountains. And there's a watering hole on the golf course that serves salads and sandwiches.

Blue Ridge Café

U.S. 29 / RUCKERSVILLE, VA. 22968
(434) 985-3633
WWW.BLUERIDGECAFE.COM

Style	Casual nice
Meals	Lunch, Monday through Saturday; dinner, seven days a week; Sunday brunch
Price Range	Moderate
Superlatives	Grilled chicken, crab cakes
Extras	Wine and beer

There are those who dream of doing things and those who do things. Chef Shawn B. Hayes falls in the latter group. In fact, he reached one of his personal goals early in 1996: to have his own business by age 30.

A graduate of the Culinary Institute of America, Hayes worked in restaurants in the Washington, D.C., area before moving to Charlottesville, where

Blue Ridge Café

his wife, Rita, was living. He has a simple philosophy: to serve good food in healthy portions in a clean, inviting atmosphere.

The restaurant is on one end of an attractive yellow building. The contemporary interior is primarily black and white with track lighting on the ceiling and small white lights around the windows and the tops of the walls. A bar on the right has ten tall chairs. About 150 guests can be seated among the three dining rooms and outdoor tables. There are two banquet rooms for special events and private parties.

The salads include a grilled blackened shrimp salad and a spinach salad with chicken tenders. Sandwiches come with chips or fries, and burgers are accompanied by fries and slaw. A stir-fry du jour, beer-battered fish, pasta primavera, and vegetable quesadillas are also available.

Chicken teriyaki, prime rib, "Swordfish Sherando," and "Pasta Thai Juan" are some of the dinner entrées.

Sunday brunch is an all-you-can-eat continental buffet with an entrée. You can choose to take your meal with or without champagne. Salmon cakes, eggs Benedict, a "Chef's Omelet," and a "Chef's Brunch Special" are some of the entrées from which to choose.

Although I couldn't pinpoint Hayes on a specialty item, his pastries definitely qualify. In fact, his original idea was to open a pastry and confection shop. I, for one, am glad he expanded his idea and opened the Blue Ridge Café. This is a nice place.

The Lafayette

U.S. 33 / STANARDSVILLE, VA. 22973
(434) 985-6345
WWW.THELAFAYETTE.COM

Style	Casual nice
Meals	Lunch, Tuesday through Saturday; dinner, Tuesday through Saturday; Sunday brunch
Price Range	Moderate
Superlatives	Mountain trout, bison specials, mountain berry flan
Extras	Full bar

Stanardsville is home to The Lafayette Hotel, whose rich history of serving travelers has been revived by two enterprising young men. In the past, travelers came to the Shenandoah National Park area for its nature and beauty. People still come for that today, along with coming to visit the wineries and universities in this region.

Whitt Ledford and Nick Spencer met while working at a resort in the area. Whitt lived in Stanardsville and drove by The Lafayette each day going to work. "Someone ought to do something with this building," he often thought.

When the opportunity presented itself, Whitt was there. Nick had by then moved to Monterey, California, but he returned to Stanardsville, and the two started a massive renovation. Today, they operate a bed-and-breakfast inn and a restaurant on the premises. Nick is the chef.

In the early days, they ordered flowers from Pat's

Floral Design in Madison. Nick married the florist, Sherry, so it's a pretty sure thing that the flowers are nice all the time.

The restaurant has two inviting dining rooms with tall windows and old-fashioned chandeliers. The tables have burgundy napkins and fresh flowers.

The soup du jour might be split pea. The best appetizer just might be the potato pancake with local smoked trout in a sour cream sauce. Among the salads are a house salad, a Caesar salad, a spinach salad, and the "Marquis Salad," which comes with smoked bacon, tomato, cheese, sweet peppers, tart apples, and grilled chicken breast. The sandwiches offered at lunch include grilled chicken, barbecued pork, grilled veggies, and thinly sliced bison. Crab cakes and fried oyster platter with sweet potato fries are also available.

The dinner menu is a creative mix of regional cuisines. The mountain trout comes with cheese herb grits, which are loved by those who don't even care for grits in general. The bison specials are popular, as are nightly specials such as pan-seared mahi-mahi with pineapple salsa and fried chicken with cream sauce.

Mountain berry flan and apple pie are among the desserts. Autumn Hill and Stone Mountain wines are featured, and The Lafayette has a private label Chardonnay made for them by Autumn Hill.

Count me among those who are glad that this Federal-style hotel building with large columns, porches, and triple-brick, 15-inch-thick walls is once again a dining and lodging landmark.

The Inwood

U.S. 15 / GORDONSVILLE, VA. 22942
(540) 832-3411

Style	Family-style
Meals	Breakfast, lunch, and dinner, seven days a week
Price Range	Inexpensive/Moderate
Superlatives	Burgers, steaks, pies
Extras	Full bar

This community got its start in 1787, when Nathaniel Gordon opened a tavern for travelers going over the Blue Ridge Mountains. The Exchange Hotel, a local landmark, was built in 1860 and within a few years was being used as a Civil War hospital. It stands today as a fine example of Greek Revival architecture.

Local resident Pamela Watson started her career in the restaurant business in the late 1950s, when she was given a Coke crate to stand on so she could wash the dishes. She was not yet 10 years old. A little more than three decades later, she bought The Inwood from her father.

The family operation doesn't stop with father and daughter. Currently, Pamela's three daughters, a sister, and a niece work at the restaurant. She's not sure where the name Inwood came from, but she's never considered changing it because, as she says, "it works."

The Inwood occupies a brick building with light-grained wood paneling on the top of the interior walls and pine on the lower half. Tan mini-blinds and dark green print valances decorate the large front windows. There are 18 booths, eight chairs at the counter, and a couple of tables.

The breakfasts here range from inexpensive selections to a deluxe combination that includes a country ham steak with eggs, potatoes, and biscuits.

Lunch features a variety of burgers and sandwiches. The ground chuck is purchased fresh every day, and the burgers are hand-pattied in the kitchen. Fish and chips, chicken and chips, country ham, sliced turkey, barbecue, and a breaded veal cutlet are also offered. Beer-battered onion rings are a popular side order.

There are more than two dozen dinner entrées. According to Pamela, The Inwood's steaks are excellent. She offers only two—New York strip and sirloin. Both are cut on the premises. Broiled swordfish, cod filet, crab cakes, fried scallops, and stuffed flounder are a few of the seafood selections. Chicken tenderloin, pork chops, veal parmigiana, spaghetti, and a fish and chicken combination plate are also offered. For lighter fare, you can order just the soup and salad bar.

The restaurant's cream pies are made in the kitchen. Depending on the day's demand, you may have a choice of coconut, chocolate, butterscotch, or banana. As for me, I'll take the homemade strawberry pie.

Toliver House

209 NORTH MAIN STREET
GORDONSVILLE, VA. 22942
(540) 832-3485

Style	Family-style
Meals	Dinner, Wednesday through Sunday; Sunday brunch
Price Range	Moderate
Superlatives	"The Toliver," fried chicken, crab cakes
Extras	Full bar

Constructed around 1870, the building that is now home to the Toliver House served as a private residence, a general store, and a nursing home prior to opening as an eatery. Mike DeCanio and Pat O'Rourke started the restaurant. The restaurant's name is a version of the surname found on the first recorded deed for the property.

There are three dining rooms in the slate-blue house. One is cream and dark green with burgundy chairs and a fruit-and-vine border around the walls. Another has light-colored paneling, mauve and cream linens, and captain's chairs. Lace curtains, sconces, tall plants in the corners, and prints on the walls add inviting touches.

The menu changes often and highlights American cuisine with Virginia fare. French onion soup, a soup du jour, chili, and Brunswick stew are offered.

The restaurant's signature dish, "The Toliver," is shrimp stuffed with lobster, then broiled. The "Gordonsville Sunday Fried Chicken Dinner" showcases fried chicken the way it was prepared

Toliver House

in the old days. Fresh whole chickens are cut in the kitchen, hand-dipped, fried golden, and served with mashed potatoes, gravy, buttermilk biscuits, and a country vegetable.

Toliver House is a homey place with a good reputation for great food and value.

ORANGE

Cape Porpoise

182 BYRD STREET / ORANGE, VA. 22960
(540) 672-0800
WWW.CAPEPORPOISELOBSTER.COM

Style	Family-style
Meals	Lunch and dinner, seven days a week; Sunday brunch. Reservations are recommended Thursday through Sunday.

Price Range	Moderate
Superlatives	Lobster, seafood fettuccini Alfredo, tiramisu
Extras	Full bar

The Cape Porpoise Lobster Company was established in the early 1970s in Kennebunkport, Maine, by the Daggett family. This family of lobster fishermen set up a restaurant and a distributorship. The mother, the late Helen Crane Daggett, was one of nine children who grew up on the family farm in Rapidian, Virginia. She married into the Maine family and was transplanted there.

Son Allen Daggett was born in Charlottesville and lived on the farm three years before moving to Maine. He had happy memories of time in Virginia and decided to expand the family enterprise back to his mother's home state. The doors of Cape Porpoise opened on July 5, 2002, and it's managed by Pat Theriault, a worldly chap with lots of restaurant experience.

The dining room is simply decorated with a nautical theme, a mural on one side, and lobster tanks near the front. Small oils lamps and burgundy napkins sit on tables covered with green-and-tan print oilcloths. The curved bar has two 32-inch televisions and a 60-inch television. The bar area has a few booths and tables with bright red tablecloths and light oak floors.

It almost goes without saying, lobster is the specialty. Lobster stew, lobster seafood rolls, lobster salad, lobster pie, just a whole Maine lobster on a platter. Steamer clams in season, Maine peel-and-eat shrimp, hot crab dip, and oysters on the half shell comprise a sampling of seafood appetizers. You can also start a meal with spicy chicken wings, onion rings, or fried mushrooms.

Lunch entrées focus on the sea with seafood quiche and the crab cake sandwich piquing my interest. A Cape griller is tuna, swordfish, or chicken breast on a toasted Kaiser roll with lettuce and tomato. French dip, classic burger, and chicken enchilada assure that everyone can find something to eat.

Clam chowder and lobster stew are usually on the menu with a chef's selection soup that changes often. The Cape Caesar salad can be topped with grilled shrimp, steak, or chicken. There are seafood, chicken, pork, and beef entrées—plain kinds of things. But the Cape Porpoise specialties look more interesting.

Seafood strudel is a unique blend of lobster, scallops, shrimp, fresh herbs, and sweet peppers inside a puff pastry, baked and served with a béchamel sauce. Lobster pie pairs lobster chunks with Newburg sauce, and the pastry on the top is in a lobster shape. It's really a cute presentation.

The wine list, like the manager, is worldly, with selections from Virginia, as well as South Africa, Germany, Italy, and other places that produce interesting wines. Pat can help you with choosing a wine to complement your meal.

Oh, and if you're craving fresh lobster or seafood and can't get to the restaurant in Orange or Kennebunkport, log on to their website and have it shipped right to your home.

The Inn at Meander Plantation

2333 NORTH JAMES MADISON HIGHWAY
LOCUST DALE, VA. 22948
(540) 672-4912
WWW.MEANDER.NET

Style	Casual nice
Meals	Dinner, Thursday through Saturday. Reservations are recommended.
Price Range	Expensive
Superlatives	Bison, white chocolate mousse crêpes
Extras	Full bar

*T*he Locust Dale post office is in a small, pre-fab building, and looks as if they can move it anytime. Perhaps they only lease the land and might need to relocate or something. According to David Van Patten, an innkeeper at The Inn at Meander Plantation, "there's not a whole lot here, but there's a lot for me."

David, you see, loves to fish, and the Robinson River and Crooked Run both come through Locust Dale. A "run," he informed me, is between a creek and a stream. So, if you like to fish, you'll love it here. Otherwise, just enjoy the pastoral beauty and sunsets.

Suzie Blanchard left her job in historic preservation, and Suzanne Thomas walked away from a journalism career in the Chicago area in 1991 to pursue the lifestyle of innkeepers at this circa 1766 plantation in the heart of Virginia. The Inn at Meander Plantation, which sits on 80 acres of rolling countryside, offers sunsets that stay in your mind long after the horizon has grown dark.

Suzie's experience has proven valuable in renovation and restoration at the inn. The eight guest rooms and suites are luxurious and romantic. Some have a private sitting area or a wood-burning fireplace. All have antiques and interesting pieces, private baths, and some are pet-friendly.

The dining room is located a step down from the spacious main entry. The old walls are painted red, and the linens are white. The floor is slate with lovely Persian rugs. Candles and fresh flowers rest on every table. It's elegant, historic, and comfortable all at once.

Dinner is *prix fixe* per person and begins with hors d'oeuvres and cocktails between 6:00 and 7:00 P.M. The first course begins around 7:00 and precedes the second, intermezzo, entrée, and the dessert courses.

Since opening in September 1992, The Inn at Meander Plantation has offered exclusively Virginia wines, beers, and microbrews. Nice nod of loyalty to the owners' newly adopted state.

Chef Paul Deigl joined the staff when they opened to the public in 2002. The food is fresh and changes with the season or whim of Chef Paul. All dinner courses have a wine suggestion, which you can buy by the glass. Two examples of first courses

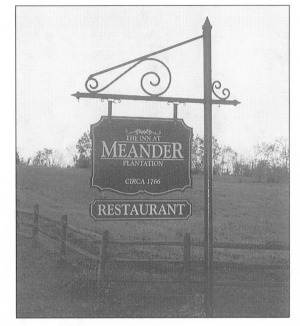

The Inn at Meander Plantation

are braised oxtail and quinoa in cabbage leaves with red wine demi-glacé and parsley oil, and fried oysters in blue corn crust, kalamata olive oil, and red pepper yogurt.

The second course is often from the salad department. While the first courses are set, there are three entrées from which to choose. Each is a complete plate such as blackened jumbo lump crab cakes with basil crème fraîche and fired leeks, green bamboo rice pilaf, and sautéed carrots with parsley oil.

A favorite dessert at The Inn at Meander Plantation is white chocolate mousse crêpes, though warm gingercake with amaretto poached pears and cinnamon whipped cream sounds divine.

Country inn cooking school is offered one week-end each month. The lessons might be about sauces, soups and stews, herbs, elegant one-dish meals, chocolate, grilling, or a host of other topics. The inn is a nice place to come, stay, relax, learn, rest, cook, and, of course, go fishing.

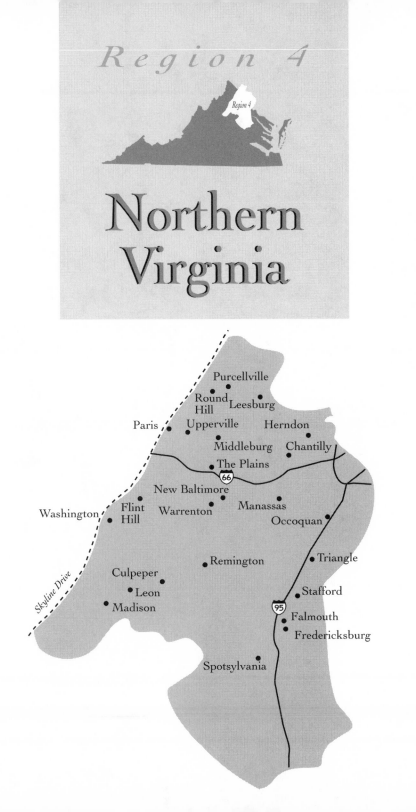

Region 4

Region 4

Northern Virginia

Purcellville

Round Hill
Leesburg

Paris

Upperville

Herndon

Middleburg
Chantilly

The Plains

66

New Baltimore

Flint Hill
Warrenton
Manassas

Washington

Occoquan

Remington
Triangle

Culpeper

Leon
Stafford

Madison
95
Falmouth

Fredericksburg

Skyline Drive

Spotsylvania

This is the region where historical tradition and contemporary living—and horses—exist in harmony. The verdant countryside is one of gentleman's farms, split-rail fences, wildflowers —and horses.

This is Virginia's hunt country. Steeplechases and fox hunts are regular weekend events, and horse breeding, training, riding, and showing are a way of life. Gift shops, restaurants, country inns, and boutiques exhibit or stock all kinds of horse-related items.

History abounds in small towns well endowed with old homes, picket fences, stone walls, and cobblestone streets. But contemporary times are nowhere more evident than in the angular architecture of the corporate and government offices that have crept west of the nation's capital.

The towns are charming. The shops are delightful. The countryside beckons. This is one of those rare growth-oriented regions that is conscientiously preserving its past.

Courthouse Café

8955 COURTHOUSE ROAD
SPOTSYLVANIA, VA. 22553
(540) 582-3302

Style	Home-style
Meals	Breakfast and lunch, seven days a week; dinner, Monday through Saturday
Price Range	Inexpensive
Superlatives	"Salt Fish Breakfast," meat loaf, bread pudding
Extras	Wine and beer

The road sign reads Spotsylvania C.H. As is the case with several other Virginia towns whose names have evolved over the years, the C.H. stands for Court House. This area is best known as the site of the Battle of Spotsylvania Court House, which took place north of town near what is now Va. 613. Here in May 1864, Union and Confederate troops battled for two weeks—sometimes for as much as 20 hours a day—in some of the most dramatic hand-to-hand combat of the Civil War. Today, the National Park Service maintains more than 5,000 acres for those who wish to learn about the battle.

At the Courthouse Café in Spotsylvania, most folks know each other. They arrive in work clothes, uniforms, or jeans—it doesn't matter. Conversations go on between patrons and waitresses, from booth to booth and even across the high front counter.

Kelli Beutel opened this restaurant in 1994, after it had been closed for about 15 years.

The seats in the Courthouse Café are bright red vinyl. Burgundy café curtains on brass rods are mounted halfway up the windows. The stained-glass hanging lamps add touches of color. Everything here is very casual—except for the cleaning team. When I visited around 7:30 P.M.—which was toward the end of the café's 14-hour day—everything was exceptionally clean.

In the morning, you can get your eggs with anything from bacon, fried bologna, or scrapple to corned beef hash, grilled pork chops, or jalapeño smoked sausage. And all the combinations come with home fries, grits, or fried apples. The "Salt Fish Breakfast" features herring that's been cleaned, filleted, and cured in salt before being soaked, breaded, frozen, and deep-fried. It's served with home fries, sliced tomatoes, and corn cakes.

Lunch is simple—a fresh soup each day, homemade chili, salads, burgers, sandwiches, and subs. You may order breakfast fare at lunch, or you can select fried chicken, grilled pork chops, a fish filet, corned beef hash, or sirloin steak.

The homemade meat loaf is popular at dinner, as is the hamburger steak dinner and the spaghetti and meatballs. Other choices include lasagna, turkey, liver and onions, veal Parmesan, and a char-broiled New York strip.

When it's time for dessert, the Courthouse Café's bread pudding ranks high on the popularity chart.

Olde Towne Steak & Seafood

1612 CAROLINE STREET
FREDERICKSBURG, VA. 22401
(540) 371-8020
WWW.OLDETOWNESTEAKANDSEAFOOD.COM

Style	Family-style
Meals	Dinner, Tuesday through Saturday
Price Range	Moderate/Expensive
Superlatives	Prime rib, prime rib, prime rib
Extras	Full bar

Some of America's most famous names are associated with Fredericksburg: Captain John Smith landed here in 1608; George Washington lived in the area from 1739 until his marriage in 1759; James Monroe had a law office here. But it is for the Battle of Fredericksburg, which took place on December 13, 1862, that the town is best known. Today, Fredericksburg's 40-block National Historic District showcases hundreds of buildings from the 18th and 19th centuries.

You can't mention Fredericksburg restaurants without hearing about Old Towne. The prime rib is described as "this thick" (picture a thumb and index finger held two inches apart) and "this big" (picture a medium-size platter).

In a brick building set back from the street, Greg and Hyon Harding have brought the concept of hands-on ownership to its height. Hyon is in the restaurant each evening greeting and seating guests and making sure everyone is content with their din-

ner. Greg has his hands full in the kitchen cooking the prime rib for which Olde Towne is so well known.

The interior is brick and wood. Captain's chairs surround tables topped with mauve-colored vinyl and oil votive candles. Artificial plants hang in copper pots and kettles. It's very crowded; wait staff and guests have to go sideways between tables. The servers wear tuxedo-style uniforms. Everyone is helpful, efficient, busy, and attentive.

Your meal begins with homemade crab soup or lobster bisque, lump crabmeat cocktail or smoked salmon, a stuffed oyster or jumbo cocktail shrimp.

Various seafood options are offered—broiled flounder stuffed with crabmeat, broiled scallops, and "Salmon Old Towne," which comes with shrimp, crabmeat, and Béarnaise sauce. Or you might enjoy stuffed lobster or lobster tail. If you love surf and turf, you can select the filet of beef paired with lobster tail, or stuffed shrimp, or the New York strip steak paired with six ounces or nine ounces of lobster tail.

The famous prime rib comes in 12- and 16-ounce portions and the filet mignon in eight- and 12-ounce portions. New York strip and Delmonico steaks are also on the menu.

Oh, and there's one lonely chicken entrée, an eight-ounce breast with Cajun spices, topped with a couple of shrimp, some crabmeat, and Béarnaise sauce.

Olde Towne's signature dessert is a hollowed-out orange filled with orange sherbet and topped with triple sec, crushed almonds, and a cherry. It's tricky to eat, as the orange turns easily under the pressure of a spoon. But there's no denying it's light and unique.

Sammy T's

801 CAROLINE STREET
FREDERICKSBURG, VA. 22401
(540) 371-2008
WWW.SAMMYTS.COM

Style	Pub
Meals	Lunch and dinner, seven days a week
Price Range	Inexpensive
Superlatives	"The Jordan," black bean cakes
Extras	Full bar

*O*wners Sammy T. and Sylvia "Sibby" Emory bought this building in 1980, some 176 years after it was built as an auction house and store. It's also been used as a post office, a residence, a gas station, and an auto supply store. Sammy T. is a retired geography professor from Mary Washington College.

The old tin ceiling has been painted a terra-cotta color. The 14 booths are made of heavy, thick wood.

Popular items at lunch are crab cake sandwich, chicken salad sandwich, and hamburgers. The black bean cakes are deep-fried beans, wheat germ, lettuce, tomato, and red onion in a pita, served with a side of hot sauce.

Most of the stuff is health oriented—falafel, an avocado melt, a bean-and-grain burger—but look closely and you'll find grilled cheese and a club sandwich. As you might expect, there's quite a selection of salads, served with homemade dressings. French fries, onion rings, and baked potatoes are also available.

The dinner entrées include chicken Parmesan, vegetarian lasagna, stuffed potatoes, quesadillas, bean burritos, and a stir-fry of broccoli, mushrooms, green peppers, and red onions.

Apple crisp, lemon chess pie, pecan pie, chocolate mousse, or rum cake can complete any meal nicely.

Smythe's Cottage

303 FAUQUIER STREET
FREDERICKSBURG, VA. 22401
(540) 373-1645
WWW.SMYTHESCOTTAGE.COM

Style	Casual nice
Meals	Lunch and dinner, Wednesday through Monday
Price Range	Moderate
Superlatives	Neat little historic house, Virginia ham biscuits, Virginia peanut soup
Extras	Full bar

*I*n this 160-year-old former blacksmith shop hangs an upside-down portrait of Ulysses S. Grant that was noted in a 1984 issue of *National Geographic*. It seems that the founder of the restaurant, Joyce Ackerman, had a great-great-grandfather who was hung by his

Smythe's Cottage

thumbs during a Civil War interrogation. The best retaliation she could think of was not only to hang Grant—a well-known bourbon imbiber—upside down but also to place him across from the bar, facing the bourbon but out of its reach.

The little house is neatly framed with a picket fence. Floors of brick and old wood, farm antiques, hanging lanterns, an old wood stove, homemade print valances, and matching menu covers give the place a rustic feel. The pen-and-ink drawings hanging in the dining rooms are the work of waiter and artist Jim Frakes. Splashes of elegance include soft classical music and servers in colonial attire. There's dining inside and out, with room for a little more than 50 when all the tables are set.

Lonnie Williams, a former chef at the Pentagon and at George Mason University, bought the restaurant in 1987. Now, his daughter Jessica Frakes owns and manages the business, having learned well from her father.

Smythe's Cottage serves an upscale version of Southern and Virginia cuisine. Peanut soup is a staple, as are such items as chicken pot pie, ham biscuits, ginger beef, and roast pork with spiced apples.

Lunch is a simple affair. Soup, salads, a quiche of the day, biscuits, and sandwiches are offered. The sandwiches—sliced breast of turkey, ham and Swiss, roast beef, tuna salad, and chicken salad among them—can be ordered half or whole or as a soup-and-sandwich combination.

Dinner entrées such as "Turkey Shortcake" (sliced turkey served on cornbread with a cheddar cheese sauce), "Braised Brace of Quail" (served with a bourbon sauce, which I guess Grant would've liked), and "Trout Boil" (rainbow trout poached with vegetables) caught my eye. All entrées come with soup or salad, a vegetable, and freshly baked bread. Children under 10 receive a half portion for half price.

FALMOUTH

Paradise Diner
268 WARRENTON ROAD (U.S. 17)
FALMOUTH, VA. 22405
(540) 372-2013

Style	Diner
Meals	Breakfast, lunch, and dinner, Tuesday through Sunday
Price Range	Inexpensive/Moderate
Superlatives	Greek omelets, chicken kabobs, stuffed shrimp
Extras	Full bar

*F*almouth was founded in 1728. During the Civil War, Walt Whitman and Clara Barton worked side by side here, treating wounded soldiers at Chatham, a Georgian-style mansion now operated by the National Park Service. Another local attraction is Belmont, the estate of painter Gari Melchers. Some of Melchers's works are displayed in the stone studio on the property.

The Paradise Diner is located on U.S. 17 about a mile north of the U.S. 1 junction. Formerly a bar, the building is a white brick place with statues of Greek gods and a flagpole flying the United States and Virginia flags. Inside, you'll find more statues, along with lots of mirrors, artificial plants, and silk flowers. The booth seats and chairs are dark blue.

At age 15, owner Jimmy Zotos traveled alone from Greece to the United States and started working as a dishwasher in the Baltimore area. From there, he moved from restaurant to restaurant, learning everything. The Paradise Diner is his third restaurant.

While this diner offers American, Italian, and Greek cuisine, Greek is definitely the strong suit. In the morning, the Greek omelet—fresh eggs, gyro meat, onions, mushrooms, tomatoes, green peppers, and feta cheese—is featured. If that's not your style, then there are hot cakes, chipped beef, and waffles.

At lunch, the sandwiches run the gamut from roast beef, pastrami, tuna salad, and chicken salad to hamburgers and subs. The "Paradise Special" has two pieces of French toast with bacon, turkey, cheese, and tomato, all grilled and served with french fries or onion rings. A barbecue platter is also offered.

Dinner entrées include steaks, beef liver, lamb chops, pork chops, spaghetti, and lasagna. The shrimp is stuffed with crabmeat and served with Béarnaise sauce. The Greek influence is felt in the souvlaki, gyros, moussaka, and shish kabobs. A popular dish is the chicken kabob—green peppers, tomatoes, onions, and chicken served on rice with chicken gravy.

The Paradise Diner has no trouble at all selling dessert. Knowing that people eat with their eyes, Jimmy has strategically placed a tall, rotating dessert display right inside the front door. It's the first thing you see, and you're not likely to forget it. The desserts aren't made at the restaurant, but they are made for the restaurant, and every one of them looks scrumptious.

If you're seated in the dining room on the right next to the inside wall, you'll find yourself next to another dessert display. This is the kind of place where it's tough to skip dessert even when you know you should.

Inn at Kelly's Ford

16589 EDWARDS SHOP ROAD
REMINGTON, VA. 22734
(540) 399-1779
WWW.INNATKELLYSFORD.COM

Style	Fine dining
Meals	Dinner, Wednesday through Sunday; Sunday brunch. Reservations are recommended.
Price Range	Expensive
Superlatives	Atmosphere, view, world-class chef
Extras	Full bar

*I*f you come from the north, you won't marvel so much at this location as you will if you drive up from Va. 3. You'll wind up and down and around the narrow, sometimes bumpy, roads, and you might be glad that you haven't eaten yet. The inn has done a great job of placing little signs at every corner or intersection where you might question which way to go.

In any event, the initial reward of getting there from Va. 3 comes when you stop and get out of the vehicle. The second reward is the awesome view across the river, where beyond the river you see horses grazing and hills in the distance.

Built circa 1779, the main house, which is now cream with dark gray trim, has been impeccably restored and renovated. It's lovely, quite upscale, and I felt uncomfortable in blue jeans, a white shirt, and blazer.

The dining room is richly furnished with mahogany or cherry spindle-back chairs, white linens, and fresh roses arranged with baby's breath and greenery. A huge stone fireplace adds warmth to the elegant atmosphere. This wonderful fireplace extends down into Pelham's Pub below, another exquisitely furnished and appointed place to relax and dine.

There are small cottage suites on the grounds and a large equestrian center with indoor and outdoor riding rings. Everything is beautiful on this 500-acre estate where the Civil War Battle of Kelly's Ford took place.

Appetizers capitalize on fresh seafood, with smoked salmon, cold jumbo crab and crayfish salad, mussels in curry sauce, and filet of trout in white-wine jelly as some of the offerings. There's always a soup du jour and Caesar salad or mesclun with goat cheese and vinaigrette.

Linguini prepared a couple ways is there for pasta lovers, and entrées might include sirloin steak in shallot sauce, lamb chop with sage jus, tilapia with garlic sauce, or shrimp in rum coconut sauce. Specials are offered often, and the desserts are homemade.

The Sunday brunch menu changes with seasons and chef's choices, but you might find pork loin au jus, sautéed trout with almond, eggs Benedict, a crayfish omelet, or beef tenderloin tips with green peppercorn sauce. Burgers, sandwiches, salads, small pizzas, and a few other enticing light meals are offered in the pub.

Overnight guest rooms and suites are in the $170 to $250 range with a full breakfast included.

Activities right here or nearby include horseback trail riding, golfing, riding a bicycle, taking a canoe ride, playing lawn games, fishing, swimming, or just gazing at the view and resting your mind.

The Bavarian Chef

U.S. 29 SOUTH OF TOWN
MADISON, VA. 22727
(540) 948-6505

Style	Casual nice
Meals	Dinner, Wednesday through Sunday. Reservations are strongly recommended.
Price Range	Moderate
Superlatives	German cuisine, veal shank
Extras	Full bar

*T*he Bavarian Chef is in a chalet-style building with lots of wood, German music, and a cozy atmosphere. It's very European with wrought-iron sconces and chandeliers, little oil lamps on the tables, and mauve-and-white linens.

Jerome Thalwitz is the owner. His father is from Bavaria, and he and Jerome have lived in the United States and in Germany. Mike Tyler, who apprenticed under a couple of the great German chefs in Virginia, worked as sous chef under Jerome until Jerome started The Bavarian Chef of Williamsburg early in 2003. Then Mike took over here as manager and chef.

The appetizers are not as German as the entrées.

There's Virginia apple-smoked trout, shrimp cocktail, cream of wild mushroom soup, and New England clam chowder for American dishes. You could start your meal with snails in beer batter Provençal or *Urgarische goulash suppe*.

Skipping over to the "Entrées" section, you'll find New York strip steak, filet mignon, and steak au poivre. But I suggest you study and select one of the German dishes. Wiener schnitzel, jager schnitzel, and the German classic, sauerbraten, are offered. *Mandel schnitzel* is a pork tenderlin coated with almonds and served in an unusual (and unusually sweet, though delicious) strawberry gin sauce. The traditional Bavarian sausage platter combines weisswurst, bauernwurst, and bratwurst with homemade sauerkraut.

Burgundy sauce and cream sauce smother several entrées, and the cordon bleu is a veal steak filled with ham and Swiss cheese. Other entrées are prepared using German customs, with breading and sauces you might not get to taste often.

You don't have to imagine what the desserts look like. The server will bring an enticing tray to your table and describe each one in a manner that makes you want a bite of each. The Black Forest cake is traditional, and one of the most popular desserts is saca torte, a flourless chocolate cake—rich and sweet. It is also low carb, but perhaps not low calorie.

The Bavarian Chef, here and I suspect also in Williamsburg, is packed, so plan ahead, make a reservation, and if you're spending the night, stay at

Ridge View B&B (www.virginia-ridgeview.com). It's just a few miles away on Route 231. It's really nice, peaceful, and relaxing, and it makes a great base from which to go shopping, antiquing, or visiting local wineries.

Pig N' Steak

WASHINGTON STREET / MADISON, VA. 22727
(540) 948-3130

Style	Home-style
Meals	Lunch and dinner, seven days a week
Price Range	Inexpensive
Superlatives	Ribs, fresh steaks, low-carb selections
Extras	Full bar

*I*t's hard to find pulled, pit-cooked barbecue that my husband, John, and I don't like. It seems, though, that the fancier the place, the worse the barbecue.

Pig N' Steak isn't very fancy, but, as the rule cited above might lead you to suspect, the barbecue is very good. Eating here may be a high-cholesterol experience, as someone in the area suggested to me, but who wants to live without one on occasion? And if you are eating low carb, this is the place to be.

The restaurant building was once a turkey farm. Inside, there's a bar to the left and a sign for those in bad need of civilizing: "No street shoes allowed on bar." You'll note the airplane made from

Budweiser cans by some patron. Straight ahead and to the right are wooden tables and vinyl chairs. In the back is a glorious mural of horses by local artist, the late Diane Perl. She finished and signed it in 1987.

Naturally, I'm going to suggest the barbecue sandwich for lunch, along with a small basket of french fries. (If you love fries and can eat a mound about the size of a football, order the small basket. Someone back in the kitchen has a generous conception of small when it comes to fries.) You can also get a cheeseburger, a chicken sandwich, a BLT loaded with bacon, a hot dog, or a rib-eye steak sandwich. Potato salad and macaroni salad are available some of the time.

For the low-carb eater, meals of char-broiled chicken with baked sweet potatoes, steamed vegetables, and low-carb bread are here for you. Appetizers include fried dill pickles, fried stuffed black olives, jalapeño peppers stuffed with cheese, and hot wings.

The barbecue platters are especially popular at dinner. They come with your choice of two items from among fries, slaw, and baked beans. The hickory-smoked ribs have been smoked a minimum of 12 hours. The "Mountaineer Platter" comes with fries, slaw, and a half-pound hamburger with all the trimmings. There are also two chicken options. And as its name suggests, Pig N' Steak is known for its steaks. They're not listed on the menu, because the selection depends on what's currently available. But rest assured that they're always fresh and never frozen.

As with most serious barbecue places, you can carry Pig N' Steak's barbecue away by the pound.

If you're a local resident, consider these folks for hosting a catered pig roast. My fond memories of pig roasts go all the way back to the mountains of Colorado, but that's another story.

LEON

The Grille at Prince Michel

PRINCE MICHEL OF VIRGINIA
U.S. 29 / LEON, VA. 22725
(800) 800-WINE
WWW.PRINCEMICHEL.COM

Style	Winery, Casual nice
Meals	Lunch, Thursday through Sunday; dinner, Wednesday through Saturday
Price Range	Moderate
Superlatives	The wine, Georgetown Farm filet mignon
Extras	Wine and beer. The winery is open every day except major holidays.

Like lots of places in Virginia, this town is so small that it has only a post office and a handful of houses. But a governor was born in the area. James Lawson Kemper was born near Leon in 1823 and moved his family to a Greek Revival home here in 1865.

The winery Prince Michel was founded in 1983 by Jean Leducq of France. It is located in an attractive brick building on the western side of U.S. 29 a few miles north of Madison. The restau-rant was established in 1992 for this stated purpose: "To offer one of life's great pleasures: the enjoyment of great wines with outstanding food."

The newly renovated dining area is off the museum, making it much more a part of the winery than the former dining room on the lower level. It's open, bright, and airy with patio dining under a trellis in pleasant weather. The linens are white, and the furniture has been made from recovered oak barrels.

Oriental rugs over gray tile, fresh flowers, candle votives, and exposed beams create a warm, inviting atmosphere. However, it's the intent that the décor not overwhelm the food. After all, you are here to eat foremost.

Cream of shiitake mushroom soup, smoked salmon pizza, and farmer's pâté of *kornichons* (French for gherkins) are good starters. Soups, salads, and sandwiches fill the lunch menu.

Dinner entrées may change, and some of them may include seared rainbow trout, crayfish étouffé, and free-range chicken with grilled polenta squares and sage cream. The Georgetown Farm filet mignon is served with shallot port-wine glaze.

The ice cream and sorbets are homemade. A ginger ice cream sandwich with chocolate fudge sounds good. You'll also find freshly baked cookies, pastries, and almond pound cake with fresh fruit compote.

Prince Michel wines are available by the glass during lunch and dinner. Someone is always available to assist with wine selection.

Besides enjoying a leisurely lunch or dinner, you must reserve time to visit the museum, view the video presentation, take the self-guided tour of the winery, and browse the gift shop.

Visiting Prince Michel shouldn't be something you do on your way to something else. It is worthy of being a destination, especially since there are now elegant one-bedroom suites for overnight stays. The decor is French Provincial, which recalls the countryside of France. With spacious living rooms, fireplaces, views, and secluded garden patios, this is good place for a getaway or vacation.

Baby Jim's

701 NORTH MAIN STREET
CULPEPER, VA. 22701
(540) 825-9212

Style	Snack bar
Meals	Breakfast and lunch, Monday through Saturday
Price Range	Inexpensive
Superlatives	Steak sandwiches, shrimp boxes, chicken boxes

Captain John Smith came to the site of Culpeper one year after the founding of Jamestown. The county was named for Lord Thomas Culpeper, the colonial governor from 1680 to 1683. The town was called Fairfax before Culpeper became the official name in 1870. Many Civil War battles were fought in and around the town, which was occupied by each side a number of times. One local farmer whose property was devastated is said to have remarked, "I hain't took no sides in this yer rebellion, but I'll be dog-garned if both sides hain't took me."

Just in case you're not familiar with weekend fun in Culpeper, here's one popular activity: back your car in front of Baby Jim's and watch the traffic go by. If you can find a parking place, that is. This local landmark is especially popular after football games and on weekend nights. Its sign was refurbished a year or so back and is identical to the original one.

Collis Jenkins III runs the place, and he knows about things to do in Culpeper because he grew up here. Not just in town, but right here at Baby Jim's, which is built on the front of the family home. Baby Jim's was the first fast-food place in town when his dad opened it on March 7, 1947. Another eight years would pass before Ray Kroc opened his first McDonald's. Collis the third figures he'll stick around for a while even though operating this friendly, old-time snack bar doesn't let him get much use out of his American University degree in real estate and urban development.

There are a few picnic tables on either side of the building and two windows inside to place your order. The interior is about the size of a house hallway, only a few feet longer.

Baby Jim's opens at 4:30 A.M. for the Washington, D.C., commuters who pop in for breakfast before joining the early rush that precedes the main rush hour. They leave with sausage and egg, ham and egg, and bacon and egg sandwiches, hash browns, and perhaps a biscuit or two. And most likely coffee.

Hamburgers, hot dogs, grilled ham and cheese sandwiches, egg sandwiches, ham salad, chicken salad, and tuna salad are among the items offered throughout the remainder of the day. The steak sandwiches are especially good. Prices top out with the shrimp platter.

There's a prominently placed sign here that reads, "No loud talking, no foul language," so be sure to mind your manners.

Hazel River Inn

195 E. DAVIS STREET
CULPEPER, VA. 22701
(540) 825-7148
WWW.HAZELRIVERINN.COM

Style	Casual nice
Meals	Lunch and dinner, Thursday through Monday. Reservations are accepted.
Price Range	Moderate/Expensive
Superlatives	Fried oysters, crab cakes, chocolate torte
Extras	Full bar

What's the harm in looking at an old house that's for sale? That's the question that passed through the minds of Peter and Karen Stogbuchner when they were in Culpeper visiting friends in 1993. Well, there was no harm done, just a relocation, change of lifestyle, and a couple of new businesses.

As you can guess, they liked the house. They bought it—a century-old place on the morningside of the Blue Ridge Mountains. They opened a small B&B the next year. Five years later, a local restaurant was abandoned. With all the equipment in place and a great downtown location, Peter and Karen purchased the restaurant and downstairs pub.

They had already been in the food business. Peter is an Austrian native and chef du cuisine, having trained in Europe and at the country club where he met Karen. She is a horticulturist from Maryland and still maintains gardens where they grow herbs, tomatoes, and other edibles used in the restaurant.

Hazel River Inn has a lovely, rustic, contemporary dining room—lovely with white-and-blue linens, cream chairs with flowered seats, and a very large brick fireplace; rustic with beams and old brick walls a century or so old; contemporary with a couple of walls painted medium green that hold some modern art.

Lunch might be a steak sandwich on French bread, a hamburger on a Kaiser roll, a grilled Reuben, or a chicken sandwich, along with some salads and Virginia smoked trout. You can even get cheese and crackers with fresh fruit or ginger barbecue shrimp.

My husband, John, fancies himself a quasi-expert on fried oysters. Obviously, we eat out a lot to write two editions of this book, and he orders fried oysters a lot. According to him, Hazel River Inn's fried oysters in the fried oyster and spinach salad are tops on his long list of oyster consumption. Another interesting appetizer is the warm lobster and spinach strudel with roasted squash.

If you move directly into the entrée section, which changes often and seasonally, you might encounter roasted Colorado rack of lamb, filet mignon, roasted rabbit, sage and rosemary Cornish hen, or mushroom-stuffed quail. They're all creative, fresh, and wonderfully prepared.

Desserts vary by the season and by the whim of chef Peter. He makes tiramisu and a very popular chocolate torte, among other things.

Before or after your meal, be sure to pop into the pub downstairs. It takes the term rustic to new heights with wood tables many inches thick; the fabulous brick fireplace; more huge, old beams; and a crooked floor. It's charming and opens directly into the parking lot. And don't forget the B&B by the same name at the same website.

It's About Thyme

128 EAST DAVIS STREET / CULPEPER, VA. 22701
(540) 825-4264

Style	Casual nice
Meals	Lunch, Monday through Saturday; dinner, Tuesday through Saturday
Price Range	Moderate
Superlatives	Atmosphere, murals
Extras	Full bar

*T*his classy place with a striped awning out front rivals any big-city spot for atmosphere. From the dark green tin ceiling to the original murals on the walls to the wood floors, It's About Thyme evokes artistic elegance.

You don't have to know much about art to recognize the characters in the impressionist murals as adaptations of those in the best of Monet and Renoir. Owner and chef John Yarnell has a lengthy history of opening restaurants. For this, his most recent acquisition, he hired Italian artist Davide Rodoquino to create the unique floor-to-ceiling scenes.

The attractive etched globe lamps were custom-made for the building when it was renovated before Yarnell moved in. Each of the wooden tables has fresh flowers, a bottle of wine, sparkling crystal, and fine silverware. Instrumental music sets the tone for Yarnell's European country cuisine.

For lunch, you can go with roasted peppers and artichoke hearts or a puff pastry sandwich. Bruschetta—a crusty bread topped with tomato, basil, and garlic and then finished with Parmesan

It's About Thyme

Kirsten's of Culpeper

219 EAST DAVIS STREET / CULPEPER, VA. 22701
(540) 829-8400

Style	Casual nice
Meals	Lunch and dinner, Tuesday through Saturday. Reservations are recommended on weekends.
Price Range	Moderate/Expensive
Superlatives	Scallops, crabmeat tart, chocolate cherry cake
Extras	Full bar

cheese—is also available, as are soups and salads. Main courses such as grilled tuna and pesto or chicken and dumplings are offered.

The dinner appetizers include portobello mushrooms and cold poached salmon. The soups might be cream of potato and turkey and pasta. For your entrée, you might try scallops served the French way—with cream, brandy, and mushrooms, topped with whipped potatoes. Roasted chicken, tuna filets, and roasted pork loin are often available. Items such as beef kidney with white onions and red wine will please the restaurant's European clientele.

Fresh desserts such as flourless chocolate torte and Key lime pie are made daily.

At the time I visited and chatted with Yarnell, he had plans to open a smoking room upstairs and to add patio dining in the alley beside the entrance. After seeing his stylistic touches inside It's About Thyme, I'd guess that any alley he creates for dining will be quite inviting and romantic.

*I*n a classy spot with rustic brick walls and a contemporary black-and-white color scheme, Kirsten's of Culpeper offers creative cuisine and impeccable service. The bar in the back corner has hanging stained-glass lamps. A few large window frames and shutters on the brick walls add a whimsical touch. The gas fireplace warms the dining-room atmosphere on chilly evenings.

Andrew Ferlazzo began his food-service career at a country club when he was 15. He worked in many fine restaurants in Florida and Virginia before deciding to strike out on his own. "Partners don't work well in this business," he had observed, "and I want to do my thing, my way."

So he found a place right here in his hometown that he could get into on his own. Andrew opened the restaurant in the fall of 2002, naming it for his infant daughter, Kirsten.

The first thing to arrive at our table, besides the

menu, was a warm, coarse-textured, grain bread with olive oil for dipping. The oil had garlic, rosemary, and special ingredients for a nice taste. Also with the bread was a small container holding a blended cream cheese with shallots, garlic, and parsley.

Exercise a little restraint with this delicious bread because there's much more to come, and it's all freshly and professionally prepared. A couple of the popular lunch items are the crimini mushroom tart with sherry cream sauce and the jumbo lump crabmeat tart with roasted red pepper coulis. Both come with a house salad.

Regular soups are cream of carrot, cumin, black bean, and bacon. A tortilla wrap comes with smoked mozzarella, spinach, peppers, and onions. There's also BLT, Monte Cristo, and fried egg sandwiches among other lunch ideas.

Dinner is a fine affair with fried oysters, the mushroom tart, a baby spinach salad, and crabmeat tart for some of the appetizers. The scallops entrée is a creative concoction of jumbo scallops with Parmesan bacon risotto, roasted tomatoes, and sautéed crimini mushrooms, corn, and spinach.

Spicy sautéed orange roughy is served with stir-fried basmati rice, olives, cherry tomatoes, and yellow squash. There's another seafood entrée with salmon, and an applewood-smoked bacon-wrapped pork medallion with Jack Daniel's sweet potato purée. Certified Angus beef® flat-iron steak comes peppercorn crusted or with herb butter and is served with garlic smashed potatoes and a specially prepared vegetable.

Kirsten's chocolate cherry cake is a favorite, and apple pecan cake, pumpkin gelato, and warmed lemon hazelnut torte are just as good because they are all homemade.

This is a really nice place with a really nice staff and terrific food. Kirsten's also does special events, holiday parties, and functions that include charity dinners. Any place that participates in charity events, especially in its early years in business, accepts a social responsibility in their community, and I think that's great.

Durango's

2610 JEFFERSON DAVIS HIGHWAY (U.S. 1)
STAFFORD, VA. 22554
(540) 720-6315

Style	Family-style
Meals	Lunch and dinner, seven days a week
Price Range	Moderate
Superlatives	Prime rib, baby back ribs
Extras	Full bar

Stafford County and the town of Stafford were named for Staffordshire, England. Just north of town is a marker noting an Indian trail that became a frontier road in 1664. More than 100 years later, George Washington traveled this road on his way to Yorktown.

Steve Estes is a native Californian who just likes steakhouses a lot. He worked in restaurants while attending Embry-Riddle University in Florida, then put in a few years with a couple of chain restaurants. He was working for an independent place when a Golden Corral restaurant closed on U.S. 1 just south of Fredericksburg. Steve consulted an atlas for a Western-sounding name, found the town of Durango in southern Colorado, and started his own Western-style steakhouse in the old Golden Corral in 1992.

Four years later, he constructed this new building on U.S. 1 just north of Stafford. It was decorated by his wife, Keri, and his mother, Sally Estes. It's very clean and very Western, with lots of wood, country-and-western music, and Western prints.

The lunch plates include your choice of meat, two fresh vegetables, and freshly baked bread. There are more than a dozen meat choices, such as "Rodeo Riblets," teriyaki steak, catfish, shrimp, a chicken breast, and pork chops. Among the dozen vegetable choices are baby carrots, baked potatoes, mashed potatoes, sweet potatoes, and rice and gravy. Burgers, roast beef sandwiches, and chicken sandwiches are also offered. You can choose from among several appetizers, soups, salads, and pasta dishes.

Dinner features lots of beef, of course. Prime rib, filet mignon, and steaks are offered, as are ribs, chops, and combination specials such as filet mignon and lobster, filet mignon and shrimp, and steak and lobster. Value is emphasized in Durango's inexpensive "Lighter Side" meals, for which you may select one meat and two vegetables; bread comes with your meal.

Durango's desserts, appropriately called "Fantas-

tic Finishes," include cherry cobbler, Key lime pie, and "Brownie Bottom Pie."

STAFFORD

The Log Cabin

1749 JEFFERSON DAVIS HIGHWAY (U.S. 1)
STAFFORD, VA. 22554
(540) 659-5067

Style	Casual nice
Meals	Dinner, seven days a week
Price Range	Moderate/Expensive
Superlatives	Crab, Cajun pasta dishes
Extras	Full bar

Besides being a charming log structure, The Log Cabin is one of the few old restaurants that have survived along U.S. 1, which used to be one of the main arteries through the state.

Darrell and Tammy Mitchell have been operating The Log Cabin—formerly an Esso station and general store—since 1979. Darrell's grandfather purchased the place in 1941, primarily for use as a dance hall. Darrell's dad, George "Slug" Summerfield Mitchell, also ran it as a bar and dance hall. His was one of the first places in the area to offer pizza. But it's Darrell and Tammy who are responsible for creating an elegant dining experience here.

The fireplace still burns real wood. The exquisite piano near the entrance dates from around 1890. The hanging lamps are definitely one of a kind. They're inverted peach baskets that Darrell bought and wired. The tablecloths are burgundy, and the chairs are basic black vinyl. The atmosphere is rustic and casual.

Crab is one of their specialties at The Log Cabin, and it comes many ways. Chef Mike Buttram, who's been here almost two decades, is emphatic that no fillers be added to the crabmeat. The restaurant's signature soup is a cream-based white crab with a hint of wine. The appetizers include a crabmeat cocktail. Crab cakes and a crab sampler are stable menu items.

Clams and spiced shrimp are popular among those who elect not to choose a crab appetizer.

Brazilian lobster tails and a lobster and steak combination are among the entrées. The "Northeast Feast" entrée features a Maine lobster, Gulf shrimp, steamed clams, and Alaskan snow crab legs. A couple of New Orleans dishes are offered—a three-seafood garlic fettuccine and shrimp Diane. The Norfolk-style seafood offerings include various combinations of crab, shrimp, lobster, and scallops. Beef lovers can select filet mignon any night or prime rib on Friday and Saturday evenings.

The most popular dessert here is "Bourbon Street Crunch," a sweet variety of chocolate pie.

TRIANGLE

The Globe and Laurel

18418 JEFFERSON DAVIS HIGHWAY (U.S. 1)
TRIANGLE, VA. 22172
(703) 221-5763

Style	Pub
Meals	Lunch, Monday through Friday; dinner, Monday through Saturday. The pub is closed on national holidays.
Price Range	Moderate
Superlatives	Military memorabilia, roast duckling à l'orange
Extras	Full bar

U.S. 1 meets two county roads at the entrance to the Marine Corps base at Quantico, forming the neat little triangle with flowers planted in it that gives this community its name. Otherwise, the town isn't much more than gas stations and a few motels and stores along U.S. 1.

Richard Spooner, a retired Marine Corps major, opened this restaurant in 1968. When asked why, he responded, "Oh, I think it's the dream of every Marine to have a little bar to swap stories."

This may have been a little bar at one time, but it's evolved into a restaurant. It's a great place to swap stories, but it's also more than that. It's a veritable museum of patches, medals, swords, crests, and other memorabilia from military units all over the world.

Dozens of little flags hang over the bar area. If Spooner knows in advance that foreign patrons are coming to dine, he sets the flag of their country with the United States flag on their table. He says they appreciate that, and I'm sure they do. Also, they might feel inclined to contribute something from their country to his collection of memorabilia.

Wooden tables are crowded in a room that can hold about 30, and a front dining room can seat another 30 or so. It's all very cozy and warm, and it's smoke-free.

There's a lot of consideration for fat intake here. The menu notes that there's only one gram of fat in the wheat bread (without butter) and two grams in the French onion soup (without croutons and cheese).

At lunch, the excellent salade niçoise has lettuce, tuna, egg, potato, artichoke hearts, hearts of palm, bell peppers, sliced mushrooms, and capers—and anchovies if you wish. The sandwiches include ham and Swiss, a Reuben, a turkey club, steak, grilled chicken breast, and barbecued beef. Each comes with the soup du jour or a garden salad.

Among the dinner entrées are a vegetarian platter, New York strip steak, roast duckling à l'orange with Grand Marnier sauce, and filet mignon with Béarnaise sauce.

Coffee, espresso, cappuccino, and a nice selection of teas are offered.

Regardless of your interest in military history and memorabilia, this is a good place to find a warm welcome and get a good meal.

OCCOQUAN

Sea Sea & Co.

201 MILL STREET / OCCOQUAN, VA. 22125
(703) 494-1365

Style	Family-style
Meals	Lunch and dinner, seven days a week

Price Range	Moderate
Superlatives	Crab cakes, "Apple Walnut Crunch"
Extras	Full bar

*H*ere's a large, bright restaurant overlooking the Occoquan River. The theme is nautical. The interior is predominantly blue and white, with lots of natural wood. There's also dining at tables on the patio, where you practically become part of the waterfront. A bridge is to the right, boats crowd a marina to the left, and sea gulls are everywhere. In short, there's no mistaking that this is a seafood restaurant.

Since each order is prepared individually, the management requests customers' patience if they have to wait a bit. As it says right on the menu, "We assure you—it will be worth it." And indeed it is.

The lunch specialties include salmon, a fried clam platter, and oysters. Among the many salad plates are chilled spicy shrimp salad and tuna salad. There's also a "Chicken Salad Supreme," a spinach salad, and a chef salad. If you'd prefer to try the chicken salad or one of the seafood salads in a sandwich, it will come with lettuce on a fresh croissant. Other sandwiches include a Reuben, hamburgers, cod, and hot ham and Swiss, all of which are served with french fries.

You have to be 21 years of age or older to order the "Oyster Shooter," an appetizer of freshly shucked oysters floating in vodka. A raw bar sampler, crab soup, crab puffs, and oysters on the half shell are some of the other appetizers. The house specialties at dinner are grilled shrimp salad, grilled chicken salad, and surf and turf—filet mignon and lobster tail. Rainbow trout amandine, stuffed shrimp, and Cajun catfish are but a few of the selections from the sea. Other entrées include barbecued baby back ribs and marinated chicken breast.

You may end your meal with Key lime pie, strawberry shortcake, or peanut butter pie, but I urge you to have Sea Sea & Co.'s most popular dessert—hot "Apple Walnut Crunch" with ice cream.

The Depot

65 SOUTH STREET / WARRENTON, VA. 20186
(540) 347-1212

Style	Casual nice
Meals	Dinner, Tuesday through Saturday. The restaurant is closed on Monday year-round and on Sunday during July and August.
Price Range	Inexpensive/Moderate
Superlatives	*Mnazzaleh*, chocolate mousse cake
Extras	Full bar

Known as Fauquier Court House when it was founded in 1760, this community was renamed Warrenton in honor of Dr. Joseph Warren, a man who helped Paul Revere begin his famous ride and who later died at the Battle of Bunker Hill. Today, one of Warrenton's attractions is the Old Jail Museum, located in one of the oldest jails in Virginia. The museum houses an interesting collection of Indian, Revolutionary War, and Civil War artifacts.

One of the town's dining attractions is The Depot. There's something appealingly nostalgic about old train depots. The original exterior of this depot is now an inside wall. Train pictures and memorabilia are tastefully arranged on narrow ledges and shelves. The cozy room to the left has a bar. The dining area in the back is a solarium-style room with a fireplace. Another dining room has a hunt theme and a fireplace. Patio dining in nice weather brings the seating to just under 80. A park with railroad cars and grassy areas has been created on the back border of the property.

Owner Karen Dorbayan grew up in the restaurant business. Her father, Charles Saah, started the Iron Gate Inn in Washington, D.C., in the 1950s. Many of Karen's recipes came from him. She and her husband, Behruze, opened The Depot in 1976 with a focus on innovative Mediterranean and American cuisine.

The Depot's signature dish, *Mnazzaleh*, is roasted eggplant with ground lamb, onions, and pine nuts. Lamb is another specialty here. You might try the braised shank of lamb or the ground lamb stuffed into cabbage rolls. Crab cakes, Venezuelan crabmeat, and calves liver are often offered.

Baklawa (spelled baklava most other places) is one of The Depot's most popular desserts. It's a delightful pastry with a taste of walnuts. But I suggest you try the "Stolen Orange Cake" in the

summer. Another time you could go with chocolate mousse cake.

Fantastico

380 BROADVIEW AVENUE
WARRENTON, VA. 20186
(540) 349-2575
WWW.FANTASTICO-INN.COM

Style	Italian
Meals	Lunch, Monday through Friday; dinner, Monday through Sunday
Price Range	Moderate
Superlatives	Homemade pasta, veal
Extras	Full bar

*T*he Oderda family moved to the United States
from Turin, Italy, in the 1980s. The parents came
first and the grown children followed.

In 1989, the family opened Fantastico in an upscale shopping center at the intersection of U.S. 17
and U.S. 211. In 1998, the restaurant moved to a
large stone building on the other side of the intersection. It is now owned by Mario Oderda and
Amilcare Strona. The dining rooms are lovely, and
there's a piano bar and 14 guest rooms, too.

The most important thing, of course, is that the
northern Italian cuisine moves with the family. The
menu items appear in Italian with English descriptions below. Grilled polenta with roasted bell peppers in a garlic sauce is one of the hot appetizers.
The arugula, radicchio, and fennel salad with

shaved Parmesan cheese and the "Insalata Giulio
Cesare" salad with croutons and Caesar dressing
are popular. A soup of the day is offered, as is a
traditional Italian mixed-vegetable soup.

The numerous pasta entrées feature a wide variety of sauces and stuffings. There's red clam sauce,
white clam sauce, pesto sauce, wine sauce, and rosemary sauce. The beef entrées number two, the
chicken entrées three, and the veal entrées more
than half a dozen. It's all very Italian.

When I dined here, the Oderdas were experi-
menting with some delectable desserts imported
from Italy, and they stock both imported tiramisu
and gelato, which are sure to satisfy the after-dinner sweet tooth.

Most of the wines are from Italy and Virginia,
and they always offer champagne for those occasions when nothing else will do.

Napoleon's

67 WATERLOO STREET
WARRENTON, VA. 20186
(540) 347-4300

Style	Casual nice
Meals	Lunch and dinner, seven days a week
Price Range	Inexpensive/Moderate
Superlatives	"French Connection," daily specials
Extras	Full bar

*N*apoleon's is a spiffy eatery with casual dining
in a solarium setting on the ground level and a more

upscale restaurant with tablecloths in the upstairs section of the house.

Built in the 1830s, the Greek Revival structure has been home to an attorney, a judge, an artist, a writer, and a general who served in both houses of Congress. At some point, it was chopped into apartments.

Philip Harway bought it in 1977 and opened Napoleon's the following year. In May 2002, Al Nosrat, a restaurateur for more than three decades, bought it. He brought a wealth of experience and his graduate degree in business.

The exterior is now white with red shutters. The terrace outside the solarium is outfitted with yellow-and-white-striped umbrellas, while the outdoor garden dining area has green umbrellas. In the booth section downstairs, the seats are burgundy and the Formica tables are coral. The atmosphere is upbeat, cheerful, and noisy. The quieter, more traditional dining room upstairs has pink walls, burgundy linens, and stemware.

The item on the menu called "French Connection" is a croissant filled with ham, Swiss cheese, and cream cheese, baked and served with fruit, and it is yummy. A quiche of the day is always available, and there are burgers, crab cake sandwiches, grilled vegetable foccacia, and other things.

Grilled chicken fettuccini pesto; beef stir-fry rigatoni; Wellington's mixed grill with a filet medallion, venison, and andouille sausage; and sautéed Virginia brook trout are some of the dinner entrées. The "Tournedos Napoleon" are sautéed tenderloin medallions with ancho pepper sauce and fried leeks.

Napoleon's

Actually, most everything on the menu sounded good, right through to the white chocolate mousse in a chocolate cup, the "Frozen Lemon Zing" with raspberry sauce, the chocolate walnut cake, and other sweet endings.

WASHINGTON
Country Café
389-A MAIN STREET / WASHINGTON, VA. 22747
(540) 675-1066

Style	Café
Meals	Breakfast, lunch, and dinner, Monday through Saturday
Price Range	Inexpensive
Superlatives	Homemade coconut cake

On the left side of this former Ford dealership is the Country Café. On the right side is the local post office. The building was renovated in the 1970s. David Huff, who has lived in Rappahannock

County all his life, bought the café in 1989. His objective: to serve good American food.

A few frying pans and coffeepots painted with country scenes hang on the walls or sit on ledges. The artist is Elizabeth Crusan of Harpers Ferry. David liked her work and bought a few pieces to decorate the café. Now, he allows her to have some of her pieces for sale here.

Breakfast runs the gamut from biscuits, croissants, and omelets to pancakes, waffles, and "Baby Cakes." The latter are small pancakes popular with children and those who want light fare.

Soups, salads, and sandwiches are offered at lunch. "Dave's Deluxe" is an eight-ounce sub with all the cheeses and meats on the premises. The "Vegetarian Delight" contains white cheeses and vegetables. The 16 lunch platters range from hot dogs, hamburgers, and grilled turkey burgers to crab cakes and shrimp baskets, all of which come with a choice of two sides.

The dinner entrées are similar to the lunch platters, though there are additional choices such as ham steak, pork chops, New York strip steak, and grilled salmon steak.

Far and away the most popular dessert is the coconut cake, made right here by David's mom. Peanut butter pie, cheesecake, cobblers, and brownies are also available. But best of all, they have cookies! It doesn't matter to me what kind. I've never met a cookie I didn't like.

The Inn at Little Washington

MIDDLE AND MAIN STREETS
WASHINGTON, VA. 22747
(540) 675-3800
WWW.THEINNATLITTLEWASHINGTON.COM

Style	Fine dining
Meals	Dinner, Wednesday through Monday year-round and Tuesday during May and October only. Reservations are required.
Price Range	Expensive
Superlatives	Lavish décor, artistic presentation
Extras	Full bar

Young people often struggle with what to do with themselves upon reaching adulthood. A common strategy is to go to college, travel in Europe, and then get back to nature—live in the country somewhere, eat granola. And stall making a decision.

This was the route for Patrick O'Connell, co-owner and chef of The Inn at Little Washington. He thought he wanted to be an actor, so he studied drama in college. Then he went to Europe, then to rural life in the Shenandoah Valley.

Reinhardt Lynch, co-owner of the restaurant, dropped in on O'Connell one day. He loved the area so much that he's never left. Together, the two started a catering business. The complications of toting food over country roads gave way to the idea of having a restaurant—people would move to the food, instead of the other way around.

Thus, in the winter of 1978, The Inn at Little

The Inn at Little Washington

Washington opened in a converted garage. O'Connell and Lynch charged $4.95 for a roasted chicken dinner in those days.

There were many struggles the first few years, not uncommon for a small business. What is uncommon, however, is what O'Connell and Lynch have since created—a restaurant and inn consistently ranked at the top of the hospitality industry and known around the world.

Today, The Inn at Little Washington is lavishly decorated with plush carpets, fringed lamps, exquisite art, antiques, and an interesting mix of fabrics and wall coverings. There's little solid color. The upholstery, the ceiling drapes, the pillows, the curtains, and the valances all have stripes, flowers, geometric patterns, or other prints. It doesn't match, but it works. Opulence abounds in the 12 guest rooms as well.

Dinner is an extravagant event. The presentations made the biggest impression on me. You'll be served edible art from hors d'oeuvres through dessert. O'Connell's aim is to pair tastes and textures, colors and contrasts that will appeal to the palate and be visually stimulating as well.

The menu changes all the time. Your entrée will not necessarily be the main attraction. It's the innovative preparation and the accompaniments that place The Inn at Little Washington in a class of its own.

To say it's expensive is an understatement. But remember, dining out is a form of entertainment and a social excursion, not merely an exercise in nourishment. Here, you enjoy an artistic culinary event in luxurious surroundings.

If you're interested in cooking well, you might consult *The Inn at Little Washington Cookbook*. The three-page introduction provides an excellent lesson on how to present food graciously and tastefully.

FLINT HILL

The Flint Hill Public House

U.S. 522
FLINT HILL, VA. 22627
(540) 675-1700
WWW.FLINTHILLPUBLICHOUSE.COM

Style	Fine dining
Meals	Lunch, Monday, Tuesday, and Thursday through Saturday; dinner, Thursday through Tuesday
Price Range	Moderate
Superlatives	Fresh meats and seafood, wine list
Extras	Full bar

John Pearson, a native of southern California, has been, in his words, a "kitchen rat" since age 17. "You name it, I've done it," he says of his restaurant experience. His wife, Denise, majored in nutrition at Louisiana Tech because she wanted to work in the food industry.

In 1991, John was working for a Washington, D.C., gourmet retailer and Denise was attending cooking school and still longing to be in the food business. He hired her. They began dating and got married in May 1994. A few months later, they started work as a chef team at The Flint Hill Public House. They purchased the business the following June, and that's where you'll find them today, making wholesome, tasty food in this rather impressive 1903 schoolhouse.

The flower gardens around the building are beautiful. The gently rolling terrain out back provides a tranquil setting for any meal. The herb and vegetable gardens bring fresh flavors and produce to your table.

If you prefer a light lunch, you can select today's soup, Caesar salad with or without grilled chicken, or rainbow trout. Sandwiches and burgers are available. The entrées might be shrimp and tasso ham Creole, pan-seared hangar steak or, pistachio-crusted chicken. An abbreviated wine and beer list accompanies the lunch menu.

The menu changes often. The evening appetizers might be a duck rillette and goat cheese tart or Vietnamese-style fried calamari. Jumbo lump crab cakes, 16-ounce rib-eye, duck breast, braised wild boar, and sesame-crusted salmon with hot-and-sour sauce and cucumber noodles are popular entrées.

Desserts are homemade and change often, but you might find crème brûlée, black chocolate espresso cake, apple crisp, or Indian pudding with grilled pineapple and toasted pound cake among the choices.

The Flint Hill Public House offers a tranquil setting in a warm, hospitable, historic building.

FLINT HILL

Four & Twenty Blackbirds

U.S. 522 / FLINT HILL, VA. 22623
(540) 675-1111
WWW.FOURANDTWENTY.COM

Style	Fine dining
Meals	Dinner, Wednesday through Saturday; Sunday brunch. Reservations are recommended.
Price Range	Moderate
Superlatives	Creative cuisine
Extras	Full bar

This small 1910 building has served as a carpentry shop, a real-estate office, a beauty shop, and a general store. It is now home to a cozy restaurant with an unusual name.

According to Vinnie DeLuise, who has owned the restaurant with his wife, Heidi Morf, since 1990, the couple was brainstorming names related to birds and nature when Four & Twenty Blackbirds was mentioned. "It was catchy and easy to remember," he said. And so it is.

The color scheme is Caribbean bold—lime green, robin's-egg blue, and pink. Linens, candles, and "lucky" bamboo adorn each table. Between the upstairs and downstairs dining areas, the restaurant can seat around 54. There are bird prints on the walls and a wonderful aquarium near the kitchen. Soft music contributes to an intimate country atmosphere that is neither stiff nor pretentious but rather comfortable and comforting.

Vinnie describes the cuisine as "New American with ethnic twists." The menu changes all the time, so most anything mentioned here won't be available when you visit, but should rather serve as an idea of the food at Four & Twenty Blackbirds.

One appetizer that has appeared from time to time is oysters baked with Southwestern chili sauce and topped with crispy cornbread and cheese. Another is a steamed vegetable and mushroom dumpling with Oriental ginger plum sauce. Another is broiled sea scallops and sage cheddar cheese puffs.

Among the entrées, you might find pan-seared, hazelnut-dusted halibut served with roasted butternut squash, caramelized Vidalia onion, and Himalayan red rice. Veal chops stuffed with Italian cheeses, a spicy Thai seafood stew, and lightly smoked grilled chicken with an apricot mustard glaze have also graced the menu.

The desserts are made from scratch. Homemade cookies are sometimes available, usually as an aside to something else, such as "Lemon Crème Caramel" with fresh strawberries.

At Four & Twenty Blackbirds, the gentle countryside, the quaint small town, and the attractive little building create a perfect backdrop for Heidi's culinary talents.

Griffin Tavern & Restaurant

659 ZACHARY TAYLOR HIGHWAY
FLINT HILL, VA. 22627
(540) 675-3227
WWW.GRIFFINTAVERN.COM

Style	Family-style and pub
Meals	Lunch and dinner, seven days a week. Reservations accepted for parties of more than eight.
Price Range	Inexpensive
Superlatives	Fish 'n' chips, Mary Frances pie
Extras	Full bar

You may think bankers work 10 to 2, but lots of them work much more. So much more that they start looking for new work. Going into the restaurant business may be a little like jumping from the pan to the fire, but when it's a dream realized, the attitude is one of joy and gratitude.

So it was with Jim and Debbie Donehey, former bankers turned restaurant and pub owners. They loved the Flint Hill area and bought land here in 1996. When an opportunity to acquire the circa 1850 Bradford House arose, they bought it and renovated it into a casual restaurant, which was less expensive than others in the area. The pub, Jim's dream, is similar to ones he patronized on visits to England.

Inside, the yellow paint with crisp white trim and floral curtains make the small dining rooms sunny. A couple of prints and maps hang on the walls. The tables are wood with small oil candles and thick, white paper napkins that feel and act like cloth.

The pub in the back is dark green with a cherry horseshoe bar, dartboard, and gold-tone, tin ceiling. The stone fireplace is warm in cool weather; the patio outside beckons on warmer days and evenings.

The menu is not extensive or cluttered with multiple word descriptions. It's simple and easy to understand, which is refreshing. Chicken wings, steamed mussels, chicken liver pâté, hummus with foccacia, mozzarella sticks, and a small pizza du jour serve as starters. And you can order chips with curry sauce, gravy, or cheese.

Garden salad; Caesar salad with chicken, shrimp, or salmon; and a spinach strawberry poppyseed salad are offered. Shepherd's pie and the fish 'n' chips are popular. Fried fish sandwiches, burgers, and macaroni and cheese will satisfy the common palate. Steve's bangers are homemade link sausages with mashed potatoes and gravy. Fried or rotisserie-cooked chicken and barbecue ribs make regular appearances on the menu.

Special dinners change weekly, according to head chef, Steve Richards. While he enjoys Asian cooking, his love is simple, home cooking. Some of the specials have been corn chowder and shrimp corn

Griffin Tavern & Restaurant

dogs for starters. Alaskan crab cake sandwiches, stuffed pork loin, and artichoke fusilli might be entrées.

Pumpkin pie and white pepper and ginger cake are specials, and regular desserts include pear shortbread crumble, gingerbread, chocolate soufflé cake, and those locally made and regionally famous Mary Frances pies.

The Griffin Tavern & Restaurant gets its name from griffins, a mythological character with the body of a lion and head and wings of an eagle. Jim collects them because they have many virtues such as vigilance, courage, and strength, and no apparent vices. That explains why they are mythological, doesn't it?

Town 'N' Country Restaurant

U.S. 29 / NEW BALTIMORE, VA. 20187
(540) 347-3614

Style	Home-style
Meals	Breakfast, lunch, and dinner, seven days a week
Price Range	Inexpensive/Moderate
Superlatives	Greek salads, steak sandwiches
Extras	Full bar

*T*he restaurant industry has one of the highest turnover rates of any business. On occasion, it reaches as high as 300 percent per year!

Not so at the Town 'N' Country, located in New Baltimore a few miles north of Warrenton. The salad cook has been on the job 29 years, another cook 24 years, and one of the night cooks 24 years also. Low turnover contributes significantly to the restaurant's consistency in food preparation.

This is a down-home kind of place built in the 1940s. You'll note the pine paneling, the red booth seats, and the oldies playing on the radio.

Breakfast is superlative. The sausage is made in the kitchen, as is the gravy. The home fries are cut from real potatoes right on the premises. Country ham, hot cakes, omelets, rib-eye steaks, and grits are some of what's available.

At lunch, you can get a crab cake sandwich, a hot turkey sandwich, a roast beef sandwich, a tuna salad sandwich, or a chicken salad sandwich. A popular choice is the steak sandwich, which comes with onion rings. There are four triple-decker sandwiches to choose from, among them the "Gladiator"—corned beef, pastrami, lettuce, and tomato. One of the three "Waist Watcher" selections combines shrimp, cottage cheese, tomato, half a peach, and half a pear on lettuce. Onion soup and the soup du jour are homemade.

At dinner, the early-bird specials include prime rib, fish and chips, eggplant parmigiana, cheese ravioli, fried clams, and New York strip steak. Among the favorites on the regular dinner menu are meat loaf, grilled ham steak, and roast beef. Lasagna, chicken cordon bleu, shrimp parmigiana, and veal cutlets are among the continental specialties.

It's hard to skip dessert when there are so many choices. Cheesecake, mousse cake, carrot cake, apple pie, meringue pies, cobblers, bread pudding, rice pudding, and a reduced-fat cherry pie are some of the offerings.

Carmello's & Little Portugal

9108 CENTER STREET
MANASSAS, VA. 20110
(703) 368-5522
WWW.CARMELLOS.COM

Style	Casual nice
Meals	Lunch, Monday through Friday; dinner, seven days a week

Price Range	Moderate
Superlatives	Nice atmosphere, daily specials
Extras	Full bar

*T*he origin of the name Manassas is uncertain. Perhaps it came from an Indian source, as many town names have, or from Manesseh, the name of a Jewish innkeeper. In any event, the town began in 1852 at the junction of two railroads. This position of importance became relevant in the Civil War, and the battles of First and Second Manassas (Bull Run) were fought here. The town became a city in 1975 and is a favorite of Civil War buffs, as well as those just meandering around the charming Old Town section. Each of the Manassas restaurants in this book is in the Old Town historic district.

Carmello's opened in the late 1980s and featured northern Italian cuisine. Alice Pires, a native of Portugal whose brother-in-law operated Carmello's, opened her restaurant, Little Portugal, in a room of Carmello's not being used by that restaurant. A few years later, they decided to combine the restaurants into one.

A white-and-burgundy theme dominates with double linens, little lamps with burgundy shades, nice cream-and-burgundy carpeting, black booth seats, and stained-glass hanging lamps.

Throughout the menu, you'll find (*I*) next to Italian dishes and (*P*) next to Portuguese items. There's a pretty even balance and lots of interesting food. For lunch appetizers, you might order *vieiras ao vinagrete* (*P*), a mix of scallops, shrimp, and anchovies in a balsamic vinaigrette, or the *calamari friti* (*I*), lightly battered squid, fried and served with marinara sauce.

Traditional Italian vegetable soup and a soup of the day are offered. Salads include *salada de fruta con queijo* (*P*), which is fresh fruits and Portuguese cheese. You can learn a little foreign language, as it's readily obvious that *insalata* is salad in Italian and *salada* is salad in Portuguese.

If you don't order a special salad, you'll get a house salad with the entrée. The lunch menu has a nice selection of veal, shrimp, pasta dishes, and smoked salmon with sun-dried tomatoes and capers in a brandy sauce over angel hair pasta topped with feta cheese.

Dinner at Carmello's is very nice. Appetizers, soups, and salads are abundant. Most of the pasta dishes are Italian, and many feature homemade pasta and cream or marinara sauces. Cheese-filled ravioli tossed with fresh lobster and served in a rosé cream sauce with Parmesan cheese sounds wonderful. A filet of cod with sautéed onions, bell peppers, and tomatoes comes with Portuguese fried potatoes.

Alice says that Portuguese cuisine is a little lighter than Italian, with less butter and no cream sauces. Some of the Portuguese entrées use zesty garlic sauce, white wine and olive oil sauce, or espresso and port wine sauce. Yum. There are several interesting chicken, veal, and beef possibilities.

Spumoni, tartufo, and gelato are offered for dessert, along with mascarpone mousse with strawberry purée.

Jake's

9412 MAIN STREET / MANASSAS, VA. 20110
(703) 330-1534
WWW.JAKESOFMANASSAS.COM

Style	Family-style
Meals	Lunch and dinner, Tuesday through Sunday; à la carte Sunday brunch
Price Range	Moderate
Superlatives	Clam chowder, fresh lobster
Extras	Full bar

John O'Brien grew up in Hull, Massachusetts, where he delivered newspapers as a young kid to a special neighbor and family friend named Jake. Jake and his cousin, Marty, started a wholesale and retail lobster business in 1949, known to the locals as Jake's. Jake added picnic tables and a small dining room in the late 1960s.

Jake died young and his wife, Dottie, ran the little business until John's family bought it in 1984. His youngest brother now runs it, along with his mother, the queen of retail, and his dad, director of charm. Those titles are on their business cards.

Like restless young people do, John went off to seek his fortune, moving to New York, Tampa, and Virginia for publishing and corporate work. However, the restaurant business stayed in his heart, and corporate work grew dull. He bought this place in December 2002, and honored his childhood mentor by naming the restaurant for him.

Jake's is housed in a corner building, which was constructed in 1906 for use as a general store. It was also used as a dentist's office until 1996 when it was converted to Brady Irish Pub, which has relocated to another site in Manassas.

The interior is heavy on oak with red or green bench upholstery or tabletops. Musical instruments and beer labels compose the primary wall décor. Old brick walls contribute to a casual, warm, comfortable atmosphere.

The clam chowder and the crab bisque are outstanding. All the fish is fresh, and John pays great attention to buying it. The lobster comes right from the wholesale business in Massachusetts. House specialties include baked scallop pie, roasted or Cajun grilled swordfish, pan-seared scallops, baked seafood casserole, Cajun-marinated catfish, and baked Boston scrod, as well as rainbow trout, baked stuffed flounder, and tilapia with crab and Old Bay hollandaise.

The over-stuffed sandwich board and gourmet burgers head up the lunch menu. Jake's fabulous soups also include a lobster bisque and soup of the day. There are generous salads such as chef, shrimp, or steak, or salmon, chicken, or swordfish Caesar. Luncheon platters of Cajun swordfish sandwich, fried scallop roll, and Carolina pulled pork sandwich come with fries and coleslaw.

Jake's fried favorites as such fish 'n' chips, New England whole belly clam platter, and deep-fried, sautéed lobster are accompanied by fries, homemade coleslaw, and Old Bay tartar sauce. A popular seafood pasta entrée combines scallops, shrimp, and fresh lobster meat in a rich Cape Cod–style lobster bisque sauce. It's garnished with fresh diced tomatoes, parsley, and fresh grated Parmesan cheese and served over tender linguine.

If fish isn't calling you, then there are chicken and vegetables in a zesty garlic marinara, New York sirloin strip steak, bourbon mustard-glazed pork chops, and rib-eye steak.

The desserts are homemade, and John will put his Key lime pie up against any other. He says, "if you don't like it, send it back and we'll finish it." You can order chocolate lava or another dessert. I'd drive out of my way for soup and Key lime pie here any time.

MANASSAS

Okra's Louisiana Bistro

9110 CENTER STREET / MANASSAS, VA. 20110
(703) 330-2729
WWW.OKRAS.COM

Style	Bistro
Meals	Lunch and dinner, Monday through Saturday
Price Range	Moderate
Superlatives	Jambalaya, red beans and rice, bananas Foster
Extras	Full bar

Originally a bank, this corner spot has been home to a series of bars throughout most of the 20th century. Charles Gilliam of Kentucky attended that state's Berea College and had a double major in business and hotel and restaurant management. He went to work for others, but bills himself as "a terrible employee."

With a good education, solid experience, and the entrepreneurial bug inside, Charles started a couple of businesses before hitting on the restaurant. Okra's opened in October 1998, and he has no regrets.

The walls are old brick with dark green trim. Each table has a bold, red oilcloth with royal blue cloth napkins, a little oil lamp, and a wine bottle for sale and for decoration.

Okra's chicken cordon bleu steps outside the norm with a N'awlins-style chicken breast on a cake of cheddar cheese baked grits, sliced tasso ham, maque choux, and homemade chicken gravy. Chili mignon offers seared cubes of filet mignon smothered in red bean chili alongside cornbread and shoestring sweet potatoes.

Tabasco mixed grill, pan-blackened catfish, chaurice-crusted salmon, boucherie chops, and pasta Diablo or pasta Creole round out the original dishes. N'awlins fare includes the really traditional Cajun entrées such as Creole jambalaya, crawfish étouffée, andouille red beans and rice, shrimp Creole, wild mushroom dirty rice, and a combination plate with your choice of any two N'awlins fare items with a mug of gumbo.

The Port Orleans salad of mixed greens tossed in citrus vinaigrette and topped with chopped dates, pecans, and crumbled bleu cheese sounds good. Oysters Rockefeller soup, gator bites, and crawfish hash are on the light fare menu section, along

Small-Town Restaurants in Virginia 187

Okra's Louisiana Bistro

with a plantation portobello mushroom, fried okra, gumbo, and pepper shrimp. Cajun popcorn is a serving of crawfish tails dipped in a special batter, flash fried, and served with tiger sauce.

Sandwiches are available at lunchtime, and the Central Grocery muffuletta heads the list. It's a hero-style sandwich that originated in 1906 at Central Grocery in New Orleans. A round loaf of crusty bread is split and filled with layers of sliced provolone, Genoa salami, and baked ham, topped with olive antipasto.

Other sandwiches are Okra's po' boy, Cajun burger, Louisiana chicken BLT, chicken salad sandwich, and soup & salad/half sandwich.

For side orders, you choose from cornbread, corn on the cob, red beans and rice, maque choux, creamy grits, mixed veggies, Cajun fries, and more.

Polish off your meal with a dessert of crème brûlée, cranberry bread pudding, pistachio praline, sweet potato pecan pie, or their most popular bananas Foster.

Charles was honored and humbled in 2001 in New Orleans when he served as a guest chef in the kitchen of Paul Prudhomme, one of the most famous chefs of our day.

MANASSAS

Philadelphia Tavern

9413 MAIN STREET / MANASSAS, VA. 20110
(703) 393-1776
WWW.PHILADELPHIATAVERN.COM

Style	Pub
Meals	Lunch and dinner, seven days a week. Reservations accepted.
Price Range	Inexpensive
Superlatives	Philly cheese steak, certified Black Angus® steaks
Extras	Full bar

*T*im Holland was a big kid, and because of his size, he was able to land a job as a bouncer at age 16. Of course, no one knew his age or that he was bouncing guys with a decade or more on him in age. But it gave him confidence and educated him about tavern management at a young age.

A Philadelphia doctor started Philadelphia Tavern, purportedly so he could get a decent Philly cheese steak sandwich when he relocated to Virginia. Tim came in as manager, then owner. The space is narrow and deep with a bar along one side and booths on the other. It used to be a liquor store with shoe repair in the back, so its current incarnation is not too far from the previous business.

According to Tim, Philadelphia Tavern is an "up-scale shot and beer joint," and that's pretty much what it looks like. The original, copper-color, tin ceiling is in place, as is the original terrazzo floor. The walls are cream over oak, with little stained-glass lamps, and a couple of globe-style street lamps. There are lots of baseball caps from police and fire departments.

Of course, the Philly cheese steaks are wonderful, but there are some pretty classy items on the menu. This is because Tim gives free reign to his cooks to experiment with ingredients and create or try new recipes. For example, you don't find Prince Edward Island mussels or baked Brie on many tavern menus. There's spinach and artichoke dip and a Pennsylvania Dutch platter of ring bologna with cheddar cheese, pickles, and jalapeño mustard.

There are nine salads, a couple of homemade soups, and tavern platters such as open-faced hot roast turkey or roast beef sandwiches; shrimp, chicken, or seafood baskets; and stuffed flounder. If you're in the mood for pasta, you'll have your pick of spaghetti and meatballs, shrimp scampi, mussels, fettuccini Alfredo, chicken Alfredo, ravioli with sausage or homemade meatballs, and a meatball and sausage combination plate.

You can order a Schmitter, which is a grilled American cheese steak with grilled salami, onion, tomato, and special dressing, or a Reuben, home-made meatballs on a steak roll, or bratwurst & kraut. Cold sandwiches include tuna salad, corned beef special, liverwurst and onions, BLT, egg salad,

and ham and cheese. South Philly hoagies or hot grinders are made with freshly sliced meats and cheeses.

The food is good, Tim and his staff are very nice, and the apple pie and chocolate mousse are home-made, too.

The Rail Stop

6478 MAIN STREET / THE PLAINS, VA. 20198
(540) 253-5644
WWW.RAILSTOPRESTAURANT.COM

Style	Family-style
Meals	Lunch, Wednesday through Saturday; dinner, Tuesday through Sunday; Sunday brunch
Price Range	Moderate
Superlatives	Grilled Black Angus strip, crème brûlée
Extras	Full bar

*T*he Rail Stop is not a rail stop, and never was. Rather, it's a cozy and inviting restaurant stop.

Chef and owner Tom Kee used to lease The Rail Stop for serving dinner when someone else owned it and did the first two meals of the day. Now Tom owns it, and he serves all kinds of folks—some in suits, some with kids, some on shopping sprees, others just meeting friends and getting a good meal.

There are several stools at the counter in the back, which practically look over the chef's shoulders. The meals are prepared expertly and efficiently in a relatively small kitchen.

The Rail Stop has lots of wood, train memorabilia, some watercolor paintings, and very clean windows. A miniature train track with a sometimes-working train runs around the front room high on the wall.

At lunch, you can get something common such as a burger, smoked turkey Reuben, or barbecue beef brisket, or something more elaborate such as a grilled shrimp club sandwich or three-cheese quesadillas. Tomato caper or couscous salads are options, along with an order of Cuban black beans.

Entrée salads are spinach with goat cheese, Cobb salad, grilled salmon niçoise, and the Rail Stop salad of grilled sirloin pieces over romaine with creamy herb dressing.

Dinner also offers the simple and the sublime with appetizers of assorted cheeses, baked herb goat cheese in phyllo, and smoked salmon on a potato cake. Calamari, Caesar, mixed green, and arugula salads are available.

A comfort-food dinner would be grilled Black Angus strip steak and garlic mashed potatoes or roasted salmon. A more adventurous choice is grilled Cuban marinated pork tenderloin with rice and black beans or roasted half lobster and lump crab cake with spinach and mushroom fondue. Chicken, lamp chops, and shrimp are also prepared with unexpected flavors, such as black olive au jus with the lamb chops.

The Rail Stop

The desserts change with the seasons. You might find crème brûlée or a caramel torte streaked with chocolate sauce. Both are tasty, both are homemade.

Sunday brunch is always a nice outing. Andouille hash, grilled eggplant Parmesan sandwich, blueberry cornmeal pancakes, the Rail Stop salad described above, and classic eggs Benedict are worthy of consideration, though there are more things.

Tom Kee is dedicated to providing great food with fresh and interesting ingredients, and The Rail Stop is a nice drive from anywhere.

Backyard Steakhouse

13999 METROTECH DRIVE
CHANTILLY, VA. 20151
(703) 802-6400

Style	Family-style
Meals	Lunch and dinner, seven days a week; Sunday brunch
Price Range	Moderate
Superlatives	"Chili Mignon," steaks, ribs
Extras	Full bar

Chantilly, a crossroads in Fairfax County, was named by a member of the famous Lee family of Westmoreland County. Richard Bland Lee, the first man from Northern Virginia elected to Congress, lived in the historic home called Sully from 1795 to 1842. When Sully was scheduled for demolition to make way for the construction of Dulles International Airport, residents of Chantilly went into action to save it. The estate is now managed by the Fairfax County Park Authority.

The Backyard Steakhouse opened in October 1996 in a corner of the little shopping strip known, appropriately enough, as Sully Place. It was recommended to me by the men at the Chevrolet dealership on the other side of U.S. 50. Perhaps it's no coincidence that Robby Qreitem, who owns the restaurant with his brother Freddy, happens to drive a Chevrolet Blazer. He also runs a pretty good place to eat.

The brothers have overlooked nothing in creating a comfortable place to dine. The walls are dark green, the trim and railings bright white, and the tables and chairs mahogany. A bar is a few steps higher than the dining room and is separated from it by a wall and a glass partition. The napkins—even at lunch—are cloth.

There's something for everyone at the midday meal. Potato skins, "Jalapeño Poppers," steamed spiced shrimp, and quesadillas are some of the appetizers. "Backyard Chili," a California salad, and a Caesar salad are also offered. You can get a traditional hamburger or a turkey burger, North Carolina barbecue, Maryland crab cakes, an "Arizona Chicken BLT," a Cajun catfish sandwich, and a Reuben. If you have a big appetite, you might opt for the Backyard's signature "Chili Mignon"—beef tips with black bean chili served over cornbread and topped with cheese, diced tomatoes, onions, and avocado.

Some of the most popular dinner entrées are shrimp scampi, pork chops, and baby back ribs. You can finish any of this with bananas Foster or "Strawberries Romanoff."

Sunday brunch features a carving station, omelet station, a variety of entrées, and spectacular desserts.

Ice House Café

760 ELDEN STREET
HERNDON, VA. 20170
(703) 437-4500
WWW.ICEHOUSECAFE.COM

Style	Casual nice
Meals	Lunch, Monday through Friday; dinner, Monday through Saturday
Price Range	Moderate
Superlatives	Fresh seafood, "Tournedos Baltimore"
Extras	Full bar

Ice House Café

Located in Herndon, one of the fastest-growing communities in Virginia, the Ice House Café is in a 50-year-old building that was originally a law office. The café's tavern was a small barbershop before being joined to the larger building.

Established in 1979, the café was taken over by Alice Dai's family in 1991. Alice is the manager of operations. This is one family that knows restaurants. It also owns La Bonne Auberge in Great Falls and Santa Fe East in Old Town Alexandria.

The Ice House is a wonderful place with a historic feel. There are old photos on the walls and white linens, green cloth napkins, and fresh carnations on the tables. Though there's seating for more than 100 patrons, the atmosphere is intimate. The patio behind the tavern was damaged in the harsh winter of 1995–96 but was redone with a dark green awning and new furniture in 1997. Patrons enjoy live jazz on weekends between 8 P.M. and midnight.

Grilled hickory-smoked pork loin and the "Chesapeake Reuben" (with crabmeat, smoked ham, slaw, Swiss cheese, and Thousand Island dressing) are two of the popular sandwiches at lunch. The entrées include beef stroganoff, fresh calf's liver, and rainbow trout.

The dinner appetizers are an interesting mix of food styles—smoked Norwegian salmon, the "Saigon Spring Roll," a Southwestern flour tortilla pizza, oysters Rockefeller. The daily specials often feature one or two fresh seafood entrées—roasted monkfish topped with crabmeat, for example. The regular entrées include "Duckling à l'Oriental," "Pork Loin à la Rome," "Trout à la Siam," Maryland lump crab cakes, and "Tournedos Baltimore"—choice beef tenderloin served with Châteaubriand sauce.

The desserts are made in-house. They might include "Raspberry Chambourd Cheesecake" with crème anglaise and the "Chocolate Sheba," a walnut dessert with chocolate mousse and dark rum.

The Russia House

790 STATION STREET
HERNDON, VA. 22070
(703) 787-8880
WWW.RUSSIAHOUSERESTAURANT.COM

Style	Fine dining
Meals	Lunch, Tuesday through Friday; dinner, seven days a week
Price Range	Moderate/Expensive
Superlatives	Borscht, caviar, Russian cuisine

You don't have to know a lot about Russia to feel it when you step inside this restaurant. The reds and gold colors, the faces in a painting or on figures, the copper-colored sheer fabric on the windows, the whimsical painting of Sputnik. It's regal, refined, romantic—Russian.

Almost everything is dark red or gold. The dining room is large, but so warmly inviting that it doesn't seem big. Each table has double white linens, white napkins, and a small lamp with a brass base and white lampshade with red trim. The carpet is red and gold. The chandeliers are fancy.

Ali and Homeyra Darugar started the restaurant here in 1992. Homeyra's mother is from Russia, so she grew up with the language, culture, and cuisine. She moved from Russia to Switzerland with her grandparents and learned lots of cooking from her grandmother. Russian czars hired many French chefs, so there is a French influence in Russian food.

Several Russian hors d'oeuvres are listed, and they offer lots of flavors of vodka such as apricot, lemon, butterscotch, and others. *Pirozhki* is puff pastry stuffed with meat, cheese, and cabbage. There are snails Russian-style, a Russia House pâté, and several versions of caviar. *Borscht*, the traditional Russian beet soup, is always available.

Salads are standard fare, and the noodle dishes feature caviar; lamb and feta cheese; mushrooms and onions; or mixed vegetables.

Lososina Alexander is broiled salmon with caviar and champagne sauce, and the *forel po-Armianski* features sautéed rainbow trout with artichoke hearts and capers. Shrimp and flounder are also among the seafood entrées.

Cabbage leaves stuffed with beef; marinated lamb on a skewer served over rice; Georgian duck with Russian-style sauerkraut; and *telyatina po-Russki*, veal medallions with cream of mushroom sauce, are some of the entrées prepared the Russian way.

There are specials every day. For the more plain palate, there's filet mignon with Béarnaise sauce, Rock Cornish hen, chicken Kiev, Châteaubriand for two, and sautéed pepper steak with peppercorn sauce.

Homeyra makes a special blend of tea that reminds her of Russia. It's interesting, and it goes well with chocolate cake. The cakes and chocolate mousse are made here. You could choose cherries jubilee or bananas Foster, too. Or you could nightcap it all with another flavored vodka.

Zeffirelli

728 PINE STREET
HERNDON, VA. 20170
(703) 318-7000
WWW.ZEFFIRELLIRISTORANTE.COM

Style	Fine dining
Meals	Lunch, Monday through Friday; dinner, seven days a week
Price Range	Moderate
Superlatives	Veal chop, linguine Cleopatra
Extras	Full bar

A dapper fellow named Nino, dressed in a fine suit with a broad smile and gentle, brown eyes, greeted my husband and me just a couple of steps inside the front door. He has that personality that makes you think he was waiting there just for you to arrive. We were seated right away in comfy, upholstered chairs at a table draped in crispy white linens with fresh flowers on top.

Delightfully bright paintings of Italian seaside towns hung on the white walls. Cheerful Italian music played in the background. I was impressed before I opened the menu.

Calamari fritti, fried squid with spicy marinara sauce, is one of the appetizers. *Funghi ripieni*, mushroom caps stuffed with back fin crabmeat, is another. Mussels, snails, fried mozzarella cheese, and shrimp wrapped in bacon also come in small, appetizer portions.

Salads, fresh homemade vegetable soup, or the soup of the day also make good beginnings for lunch or dinner. Pasta, veal, chicken, vegetables, and filet mignon are prepared in a variety of ways for a variety of flavors and interesting tastes.

The pasta is homemade at Zeffirelli, and if you order the tortellini stuffed with cheese, you may choose either a cream sauce or fresh tomato sauce. *The cannelloni fiorentina* is crêpes of pasta filled with spinach and ground veal, baked in cream sauce.

Seafood lunch options include sea scallops, shrimp, Norwegian salmon, and a medley of shrimp, lobster meat, and scallops in a mild tomato sauce.

Like the lunch menu, dinner entrées run the gamut of seafood, veal prepared lots of ways, chicken, and a couple of grilled beef items. The linguine Cleopatra is an exquisite blend of lobster, shrimp, scallops, and mussels in a champagne and lobster sauce.

Homemade ravioli may be ordered filled with sausage and spinach or stuffed with fresh lobster and leeks. A new twist on pasta would be the *tortellini alla panna*, ringlets of fresh pasta filled with meat and simmered in fresh whipping cream. Sauces for the chicken dishes include a lemon and wine sauce, balsamic sauce, and a Marsala wine and mushroom sauce.

If you missed your breakfast, you might want *linguini carbonara*, traditional Roman pasta with bacon, eggs, onions, and Parmesan cheese.

The choices are vast. The aroma is enticing. The atmosphere is casually upscale. The staff is warmly professional. And they have tiramisu on the dessert list, along with dark and white chocolate mousse cake, crème brûlée, spumoni ice cream, and others.

The Coach Stop

9 EAST WASHINGTON STREET
MIDDLEBURG, VA. 22117
(703) 687-5515

Style	Home-style
Meals	Breakfast, lunch, and dinner, seven days a week
Price Range	Moderate
Superlatives	Hamburgers, prime rib, fresh seafood
Extras	Full bar

This town was originally called Chinn's Crossroads after a Mr. Chinn, who started the local tavern. The village was established in 1787 by Leven Powell, a lieutenant colonel in the Revolutionary War. Middleburg was eventually chosen as the name because of the town's location midway between Winchester and Alexandria. Fox hunting and steeplechasing have grown so popular around here since the turn of the 20th century that Middleburg is sometimes called "the Nation's Horse and Hunt Capital."

Michael Tate, a Middleburg native, started working at The Coach Stop when he was 15. He later went to Virginia Tech and majored in aerospace engineering, only to discover after three months on a job that he didn't care for it. His brother Mark majored in biology at Randolph-Macon and worked in sales for about 18 months. The two returned to Middleburg, bought The Coach Stop in 1988, and have never regretted it.

It's a popular, simple restaurant with stools at a counter along the left side, circular booths on the right wall, and tables and chairs in the middle. Horse and hunt photos are on all the walls. A single rose on each table adds a touch of class.

In the morning, you can have fresh-squeezed orange juice, homemade sausage, fresh eggs, creamed chipped beef on homemade buttermilk biscuits, eggs Benedict, or a "Horseman's Special"—two eggs, a couple slices of bacon, hash browns, toast, juice, and coffee or tea.

Hummus is served as an appetizer at lunch and dinner. Cream of peanut soup is a regular item. Among the salads are a chicken salad, tuna salad, and a pasta salad platter. The vegetarian sandwich and the crab cakes on a toasted bun are two of the locals' favorites for lunch. Willard Scott of NBC's *Today* show has been to The Coach Stop more than once and has stated his opinion that the hamburgers served here are "the best." Side dishes for lunch include pan-fried apples, applesauce, corn pudding, mashed sweet potatoes, and steamed rice.

According to Michael, an unusual choice that's surprisingly popular at dinner is the wild rice, orzo, and lentils. Tournedos of beef, roast turkey, Maryland-style crab cakes, broiled salmon, and grilled pork chops with apple currant chutney are some of the regular entrées. The Coach Stop offers soft-shell crabs in season, and shadroe, which is shad fish eggs, sautéed with bacon and capers.

Almost any item here with turkey in it is guaranteed to be fresh and good. The chef cooks two fresh turkeys every day.

You can wind up your meal with raspberry or strawberry pie or bread pudding.

Hidden Horse Tavern

7 WEST WASHINGTON STREET
MIDDLEBURG, VA. 20118
(540) 687-3828

Style	Casual nice
Meals	Dinner, seven days a week; Sunday brunch.
Price Range	Moderate/Expensive
Superlatives	Cozy atmosphere, fresh seafood
Extras	Full bar

*T*he definition of "cozy" in *The New Oxford American Dictionary* is "a feeling of comfort, warmth, and relaxation" as in "a cozy cabin tucked away in the trees." The Hidden Horse Tavern is cozy. The word "hidden" evokes the idea that there is something to discover. The side street entrance contributes to the discovery aspect.

Low ceilings and thick, stone walls more than two centuries old, which are painted white, enhance the cozy environment. There are small oil candles and white linens under glass on each table. The chairs are blue with rush splint seats, and the curtains are blue-checkered.

The dining room you enter is non-smoking. A few steps up and back are the smoking dining room and a seven-stool bar. There are some prints, a large Lee Marvin poster, and lots of framed photos, mostly of customers.

Jay Trier was born and raised in Washington, D.C. He came to Middleburg for a weekend in the mid-1970s and loved it. He moved and proceeded to work his way through most of the local restaurants—some still here, others long gone.

As he puts it, "I got tired of getting fired," so he opened the Hidden Horse Tavern. And then, he laughs, "I learned how much I didn't know." After 13 years in the business, he's not tired, and he can't get fired. There's always more stuff to learn, he's discovered, and he loves it here still.

The food was great. The menu isn't terribly exciting with six of the seven entrées served "with rice and vegetables." Only the steak came with a potato. However, I asked for and received potatoes with the crab cakes, so there's a little flexibility, at least on a mid-week night in November. There are specials every day, too.

After I completed writing this information about the Hidden Horse Tavern, I noticed that Jay's business card says "cozy atmosphere in a 200-year-old building." And I was sure the "cozy" diatribe above was all my idea. And it was [my idea], and it is [a cozy place]. Good food, too!

Red Fox Inn

2 EAST WASHINGTON STREET
MIDDLEBURG, VA. 20118
(800) 223-1728
WWW.REDFOX.COM

Style	Fine dining
Meals	Lunch, Monday through Saturday; dinner, seven days a week; Sunday brunch
Price Range	Moderate/Expensive
Superlatives	Peanut soup, crab cakes
Extras	Full bar

Red Fox Inn

George Washington wasn't even born when this place opened as Mr. Chinn's Ordinary in 1728. The route in front went east to Alexandria and west to what was then the frontier town of Winchester. In 1812, the ordinary was remodeled and renamed the Beveridge House. It served as a Confederate hospital during the Civil War. Renamed the Middleburg Inn in 1887 and the Red Fox Inn half a century later, the property now includes three nearby historic buildings as well as the main structure.

The dining rooms are historically authentic—low ceilings, fieldstone walls, wooden beams, fireplaces, pierced-tin sconces. The tables have cloth napkins and candles.

At Sunday brunch, you can get French toast, Belgian waffles, and eggs Benedict. One of the favorite choices is "Eggs Chesapeake"—poached eggs with jumbo lump crabmeat and hollandaise sauce on an English muffin, served with home fries.

The lunch appetizers include crab and artichoke casserole. Among the popular sandwiches are a crab cake sandwich and the "Grilled Applewood-Smoked Chicken Sandwich." Fish and chips, beef stroganoff, and grilled salmon filet with honey-mustard glaze are some other choices.

Grilled lamb chops, filet mignon, crab cakes, and grilled duck breast are among the evening options. Specials featuring fresh fish, fresh fowl, and fresh beef are created every day by the culinary staff.

Patrons may reserve overnight accommodations in any of the four historic buildings. Fresh flowers, plush bathrobes, and bedside sweets enhance the romantic atmosphere of the guest rooms.

1763 Inn

U.S. 50 / UPPERVILLE, VA. 20184
(800) 669-1763
WWW.1763INN.COM

Style	Casual nice
Meals	Lunch, Saturday; dinner, Wednesday through Saturday; Sunday brunch
Price Range	Moderate/Expensive
Superlatives	"Hot Love" dessert
Extras	Full bar

*U*pperville could be called "Horseville" for its beautiful horse farms. Most of the goings-on here involve horses. For example, the Annual Stable Tour is held the last weekend in May and the Upperville Colt and Horse Show the first week in June.

The name this magnificent old inn bears today recalls its origin well over two centuries ago. The original section of the main house was built in 1763. The inn sits on 50 acres of rolling land and forest.

Purchased in 1970 by Uta and Don Kirchner, the property was renovated into an elegant country inn. Their son, Bernie, and his wife, Megan, bought the inn in May 2003 and changed the focus from German-American to casual, more continental cuisine.

You'll find Oriental rugs, fine art, oak tables and chairs, and lots of small brass animals. The 1763 Inn is a refined country manor where comfort and a casual atmosphere prevail. There are several dining areas, some overlooking the grounds and the pond behind the house, others are more intimate rooms. All are cozy and inviting.

The menu is changed due to market availability, seasonal produce and game, so you may be surprised by a local or regional special. Generally, there's soup du jour and the 1763 salad of roasted portobellos, almonds, Stilton bleu cheese, and house balsamic vinaigrette. Appetizers might include mussels or other fresh fish.

The lunch menu reflects Bernie's German roots with kassler, bratwurst, and sauerbraten, though there are also omelets, other salads, and grilled chicken. Dinner entrées often presented feature herb-roasted chicken, a vegetarian dish with angel hair pasta, filet of cod, char-grilled pork loin, or a New York strip steak.

Desserts are lovely. "Hot Love" is a dessert of vanilla ice cream with hot raspberry sauce. Or you can choose apple strudel, bittersweet chocolate mousse, or flourless chocolate torte.

For those who wish to stay overnight, there are guest rooms in the main house, in a duplex cottage, in a restored barn, in log cabins, and in the carriage house. Factor in the lovely grounds and it all adds up to a superb getaway spot.

Hunter's Head

9048 JOHN MOSBY HIGHWAY (U.S. 50)
UPPERVILLE, VA. 20184
(540) 592-9020

Style	Casual nice
Meals	Lunch, Tuesday through Saturday; dinner, Tuesday through Sunday
Price Range	Inexpensive/Moderate
Superlatives	Organic meats, fruits, and vegetables
Extras	Full bar

*H*unter's Head is a uniquely charming, English-style pub and restaurant. In the old English pub manner, you place your drink and dinner order with the bartender over a Dutch door, and you are given a small, wood block with a number. This is placed on your table so meals can be delivered to the proper place, and charges can be collected under your number.

The dining rooms' wood floors have that pitch that attests to centuries of foot traffic. The interior hand-hewn logs and mud between 'em also point to construction techniques of long ago. Open-flame candles adorn the wooden tables, and real wood fires burn in centuries-old stone fireplaces.

Amidst this delightful and historical atmosphere, one might expect the bartender to scrawl your order on an old piece of slate and carry it to the kitchen. But alas, the man turns 90 degrees to a high-tech, flat-screen, digital dining and point-of-sale system and quickly taps this box and that box on the touch screen to submit your order. The contrast made me smile.

Hunter's Head serves the freshest, natural, most flavorful, and wholesome food purchased from Ayrshire Farm just up the road. The farm raises 100% organic meats and produce and is certified with the new USDA organic certification. This means premium, heirloom, locally grown produce and meats—beef, chicken, and pork.

The bar menu is available all the time and features chicken pot pie, Ayrshire burger, shepherd's pie, and chicken liver pâté with the organic meats. Three-cheese fondue comes with bread and vegetables, but the staff was gracious about serving it, at my request, with apples, their wonderful crusty, fresh bread, and carrots. The bread had been lightly toasted and the baby carrots were warm and cooked al dente.

Lunch salads include a strawberry spinach salad; mixed greens with goat cheese, apples and walnuts; a Cobb salad; and a couple others. Lobster club sandwich with bacon and avocado or a smoked salmon and bacon sandwich are also offered. Pork barbecue, vegetable lasagna, and grilled steak and other sandwiches come with chips, pickles, lettuce, and tomatoes.

Evening dinner appetizers might be steamed artichoke, seafood soup du jour, or steamed asparagus. Entrées such as grilled pork chops, one-half baked chicken, crab cakes, grilled salmon, or tuna steak are accompanied by a potato and fresh, seasonal vegetables.

The desserts are homemade, so just pick one. They all look tasty, and you'll see them as you walk up to place your drink and dinner order. Homemade pies, cakes, crème brûlée, and English custards change with the availability of ingredients and seasons.

The servers are not assigned to sections or tables, which is in your favor because everyone on the wait staff who walks by your table glances over to see if you need a drink refreshed, a plate cleared, or dessert ordered. They are so friendly and happy. The whole place is friendly and happy. Hunter's Head is the kind of place you'll enjoy any time, any season.

PARIS

Ashby Inn
692 FEDERAL STREET / PARIS, VA. 20130
(540) 592-3900
WWW.ASHBYINN.COM

Style	Fine dining
Meals	Dinner, Wednesday through Saturday; Sunday brunch. Reservations are strongly recommended.
Price Range	Moderate/Expensive
Superlatives	Duck pot pie, vanilla crème brûlée
Extras	Full bar

*P*aris, which counts its population in two digits, i.e., less than 100 people, lies in the rolling Blue Ridge foothills. John and Roma Sherman left Washington, D.C., jobs in advertising and politics to renovate and create The Ashby Inn. The house

Ashby Inn

was built as a residence in 1829. They preserved the early architecture during the renovation, which created charming guest rooms upstairs and dining rooms on the main floor and outdoor patio.

The library is on the right as you enter. Most of the floors are the original wood. Some of the floors have stenciled oilcloths on them. A peach-colored dining room with seven tables and oversized liquor ad posters is across from the library. The hall walls are gold. Walking forward and down six steps takes you into a smaller dining area with five black booths and floral paintings.

From this dining room, you can take seven more steps down into the taproom. Birds, decoys, and antlers make up part of the décor. A small service bar is located here. Sconces and track lights lend soft illumination, and the eight or so tables are very inviting.

From the outdoor patio, you will relish the pastoral countryside and quiet of such a small town.

The Shermans have been motivated more by

tradition than trend in their cuisine. Seasonal produce and game play a large part in menu creation, and all the bread and desserts are homemade. Their own gardens supply lots of the produce, herbs, and fresh flowers.

As the menu changes often, it's hard to pinpoint specific food items. Sometimes you'll find lobster bisque; Caesar salad; a fennel, pear, and bleu cheese salad; lobster risotto; or mussels à la mariniere for appetizers.

Main courses that make repeat appearances include prune-stuffed pork loin on celery root purée with red onion marmalade and pan jus. Duck pot pie, rib-eye au poivre, fresh cod, and herb-roasted chicken are possibilities. Accompaniments might be garlic mashed potatoes, a polenta cake, pommes frites, and other delightful treats such as puff pastry or sherry cream sauce.

Desserts are little works of art with food as the medium. A recent dessert menu included vanilla crème brûlée, red wine spice poached pear, chocolate pistachio and candied cherry terrine, pumpkin cheesecake, and apple and cranberry crisp.

For a fine dinner, The Ashby Inn ranks very high. For a getaway, it's higher than very high. It's classy, simple, historical, and lovely all bundled together.

Doc's BBQ

1316 JOHN MOSBY HIGHWAY
PARIS, VA. 20130
(540) 837-9188

Style	Home-style
Meals	Breakfast, lunch, and dinner, seven days a week
Price Range	Inexpensive/Moderate
Superlatives	Barbecue beef, homemade pie and cake
Extras	Beer

My husband John was driving west on U.S. 50/17 just west of the small hamlet of Paris. As we started down the mountain from Ashby Gap, I was looking straight ahead. Although he was driving, John was apparently not looking ahead, because he noticed the Doc's BBQ sign and building tucked back from the road on the right.

He took a U-turn at the next median break, and we went back to this small, single-story combination convenience store and restaurant. I noticed the portable barbecue pit on wheels and thought someone must do some catering.

Inside, there are four stools at a counter near the door and nine tables in the back. It's yellow with white trim behind the counter, and knotty pine most everywhere else. The floors are wood. Front picture windows let in lots of light.

The convenience store part sells some chips, mustard, tomato soup, gloves, motor oil, newspapers, aspirin, canned and boxed goods, a little of a lot of different things.

We received an exceptionally warm and friendly welcome from Bonnie McIntosh, the waitress and cashier of the moment. I looked over the breakfast menu of eggs, bacon, sausage gravy, the usual stuff, and nothing seemed appealing.

I love beef barbecue, even though I don't usually have it for breakfast. Bonnie was delighted to take the barbecue order because she said Doc makes the best beef barbecue. Doc is the owner, John Behlier, and he's not really a doctor. He and a veterinarian buddy started the barbecue business and named it Doc's. John owns the Upperville Country Store and Aldie Country Store, where you'll also find Doc's BBQ.

The beef barbecue is everything Bonnie promised—tasty and tender, really tender. It's fantastic and good for breakfast. You can also order Texas pork barbecue and North Carolina barbecue, as well as burgers, sandwiches, salads, and Sonja's homemade baked beans, coleslaw, and potato salad. Sonja is John's wife.

The barbecue sandwiches and dinners are the evening headliners, and you can get pizza and wings. The best deal is probably the sampler with three ribs, one quarter chicken, your choice of barbecue, baked beans, coleslaw, or potato salad.

Follow all that with homemade cake or pie, and you'll be happy you stopped here. Don't drive too fast going west, but perhaps the passenger, not the driver, should be the lookout scout for Doc's BBQ.

Hill High Orchard

35246 HARRY BYRD HIGHWAY (VA. 7)
ROUND HILL, VA. 20141
(540) 338-9113

Style	Farm market
Meals	Breakfast and lunch, seven days a week
Price Range	Inexpensive
Superlatives	Pie, pie, pie
Extras	Fresh produce, gift shop

On the north side of Va. 7, less than a mile from the turn-off for Business 7 into the town of Round Hill, there's an old, red covered wagon with a sign that reads "Hill High Orchard." Inside the building to the right is the fresh produce, along with rows of jams, jellies, preserves, marmalades, honey, stick candy, bean soup mix, country hams in cloth wrap, butters such as apple butter and pumpkin butter, and an eclectic gift assortment of gnomes, candles, rolling pins, and country things.

Ron and Kate Heimburger have operated Hill High since 1993, and it's been in business since the 1940s. Back then, the orchards were behind the building, and farmland encircled all three sides of the little market. Now, most everything comes fresh from the Shenandoah Valley, as the orchards have succumbed to subdivision development.

To the left of the entry is the bakery and deli where you can get a breakfast of English muffin with eggs, cheese, and your choice of sausage, bacon, or country ham, or chopped-beef gravy on biscuits. These things are served all day. More lunch oriented are the chili, fresh soups such as cream of broccoli or cream of potato, barbecue, BLTs, burgers, chicken salad, deli salad platters, and deli cold plates. Deli meats and cheeses are sold by the pound, too.

There are four tables with white tops and wood chairs on a linoleum floor. Green Mountain coffee is featured, and there is a variety of flavored teas from which to choose.

Hill High Orchard is known for its pies. People order wholesale from here and others buy just a slice. The selection is staggering. Apple, apple caramel walnut, blackberry, blueberry, blueberry cream cheese, Boston cream, cherry, coconut cream, coconut custard, five fruit, Dutch apple, French apple, Key lime, chocolate meringue, lemon meringue, mince, peach, pecan, pumpkin, red raspberry, rhubarb, sweet potato, strawberry rhubarb, French silk, lemon crunch, carrot cake (yes, that's carrot cake pie), and more.

Sugar-free pies include apple, wild berry, and cherry. And we're not done yet. There's peach crunch, cherry crunch, apple dumpling, cherry cheesecake, cranapple, egg custard, and occasionally, other kinds of pie, as if there are many others!

Past the deli area is another small room with Christmas ornaments and decorations and more country things.

Ron says they are always open, even on Thanksgiving and Christmas. "We don't make any money

those days. Most people just stop to use the restrooms, but we have lots of fun anyway."

There are outdoor picnic tables and a large pond where kids come to fish and feed ducks. "Anyone can come up to the pond and enjoy it outside here," explained Kate. It's apparent that Ron and Kate are not the type of business owners who get frazzled over little things. They are as charming as the whole place.

ROUND HILL

Round Hill Diner
VA. 7 AND VA. 719 / ROUND HILL, VA. 20142
(540) 338-3663

Style	Café
Meals	Breakfast and lunch, seven days a week
Price Range	Inexpensive
Superlatives	Blueberry hot cakes, meat loaf

For some reason, Round Hill just sounds like a small town, and indeed it is. The name comes from a local hill that was surveyed in 1725 and later served as an observation point for both armies during the Civil War. The town was incorporated in 1900.

The Round Hill Diner is located in a little building just to the left of and slightly back from an Amoco station. Looking for a challenge, owner Joan Farris took over the fledgling café in 1992. She had worked for the previous owner and decided to venture out when the opportunity presented itself.

The small eatery seats around 40 and serves breakfast whenever it's open, except that hot cakes are not made after 1:30 P.M. Joan says that's because the grill needs time to cool before the place closes. "You can make a hamburger in a skillet then, but the temperature in a skillet is not right for hot cakes," she explained.

The blueberry hot cakes are mighty popular. You can also get bacon, eggs, omelets, and other breakfast fare.

Pork barbecue, sandwiches, and hamburgers hand-pattied on the premises are offered at lunch. The most popular of the daily specials is the meat loaf, served on Thursdays. Other specials include chicken cordon bleu and hot turkey and hot roast beef sandwiches.

All the soups—such as vegetable beef and navy bean—are homemade. Pie is the dessert of choice with pumpkin, coconut cream, apple, blackberry, and others depending on the time of year.

The Round Hill Diner is a small, simple place with old-fashioned country cooking.

Bacchus Café

9E CATOCTIN CIRCLE SW
(VILLAGE SQUARE SHOPPING CENTER)
LEESBURG, VA. 20175
(703) 779-2222
WWW.BACCHUSCAFE.COM

Style	Casual nice
Meals	Lunch and dinner, Monday through Saturday. Reservations are recommended.
Price Range	Inexpensive/Moderate
Superlatives	Calamari, couscous
Extras	Full bar

Andy Ghuzlan, from Syria, and Sheryl Weitzel, from Philadelphia, met while working at a restaurant. Deciding they could partner well on their own, they pooled resources and opened Andy's Pizza & Subs in 1989.

As Leesburg grew, Sheryl said they decided "Leesburgers needed a comfortable place with upscale food at prices that were not astronomical." And Bacchus was conceived and opened a couple of years later.

Warm yellow walls, wrought-iron chandeliers, and oak floors create an inviting atmosphere, but it's the flowers that will capture your senses. A tall vase of gorgeous, colorful flowers greets you near the front entrance. There's another bouquet in the ladies restroom and another near the bar. The flowers are very elegant, and I understand when they are delivered, the whole place smells like a flower garden.

Bacchus has an extensive stock of fine wines from

around the world, which makes sense since Bacchus is the god of wine. There's a featured wine, selected for taste, quality, and availability, on each table.

If you're in the mood for an appetizer, you can choose from many things such as bruschetta, eggplant marinara, hummus, calamari, beef carpaccio, or vegetarian mezze, which is spinach pie with hummus, baba gannouj, stuffed grape leaves, and Mediterranean salad in a warm pita.

There's a soup of the day and minestrone soup and gazpacho are always available. Salads include Greek, antipasto, tomato-mozzarella, grilled steak, and salad niçoise. Lunch pizzas have 12-inch diameters and come with red or white sauce with grilled vegetables, Italian meats, grilled chicken, or all ingredients.

Sandwiches include the American cheeseburger, grilled salmon, French dip, Italian cold cut, open-faced steak and cheese, a prosciutto panini, and tasso (ham) panini. Entrées of angel hair with marinara or white clam sauce, vegetable lasagna, and chicken Parmesan are offered with other lunch dishes.

Time-saver lunches are available Monday through Friday. A house salad or Caesar salad with or without chicken, soup, and a soft drink are examples. Another is a half sandwich with side, soup, and soft drink.

The dinner menu is more comprehensive. Pasta entrées include rigatoni with Italian sausage ragout, portobello ravioli, linguine with clams, eggplant parmigiana, and penne salmon rosé. Gorgonzola breaded chicken is coated and baked with bread crumbs and Gorgonzola cheese, then served over mashed, red potatoes and steamed spinach in a light cream sauce.

Rib-eye steak, duck breast, grilled filet, veal chops, and shrimp are available, along with a kabob sampler of your choice. If you are uncertain about the food or wine, ask for Eric Foxx-Nettnin. He's the executive chef, and he's willing to come to your table to offer explanation and assistance.

Tiramisu and cheesecake are optional meal endings, and they don't need much explanation. I haven't yet met a tiramisu I did not like.

Eiffel Tower Café

107 LOUDOUN STREET SW
LEESBURG, VA. 20175
(703) 777-5142
WWW.EIFFELTOWERCAFE.COM

Style	Casual nice
Meals	Lunch, seven days a week; dinner, Monday through Saturday
Price Range	Moderate/Expensive
Superlatives	French cuisine, vanilla crème brûlée
Extras	Full bar

Madeleine Sosnitsky came to the United States from France with her husband, Pierre, in 1969. They had a successful, French restaurant in northern Virginia for more than 18 years. Madeleine opened Eiffel Tower Café in a circa 1850s house late in 1997.

Eiffel Tower Café

The entrance is on the side and can be tricky to find. The parking lot behind the building next door (located toward downtown) is available after 5 P.M. and on weekends, and there's a public parking lot across the street.

The interior is charming with pink walls, small and large posters (some with the Eiffel Tower), chef and mâitre d' plates, and some of Madeleine's father's art. He was a well-known Polish artist.

The floors are hardwood, the linens are white over light mauve. Little oil lamps with mauve shades complement the recessed ceiling lights and natural light coming in the side windows. Fine china and crystal are the standard.

The music is French, and half the customers were conversing in French the afternoon I was there. *C'est très chic.*

The menus change four times a year to take advantage of fresh produce, game, and seasonal abundance. Some of the lunches might be a half-dozen escargots with parsley butter; warm goat cheese in puff pastry on a bed of baby spinach; grilled trout with rice Pilav; seasonal vegetables and a lemon capers sauce; or chicken fricassee Basquaise with mashed potatoes. Sea scallops and filet of salmon are often offered, along with a quiche of the day.

Either a pan-seared duck foie gras with mango and honey lemon sauce or the sautéed calamari with pistachio, shallots, garlic, and tomatoes with cherry bandit dressing might be an appealing start to a romantic, evening dinner.

Entrées developed by trained chefs seek to blend traditional and modern cuisine and preparation styles to satisfy the most discriminating palates. Filet of venison is served with sauce Grand Veneur. Rack of lamb may be accented with garlic cream, rosemary jus, and tomatoes Provençal.

Fresh seafood might be rockfish, sautéed with braised Belgium endives and lemon polenta or grilled pepper tuna steak. All dinners come with seasonal vegetables and a chef's special selection.

Eiffel Tower Café's signature dessert is vanilla crème brûlée, and I've heard that all the desserts are almost too beautiful to eat. The key word there is "almost." Admire, then enjoy. *Bon appetit!*

Lightfoot

13 NORTH KING STREET
LEESBURG, VA. 20176
(703) 771-2233
WWW.LIGHTFOOTRESTAURANT.COM

Style	Fine dining
Meals	Lunch and dinner, seven days a week
Price Range	Moderate/expensive
Superlatives	"Blue Ridge Spinach Salad," "Mocha Ya Ya"
Extras	Full bar

Lightfoot has moved from modest, contemporary quarters to an elegant, almost intimidating, former bank building. In 1999, the Romanesque Revival style was restored to its grandeur, and the restaurant expanded considerably with new banquet rooms, a bridal suite, and a piano bar.

Though she'd planned a career in food service, Ingrid Gustavson had no intention of operating a restaurant. After graduating from the Culinary Institute of America, she started a small catering business. As the business grew, her sister Carrie helped deliver, set up, and serve on her lunch hours and weekends. The sisters finally decided to try their hand at running a restaurant. They opened in 1993.

You'll find a "Day Menu," a "Bar Menu," and a "Night Menu" at Lightfoot. The items change frequently.

The "Day Menu" features salads and sandwiches. Among the salads, the "Blue Ridge Spinach Salad" takes top billing. The California Caesar has the tra-ditional makings, plus grilled chicken breast, Gulf shrimp, and sun-dried tomatoes. The "Chinatown Salad" combines grilled chicken, crispy Chinese noodles, carrots, bean sprouts, water chestnuts, snow peas, scallions, fresh greens, and peanut dressing. The "Groovy Meat Loaf Sandwich" is meat loaf, tomato, onion, watercress, and red Thai curry mayonnaise on a toasted baguette. The grilled eggplant sandwich comes open-faced on homemade herb bread.

The "Night Menu" appetizers might include crab and shrimp cake and Peking duck quesadilla. Soup is headlined with spicy creamy tomato, and salads feature fresh greens. Entrées include filet mignon, free-range tarragon-crusted chicken, seared scallops, lamb T-bones, China moon pork, and creamy feta risotto, all innovatively prepared and served with complementary foods and flavors.

The bar menu sports soups, appetizers, sandwiches, and salads. Desserts are generous in size and delicious to eat. The house specialty, "Mocha Ya Ya," is a flourless chocolate torte. I ordered it along with a cheese appetizer this visit, and called it lunch. It's dense and tasty, and I justified my decision by calling it a low-carb meal. Which it was. High in sugar, perhaps, but low carb just the same.

Tuscarora Mill

203 HARRISON STREET SE
LEESBURG, VA. 20175
(703) 771-9300

Style	Fine dining
Meals	Lunch and dinner, seven days a week
Price Range	Moderate/Expensive
Superlatives	Atmosphere, salmon, roasted rack of lamb
Extras	Full bar

*T*he Tuscarora Mill became a "must" for this book when it was repeatedly recommended to me by people from Northern Virginia and Maryland.

The gristmill was constructed in 1899. After its days as a mill were over, the building housed a general store until December 1984. The restaurant opened the following year.

You'll immediately notice the great wooden beams, which were needed to support as much as 300 tons of grain. Old belts and pulleys are still in evidence also. The restaurant boasts a tasteful decorating scheme with whimsical touches. Big globe-style street lamps are mounted on vertical beams. Quilts and tapestries hang high on the walls. Fresh flowers are on each table, and instrumental or classical music plays in the background. It's all inviting, rustic, and elegant at the same time.

For starters, you might choose sautéed calamari, baked oysters, spring rolls, corn chowder, or sautéed medallions of lobster. The tossed salad has organic greens, and a warm pistachio-crusted goat cheese salad comes with aged sherry vinaigrette.

Grilled beef tenderloin, shrimp and grits, eggplant Barcelona, and roasted Long Island duckling are among the entrées. You may also choose from smoked chicken pasta or Gulf shrimp pasta, grilled pork chops, and baked rainbow trout stuffed with crab. Sides include tobacco onions, whipped or scalloped potatoes, broccoli, green beans, angel hair pasta, and stir-fried vegetables.

And you just might be lucky enough to find cheesecake and chocolate torte among the desserts, all of which are made in-house.

Candelora's

VA. 7 / PURCELLVILLE, VA. 22132
(540) 338-2075

Style	Fine dining/Pub
Meals	Lunch, Tuesday through Saturday; dinner, Tuesday through Sunday
Price Range	Moderate
Superlatives	Waitresses, mussels, roasted rack of lamb
Extras	Full bar

*H*ealthy people like to get on their bicycles in Alexandria and pedal 45 miles to Purcellville, dubbed "Everyone's Hometown." The town began taking shape because it was on the road between Leesburg and Winchester. Prosperity ensued when the railroad came in 1874. The bicycle path runs on the old railroad bed.

When you see the golf course on the southern side of Va. 7, slow down and look for Candelora's. It's located in the middle where you park for the driving range. The two-story yellow building is nestled among oak and maple trees.

Built around 1915, this house became an inn in the 1930s and a restaurant a couple of decades later. Candelora's opened in 1993 in Lovettsville and moved here to Purcellville in 1999. Owner Fred Petrello comes from a family of cooks.

The beautiful dining room on the main floor has yellow walls, white trim, and draperies with a black print. The fireplace burns real wood. The rustic pub downstairs has cream cloth napkins on dark green tables. There's room here for another 35 people. The patio out back has a nice awning and wrought-iron furniture. The pub menu is in effect on the patio.

The staff at Candelora's, like Ashley Holt and Kyle Waters, are exceptionally cordial, helpful, and knowledgeable. They'll be happy to recommend an appetizer such as portobellase goat cheese or calamari marinara. Entrées run from grilled lamb chops, pork fennel sausage, and broiled shrimp to the popular *pollo con fussilli*, which is sliced chicken in sweet balsamic caramelized-onion sauce with goat cheese over fussilli, and *agnello con erbe*, which translates to roasted rack of lamb with portobello mushrooms and roasted potatoes.

Spumoni is a house special for dessert, along with cannolis, chocolate soufflé, tiramisu, and chocolate or cappuccino tartufo.

The chef graciously accommodates most special requests. The serving staff will assist you in any way. They are super nice. *Bouno appeti'to.*

Cate's Restaurant
U.S. 7 BUSINESS
PURCELLVILLE, VA. 22132
(540) 338-7072

Style	Home-style
Meals	Lunch and dinner, Monday through Saturday
Price Range	Inexpensive
Superlatives	Maryland fried chicken, fish 'n' chips
Extras	Wine and beer

*E*velyn Comandoras lived in Massachusetts most of her life. After her daughter, Tori, got married, moved to Virginia, and had a couple of children, Evelyn couldn't bear being so far from them.

Before Evelyn signed the contract to buy the restaurant property, her best friend, Susan Livesey called from her Oswego, New York, home and said, "I've named your restaurant." Susan, you see, has a restaurant named Rudy's, but she got the name with the restaurant. This time she took it upon herself to name Evelyn's place, even though the paperwork was not final.

And it all materialized. Cate's opened in 1997. The "C" and "A" are for Evelyn's granddaughters,

Small-Town Restaurants in Virginia 209

Courtney and Alexandra. "T" is for Tori and "E" is for Evelyn. Nice work, Susan! It's a family business run by mother and daughter.

It's cute from the road after dark because you see into the dining area through the glass front. Little lamps with cream lampshades rest on every table, and it appears warmly inviting.

They make their own pulled pork barbecue and serve it with a tangy mustard sauce. The chunky, chicken salad and tuna salad are homemade and served on your choice of bread. Or you can order the salad and a side of freshly baked white or wheat bread.

For comfort food, the roast beef is slow roasted, thinly sliced, and served on a Portuguese roll with mashed potatoes and gravy. Macaroni and cheese, burgers, BLTs, grilled cheese and grilled chicken sandwiches, and jumbo hot dogs (plain, with chili, or with chili and bacon) are also lunch options.

There's a fresh soup of the day and several salads such as spinach and Caesar, which you can order as a salad complement to a meal or as an entrée salad by adding chicken or shrimp.

Vegetable trio sampler, Italian buffalo wings, Santa Fe chicken egg rolls, and buffalo shrimp are some of the appetizers. Beef stroganoff, shrimp Florentine, liver and onions, and grilled pork chops are among the entrées. The old-style pot roast is slow roasted until tender and marinated in its own juices. Spring chicken piccata is pan-seared chicken breast sautéed with capers, mushrooms, onions, and lemon, served over pasta.

The desserts change often, so you'll have to ask. The water, coffee, and soda machines are all on filtered water systems.

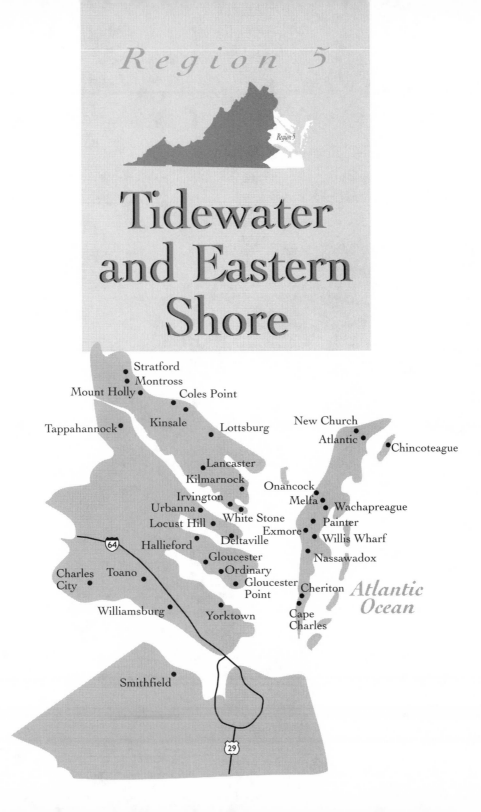

Region 5

Region 5

Tidewater
and Eastern
Shore

Stratford
Montross
Mount Holly
Coles Point
Tappahannock
Kinsale
Lottsburg
New Church
Atlantic
Chincoteague
Lancaster
Kilmarnock
Onancock
Irvington
Melfa
Wachapreague
Urbanna
White Stone
Painter
Locust Hill
Exmore
Hallieford
Deltaville
Willis Wharf
Gloucester
Nassawadox
Charles
City
Toano
Ordinary
Gloucester
Point
Cheriton
Atlantic
Ocean
Williamsburg
Yorktown
Cape
Charles
Smithfield

64

29

"Water, water everywhere" comes to mind in this part of Virginia. So do the romance of sunsets, the taste of fresh fish, and the aroma of salt air. The land is flat and the small-town people are sincere, wholesome, and hardworking.

Much more farming is done here than you might expect. In some spots, wheat fields stretch as far as the eye can see. And fishing is big business, of course. This is also the leading tourist region in the state. Quaint fishing villages, bed-and-breakfasts in renovated historic homes, day and evening cruises, and clamming and crabbing adventures are all here to enjoy.

You don't have to go far to get off the beaten path on the Eastern Shore. Water is never more than a few miles off either side of U.S. 13, which serves as the beaten path in this area. More than a dozen barrier islands under the administration of the Nature Conservancy offer some of the most remote and most rewarding bird-watching anywhere. And up and down the peninsulas are little villages and restaurants that will entice you to visit, if only for a weekend, a day or an hour.

Stratford Hall

485 GREAT HOUSE ROAD
STRATFORD, VA. 22558
(804) 493-8038
WWW.STRATFORDHALL.ORG

Style	Family-style
Meals	Lunch, seven days a week
Price Range	Moderate
Superlatives	Ginger cookies, crab cakes, apple Betty
Extras	Wine and beer

*T*his ancestral home of the remarkable Lee family is a 1700-acre plantation on the Potomac River. The paper place mat found at each seat in the Log Cabin dining room shows 28 sites on the grounds. Some of the things listed include the administration building, executive director's house, and a farm manager's house. But other places look more interesting, such as a trail to the spring, East garden, coach house and stable, kitchen and laundry, northeast dependency and northwest dependency, and the great house itself.

The Stratford Plantation entrance is less than three miles off Va. 3 down Va. 214. You do not have to pay admission to go for lunch.

The inside dining room is small compared to the screened porch on the back, which has Plexiglas over the screens in cooler months for year-round use. It's a lot like sitting in the woods out there, encircled as you are by a tall forest on three sides. The room is filled with natural daylight, though there are chandeliers in the interior dining area.

The tables and chairs are wood. Everything is wood except the food, dishes, and utensils. It's like an upscale camp atmosphere.

The menu is simple with six choices on the lighter fare side, along with the plantation bean soup and cream of crab soup. Biscuits, cornbread, and coleslaw are homemade. There's a two-egg omelet, tuna or chicken cold-plate salad, fried or broiled filet of flounder, fried oysters, and a chef salad topped with sliced chicken breast or country ham.

On the slow drive in, we passed a car coming out with the driver's window down. The lady driver smiled, waved, and hollered, "Have the crab cakes with a bottle of Michelob!" There was a satisfied customer.

Plantation dinners offer a more comprehensive meal such as southern fried chicken, marinated pork tenderloin, Virginia country ham, and fried oyster platter. The dinners come with two vegetables, hot biscuits and cornbread with plantation preserves.

Their special dessert is apple Betty with ice cream. They also offer ice cream alone and ice cream pie. The day I was there, they had Key lime pie, which was good.

Stratford Plantation is loaded with beauty, quiet, history, and the enduring legacy of an American family that helped shape our nation across centuries. The dining room is available for some holiday and group dinners. Weddings, receptions, and meetings are held on the grounds, and overnight accommodations are available.

Friends of Stratford is a support group that contributes significantly to the educational programs and historic preservation of this magnificent estate. Check out the website for information if you wish to be involved in this worthy endeavor. At the very least, go for lunch.

The Inn at Montross

21 POLK STREET / MONTROSS, VA. 22520
(804) 493-0573
WWW.INNATMONTROSS.COM

Style	Casual nice
Meals	Breakfast for lodging guests only; lunch, seasonal; dinner, Friday through Tuesday. Reservations are accepted.
Price Range	Moderate
Superlatives	Hand-cut steaks, veal chops, rack of lamb
Extras	Full bar

Scott Massidda and Cindy Brigman met on the second day of class at the Metropolitan Art Institute of Atlanta in the fall of 1995. Two years later, they joined forces and bought The Inn at Montross. It's a charming place steeped in history.

The original pub in the back was established in 1683 by the justices of the county under the condition that the owner, John Minor, "sell or otherwise dispose of no wine, spirits, cider or other strong liquors during the term of ye session of said court." The property changed hands around 1730 and burned in 1790.

A new building was constructed on the original foundation, and that's what you see today. The red hardwood pine throughout is more than two centuries old. The colonial décor is a neat complement of wallpaper, chair rails, wood, old brick, and cream paint.

There are a few cozy dining rooms with rich-grained oak tables and chairs, white linens, dried flowers, and small candles. Large windows, sconces on the walls, and some recessed lighting provide illumination.

Scott and Cindy, both certified chefs, developed the menu as a chophouse with landlubber's entrées the primary focus. They also own the Mount Holly Steamboat Inn a few miles away on water, and that menu centers on seafood.

The beef is the freshest available and hand-cut on the premises. Appetizers, salads, and soups are offered, along with entrées such as New York strip, prime rib, crab cakes, and rockfish topped with crab imperial. The creamy chicken Alfredo dish of chicken and pasta is combined with a rich, house béchamel for one of the best Alfredo sauces you've ever tasted.

Dinners come with a trip to the salad bar and your choice of red-skin mashed potatoes or wild rice pilaf. You can follow your meal with homemade cheesecake.

If you're cruising the Rappahannock River out

of Fredericksburg or Tappahannock on *The City of Fredericksburg* paddle wheeler or the *Capt. Thomas* cruise boat, you'll taste Scott and Cindy's creative cuisine as they cater the lunch and dinner cruises.

The Inn at Montross is a lovely restaurant and inn in a peaceful, small town. Come for the night, and you can bring your little dog, too!

Yesterday's

15220 KINGS HIGHWAY (VA. 3)
MONTROSS, VA. 22520
(804) 493-0718

Style	Family-style
Meals	Lunch and dinner, Tuesday through Sunday. Reservations are accepted.
Price Range	Inexpensive/Moderate
Superlatives	Prime rib, fresh seafood
Extras	Full bar (service only)

*B*ruce Newbold, originally from Florida, and Daniel Vaughn, hailing from Washington, D.C., have combined restaurant experience totaling more than six decades. They obviously learned a lot along the way because their restaurant, Yesterday's, is packed most days.

It's in a green-and-white building with umbrella patio tables on a front deck and the front lawn. The interior is also green, with pine wainscoting and a variety of old photos, including one of John F. Kennedy. It's neat and clean, with fresh flowers on the tables.

Newbold and Vaughn's first Yesterday's opened in Fredericksburg in 1986. It was sold, and they opened this one in 1993. Bruce is convinced their success is due to buying the freshest food available, roasting all their meats, and making most of the menu from scratch. I'll bet good service, fair prices, and the friendly atmosphere also contribute to the restaurant's popularity.

For the light appetite, Yesterday's offers grilled, sliced chicken; a six-ounce chopped sirloin patty; or six ounces of broiled fresh fish. Mexican suggestions include nachos, a taco salad, a chicken quesadilla, and a fajita wrap. Cheese ravioli, lasagna, spaghetti, and chicken Parmesan satisfy the Italian appetite.

A cup of homemade soup is part of the sandwich package along with your choice of potato. The soups vary between crab bisque, crab vegetable, potato, navy bean, split pea, and others. Prime rib, crab cakes, and grilled chicken all come in sandwich form.

Fresh seafood is a specialty, and you can usually find shrimp, scallops, flounder, seafood gumbo, crab legs, stuffed fish, and variety platters. Some of the everyday favorites are baked meat loaf, liver and onions, Delmonico steak, pot roast, pork chops, mesquite chicken, and country-fried steak.

Daily specials are comprehensive meals, often combination plates, including potato, vegetable, and honey wheat bread made especially for Yesterday's. Prime rib and fresh fried oysters is one pairing. Another is a five-ounce cut of prime rib with a cluster of steamed Alaskan crab legs and five golden fried shrimp.

Desserts are homemade and very popular. Bread pudding, rice pudding, chocolate ganache cheesecake, turtle cheesecake, and others are there for a sweet ending.

When Bruce and Daniel opened the first Yesterday's, they accepted and followed this well-intentioned advice: "Give good food and value." Their receptivity to this nugget of advice, coupled with their experience in the food industry, has brought the local and traveling public exactly that: good food and value.

Mount Holly Steamboat Inn

VA. 202 / MOUNT HOLLY, VA. 22524
(804) 472-3336

Style	Casual nice
Meals	Dinner, five to seven days a week, seasonal; Sunday brunch
Price Range	Moderate/Expensive
Superlatives	Soft-shell crabs, Key lime pie
Extras	Full bar

*T*here really isn't a village of Mount Holly. The nearest town is Montross, four miles away. But it wouldn't be fair to say there's nothing here. There's a one-room brick post office. There's a farm implement dealer occupying two corners of the intersection of Va. 202 and a county road. There's nearby Nomini Baptist Church, whose current brick sanctuary, built in 1858, replaced a meeting house erected in 1790. And until 1996, there was a combination gas station, convenience store, and auto repair place. But it blew up one day—something about fumes inside the building.

Mount Holly House, as Mount Holly Steamboat Inn was originally called, was built in 1876 to serve travelers and merchants on the Nomini Creek steamboat route to and from Washington, D.C.

As with many historical properties, there's always renovation going on here. The main dining room is bright and contemporary. The entire wall facing the water is glass. The furniture is rich-grained oak.

Chef couple Scott Massidda and Cindy Brigman own this property as well as The Inn at Montross in town. Generally speaking, Mount Holly focuses on seafood, while the other inn features fine beef, hand-cut in the kitchen.

Dinner here may start with mushroom caps stuffed with crab imperial or oysters and ham. The seafood dinners include "Crab Norfolk," rockfish, stuffed rainbow trout, fried oysters, baked salmon, and soft-shell crabs, which are caught in the water right in front of the inn. The house specialties are a deluxe seafood platter (lobster tail, a crab cake, shrimp, a soft-shell crab, and fried oysters) and a solo entrée of crab legs. All meals come with salad, dinner rolls, potato or rice, and the vegetable of the day.

Desserts such as Key lime pie, chocolate truffle

cake, and a variety of cheesecakes are created by this talented pair of chefs.

Sunday brunch is an all-you-can-eat buffet that includes poached salmon, spicy shrimp, baked ham, crab salad, and many other things. The chefs will prepare omelets and eggs to order as you watch. Pasta, waffle, and carving stations are also set up.

Sailboats and motorboats are welcome at the beautiful, 12-slip pier. And pets are welcome in each of the five guest rooms.

COLES POINT

The Driftwood

VA. 612 / COLES POINT, VA. 22442
(804) 472-3892

Style	Home-style
Meals	Lunch and dinner, Tuesday through Sunday
Price Range	Inexpensive/Moderate
Superlatives	Seafood, steaks, home-cooked vegetables
Extras	Full bar

One of the many small harbors in Westmoreland County, Coles Point sits on the southern side of the Potomac River at the tip of a peninsula and at the end of Va. 612. It's little surprise that two of the annual events at this village at the end of the land are a spring sailboat race and a rockfish tournament.

There's a burgundy sign out front reading *The Driftwood*. There's also a good-sized red-and-white sign on top of the building.

It's a small, square brick building with windows in the front. The carpeting is gray and burgundy, the tablecloths burgundy, and the walls in the front dining room gray and white. The little back room has wood paneling. The place is so clean that a repairman once commented that it was the first time he hadn't felt the need to brush off his pants after lying on the floor to fix something.

In 1993, Spencer and Pam Standbridge bought the restaurant from Pam's parents, who'd started it 13 years earlier. It's very popular among locals. Pam says one reason is consistency.

At lunch, Spencer and Pam serve sandwiches, burgers, platters, fried fish, and homemade crab cakes, among other things.

At dinner, steaks, seafood, and daily specials such as lobster tail stuffed with crabmeat are featured.

The vegetables are all fresh and home-cooked. People practically stand in line for them. The bread is baked on the premises, and all the desserts are homemade as well.

The Driftwood is the type of place that emphasizes value. You pay a fair price for a good meal in impeccably clean surroundings. The friendly people are a free—but highly appreciated—bonus.

The Backdraft

7415 OLDHAMS ROAD / KINSALE, VA. 22488
(804) 472-4200
WWW.THEBACKDRAFT.COM

Style	Family-style
Meals	Lunch and dinner, Tuesday through Saturday; lunch only on Sunday. Reservations are accepted, except on Wednesdays.
Price Range	Inexpensive
Superlatives	Crab cakes, crab soup, prime rib
Extras	Full bar

You don't need to be a rocket scientist to guess that this restaurant is owned by a firefighter. In this case, retired firefighter Jay Genest. Jay had the restaurant at The Mooring for three years before moving here in mid-2003. In order to keep his staff busy during the transition, Jay employed them to renovate, paint, install equipment, and set up the new place.

The square, brick building is painted fire engine red. Through the front doors is the gray-and-white dining room with black linens on the tables. Local artists Doc Dugan and Teresa Edwards display and sell their art here—Doc has the prints; the oil paintings are Teresa's.

There's a garage door on the left side of the dining room. Jay looked at a couple of doors to put here and settled on the garage door for practicality and expense. It lends to the firefighting theme, though the theme is mostly in the name.

The bar area in the back is twice the size of the dining room, and it's much more colorful and lively. Since the food here is excellent, and there's a wide variety of customers, Jay has made a point to keep the dining room low-key for the lower-key clientele such as families and seniors. After dining hours some nights, the garage door is opened, and the space is full for entertainment and music.

As the food appeals to everyone, so does the entertainment—on at least one night. There's a DJ night, a classic rock night, a karaoke evening, and sometimes live bands.

Jay says there's a line out the door every Wednesday for the chicken wings. My husband ate a whole basket of them. If they are half as good as the ribs and the crab cake, I'd stand in line. Since I was there on a Wednesday, I actually got leftover ribs from Tuesday's all-you-can-eat special. I'd stand in line for those, too. The crab cake was simply luscious (and worth standing in line for!).

Other things on the lunch menu include their special crab soup, Backdraft chili, taco salad, Cobb salad, a fried shrimp basket, cheese quesadilla, crab legs, and chili mac—a large serving of macaroni topped with chili, cheese, and onions.

The crab cake is dubbed the best in all Virginia, and I concur. There are also burgers, BLTs, Reubens, triple-decker clubs, and daily specials.

There are six entrées and a daily special for dinner. Tuesday, you now know, is all-you-can-eat ribs; Wednesday is wingdings; Thursday, steamed shrimp; Friday, prime rib; Saturday, ask your server for the special as it varies.

Every evening, you can order crab cakes, prime rib, filet mignon, fried shrimp, a catch of the day, and chicken Alfredo. The Backdraft is a real find for great food.

Lowery's

U.S. 17 AND U.S. 360
TAPPAHANNOCK, VA. 22560
(804) 443-2800

Style	Family-style
Meals	Lunch and dinner, every day except Christmas
Price Range	Inexpensive/Moderate
Superlatives	Local seafood, crab cakes, hot fudge cake
Extras	Wine and beer

*T*he town called Tappahannock lies on the river called the Rappahannock. The two names are variations on an Indian word meaning "on the rise and fall of water." Among the buildings in Tappahannock's 12-block historic district are the Scots Arms Tavern (built around 1680), the Ritchie House (built around 1706), and the Debtor's Prison (built before 1769).

A full parking lot and people waiting in line at a restaurant that seats more than 300 are sure signs that something is being done right. That's certainly the case with Lowery's, which has been feeding the Tappahannock crowd since 1938.

William Lowery III and his brother Robert now manage the restaurant started by their parents. William Lowery IV, affectionately known as "Duby," is the first member of the third generation to help run the business.

The décor is family friendly. The paper place mats have a travel guide to the area that includes town history, distances to places such as Baltimore and Williamsburg, local historic sites, and a map of the original town grid.

To say the menu is comprehensive is an understatement. At lunch, the sandwiches range from burgers and barbecue to chicken, fish, and rib-eye steak. You can also get an oyster burger or a crab burger. The lunch specials include things such as a hot roast beef sandwich with mashed potatoes and gravy and chicken with mashed potatoes.

The dinner menu is several pages long. There are hot appetizers, cold appetizers, and specialty appetizers. Listed under "Favorites" are broiled crab cakes, shrimp stuffed with crabmeat, a seafood platter, and a half-pound of tenderloin. Such entrées as fried chicken and deviled crabs are listed under "Old Standbys." More than 20 seafood entrées and combinations are on the menu. Char-broiled steaks are available, as is a steak and seafood combination meal. There are also numerous listings for chef's suggestions, hot sandwiches, children's meals, salads, and cold plates. If this isn't enough of a choice, there are specials on little pieces of paper clipped inside your menu.

More than a dozen desserts are offered—pies, hot fudge cake, peach cobbler, dessert of the day. If you don't have room right after your meal, you're welcome to buy a whole pie and take it home.

After you've been here, you'll understand why the parking lot is full and why so many people eat at Lowery's.

Café Lotté

2816 NORTHUMBERLAND HIGHWAY
LOTTSBURG, VA. 22511
(804) 529-5938
WWW.NORTHERNNECKTODAY.COM

Style	Home-style
Meals	Lunch, Monday through Saturday; dinner, Friday and Saturday
Price Range	Inexpensive
Superlatives	Gumbo, homemade desserts, baby back rib soup
Extras	Beer and wine, gift shop

*T*his is one of those worth-the-drive-out-of-your-way places for good, homemade food and an interesting, eclectic gift shop. The official name is The Little People's Guild and Café Lotté. Owners Marty and Joyce Stewart started carving small figures years ago and selling them at craft fairs.

Marty was Army Special Ops, then a defense contractor in the nation's capital. He and Joyce bought a weekend home here in Northumberland County in 1993. The relaxing pace and the fishing agreed with them. As it got harder to make the drive back to the city, they looked for a reason to stay.

In 1995, they bought this circa 1895 building,

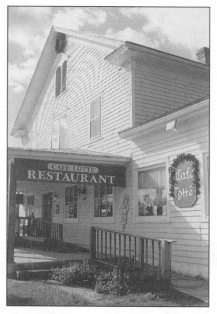

Café Lotté

which served as the local post office in the 1920s. You can see the dip in the original floor where the postman stood. Marty makes a mean gumbo, and Joyce is a terrific cook. With the little people standing sentry in a newly arranged gift shop, the Stewarts opened a coffee shop, which is today's Café Lotté restaurant.

The gift shop is everywhere you turn in each room. About 60% of the prints, carvings, tote bags, antique dishes, nautical trinkets, and assorted crafts are for sale on consignment from local and regional artists. Things are reasonably priced and of very nice quality.

Dark green linens with a big checkered napkin rest under glass on each of the 12 tables, several of which are located in the gift-shop rooms. There's a small, ceramic lamp on each table.

The meats are smoked on the premises—turkey, pork, beef, salmon, and others. Joyce cooks and pulls the pork, and it's tender and tasty. The barbecue sandwiches are served on a round French roll with Café Lotté's own barbecue sauce on the side. Other sandwiches include a Reuben on rye, cheese steak, gourmet club, and smoked ham or turkey with Swiss cheese.

The chicken salad is homemade, as are Marty's soups and gumbos. You can create your own platter lunch by adding servings of coleslaw, potato salad, smokey baked beans, fries, pasta salad, or extra onions and tomato.

The weekend dinners may feature frog legs, pork ribs, crab quiche, or other interesting entrées with potatoes, pasta salad, fries, coleslaw, or other side dishes prepared at the whim of this talented, cooking couple.

Save room for Joyce's homemade desserts. They change often and her favorites are orange crunch cake, bread pudding with bourbon, chocolate cherry crunch, and the cheesecakes. You might say they are all her favorites. She loves to make dessert, and you'll equally love consuming any one of them.

Conrad's Upper Deck

1947 ROCKY NECK ROAD / LANCASTER, VA.
22503
(804) 462-7400

Style	Family-style
Meals	Dinner, Friday and Saturday from March through October. Credit cards are not accepted.
Price Range	Inexpensive/Moderate
Superlatives	View, seafood
Extras	Full bar

*I*solated at the end of a back road on the Rappahannock River and Greenvale Creek, Conrad's Upper Deck is no secret to Lancaster County residents and regular visitors to the Northern Neck. They flock here by car, van, motor home, pickup, and powerboat, parking in the oyster-shell lot or tying up at the bulkhead. Conrad's is easy to find from River Road (Va. 354) at Mollusk. Just turn onto Rocky Neck Road and drive two miles to the end.

The place is a special treat, since it's open only two nights, and then only for part of the year. It seats 110 in two dining rooms and is especially popular for birthdays. Make sure you bring cash, since Conrad's does not accept credit cards.

The restaurant sits atop E. J. Conrad & Sons, a wholesale seafood operation that has been in business since 1935. Milton Conrad bought the business from his father in 1972 and opened the restaurant in the early 1980s.

Conrad's features an all-you-can-eat buffet of steamed shrimp, fried scallops, oysters, clams, crab balls, baked fish, fried chicken, corn on the cob, vegetables, and hush puppies. The piping-hot clam chowder is excellent.

You can also order off the menu. The menu selections are generous and include two vegetables or a trip to the salad bar. Some popular entrées are the seafood platter, fried flounder stuffed with crabmeat, two pounds of snow crab legs, and the "Pick Three"—your choice of three from among oysters, fish, popcorn shrimp, scallops, clams strips, and crab balls. Beef and chicken entrées are also on the menu, as is a selection of foods for children under six—burgers, fries, chicken tenders.

Local patrons claim never to have room for dessert. Still, you'll sometimes catch them succumbing to a slice of Gale Conrad's homemade German chocolate pie.

Lee's

30 MAIN STREET / KILMARNOCK, VA. 22482
(804) 435-1255

Style	Home-style
Meals	Breakfast, lunch, and dinner, Monday through Saturday
Price Range	Inexpensive
Superlatives	Fried shrimp, fried chicken, homemade pies

*T*his is a classic family business. Brothers Bill and Jerry Lee operate it with brother-in-law Steve Smith. The brothers' father, Foster Lee, bought it in the 1940s from his father, who opened it in 1939.

It's clean and simple. The booth benches, drapes, and carpets are bluish green. There's pine paneling on the bottom half of the walls and white stucco on the top. A wonderful sailing mural—purportedly painted by an Indian fellow for a six-pack of beer—fills one wall.

Two of the breakfast specials—appropriately dubbed "Special No. 1" and "Special No. 2"—are, respectively, a ham omelet and a cheese omelet, either of which comes with juice, grits, toast, and coffee. Eggs, pancakes, breakfast meats, cereal, oatmeal, biscuits with hot apple butter, and juices are also available.

Sandwiches, burgers, tuna salad, chicken salad, crab cakes, oyster cakes, and chicken croquettes are among the offerings at lunch.

Dinner comes with two vegetables and rolls. You'll note that the word "Vegetables" is in quotes on the menu, presumably because the list includes macaroni and cheese and applesauce as well as pickled beets, stewed tomatoes, slaw, mashed potatoes, and other things. Most of the entrées are seafood dishes—crab cakes, oysters, fried scallops, broiled scallops, and trout. Hamburgers, pepper steak, beef liver, and chopped beef are also available. The fried chicken and fried shrimp are the most popular choices among the locals.

And the homemade pies are good enough reason

for coming in all by themselves. Coconut cream pie, pineapple cream pie, sweet potato pie, and apple pie are some of the favorites.

Smokin' Joe's Bar-B-Que

55 IRVINGTON ROAD
KILMARNOCK, VA. 22482
(804) 435-6000

Style	Family-style
Meals	Lunch and dinner, Monday through Saturday
Price Range	Inexpensive
Superlative	Ribs, ribs, ribs

*I*t's clear from the first bite that Rick Moss, the owner, knows something about making barbecue. It appears, during lunchtime anyway, that as many ribs go out the door in take-out bags as stay with the diners inside or on the patio.

If you come to Irvington Road from the main street of Kilmarnock, you'll have to look backwards on your left about a block after you turn onto Irvington Road. Look for the wood-and-lattice patio and the American flag on the street side. It used to be a gas station. Slow down. You don't want to miss these ribs.

Rick Moss hails from the D.C. area and spent time as a kid out here on the Northern Neck, crabbin' and fishin'. After graduating from George Mason University, Rick got a job inspecting shellfish. He later worked as a social worker.

All along the way, Rick held to his tenet that really good barbecue has more to do with the meat than the sauce. To prove his point, he started Smokin' Joe's. At first it was open one day, Saturday. Three months later, he opened three days a week, and finally he quit his day job and opened six days. He can barely make enough barbecue to serve everyone, and most days, he sells out.

The pork and chicken are covered only in a dry rub, never any salt. There's a touch of salt on the beef brisket. The meat is smoked and pulled on the property. You can also get smoked turkey, smoked burgers, a combo platter, and sides such as baked beans, macaroni and cheese, deviled eggs, coleslaw, potato salad, and collard greens.

In 2000, another Smokin' Joe's opened in Hampton. It's run by his oldest daughter, Stacey. She attended Virginia Tech, which explains the "Go Hokies" on the blackboard at Smokin' Joe's. And there's this friendly reminder next to a hand-drawn doggie: "also do not forget free bones."

Rick named the restaurant for his dad, Joe, because he thought Smokin' Joe's rolled out better than Smokin' Rick's. I would agree with that.

The Main Dining Room

THE TIDES INN
VA. 709 / IRVINGTON, VA. 22480
(804) 438-5000
WWW.TIDESINN.COM

Style	Resort
Meals	Breakfast and dinner, seven days a week. Reservations are required for dinner. Jackets are required for men after 5:30 P.M. Closed January 1 to mid-March
Price Range	Moderate
Superlatives	Prime rib, rack of lamb, veal chops
Extras	Full bar

*I*rvington is a neat, tidy town of well-kept homes, shops, and yards. One of its historic sites is Christ Church, completed in 1735 and unchanged since. The old church has a three-tiered pulpit and high-backed pews.

The main dining room at The Tides is done in cream and burgundy with an awesome water view. All plush armchairs invite you to stay for a meal. It exudes an air of casual elegance. The Chesapeake Club next door is a classy pub with lunch and dinner served daily.

E. A. Stephens, Jr., the previous owner, was seven years old when his parents built The Tides Inn. They lived on the other side of town (which, once you've been to Irvington, you'll realize is a whole mile or so away). Stephens never ran out of food ideas because he was an avid collector of menus. Sedona Resort Management acquired the property in April 2000, and there's still a lot of great cuisine and innovative food served.

Breakfast in a Glass is on the "To your health" section of the morning menu. It's an energizing parfait with layers of yogurt, honey, strawberry, and bananas with wheat germ, granola, walnuts, and fresh cream. The spa omelet, seasonal fruit platter, and oatmeal are in the same category.

Fret not, however, if you choose to start your day hearty. You can order eggs Benedict, a Belgian waffle, buttermilk pancakes, Scottish smoked salmon, French toast, a crab and country ham omelet, and more.

Lunch features soups, salads, and sandwiches and light entrées in this delightful setting.

Dinner appetizers include she-crab soup au sherry, *oysters vol-au-vent* (in puff pastry with lobster cream), vanilla shrimp and blue crab martini (no alcohol).

"Health focus" entrées include the fresh catch and lasagna of roasted and grilled vegetables. Lavender honey duckling, braised Colorado lamb shank, seared ahi tuna, a venison chop, crab cakes, and local rockfish are prepared to order.

Desserts are homemade right here and include a chocolate torte, vanilla bean crème brûlée, banana baked Alaska, and butterscotch brownie sundae.

The Tides Inn is a four-diamond waterfront resort with golf, a marina, river cruises, tennis, a fitness center, and delightful shops.

Trick Dog Café

4357 IRVINGTON ROAD / IRVINGTON, VA. 22480
(804) 438-1055
WWW.TRICKDOGCAFE.COM

Style	Casual nice
Meals	Dinner, Tuesday through Sunday; Sunday brunch
Price Range	Moderate
Superlatives	Crab cakes, calamari
Extras	Full bar

The Trick Dog Café is in a neat, little row of cute cottages with flowers and picket fences. It is one of Bill Westbrook's enterprises. Bill came to Irvington in the early 1980s looking for a place to go sailing. In 1996, he bought a run-down place and renovated it into The Hope & Glory Inn. Now he had a place to stay, but he needed a place to eat and something to do.

So he built these tidy cottages for a restaurant and shops. He is also the entrepreneur behind the new White Fences Winery up the road. The grapes are in, the buildings will go up in 2004, and the winery will open in 2005.

Trick Dog Café is a contemporary restaurant, which opened right here in its cottage in 1999. The black, white, and red décor works well within the gold-painted walls. The tables have white linens with white paper on top. A container of crayons sits in the middle of each table, next to the tall, thin bottle of Voss water.

Departing from the dining room color scheme, there are more than a dozen orange stools at the redwood bar. You can eat at the bar, but there are no crayons there.

Chef Joe Merolli, schooled at the French Culinary Institute in New York, came by way of Arizona, North Carolina, Georgia, and Richmond, Virginia. His favorite food to work with is seafood. Because he insists on great seafood, much of it is flown in daily from Maine. He thinks the best appetizer is fried calamari, but concedes they are all good. Warm Asian ginger beef salad, duck rillete egg rolls, Maine lobster empanadas, and wild rice stuffed quail are some of the other appetizers.

The main courses cover the main meats, fowl and fish. Steak au poivre with crushed peppercorns, shoestring potatoes, and green peppercorn sauce is

Trick Dog Café

very popular. Soy butter-glazed tuna, pan-fried rainbow trout with andouille grits, and the Trick Dog crab cakes will entice the seafood lovers.

Toasted coriander-crusted duck breast and Cajun chicken are sure to please those with a bent toward fowl. There are specials every evening—creative dishes from Chef Joe that take advantage of seasonal ingredients. Some specials have been blackened flounder with Creole basmati rice and pan-seared rockfish with Indian-spiced roasted red potatoes.

Joe also makes the desserts—things such as chocolate Godiva cake, bread pudding, mocha freeze, and pumpkin cheesecake.

The motto of Trick Dog Café is "sit and stay." When they're closed, the sign notes, "sleeping." And at the bottom of the specials menu, you'll read "bark if you want a T-shirt, $20."

Rocket Billy's

WHITE STONE

Rocket Billy's

851 RAPPAHANNOCK AVENUE
WHITE STONE, VA. 22578
(804) 435-7040

Style	Drive-in
Meals	Breakfast and lunch, Monday through Saturday
Price Range	Inexpensive
Superlatives	Crab cakes, seafood bisque, barbecue

*B*illy and Barbara Ancarrow retired from the restaurant business in 1996. On a North Carolina vacation, they saw a 16-foot trailer in a field. It would look like a camper to most folks. To Billy and Barbara, it spelled o-p-p-o-r-t-u-n-i-t-y, so they bought it. Retirement, you see, just didn't suit them.

Billy tore out the inside and compactly retrofitted it to perform every function one would find in a standard, much larger, commercial kitchen. Barbara loves the fact that, standing in one spot, everything she needs is within an arm's reach—the grill, the deep-fat fryer, food, utensils, a small sink. She could have her feet in concrete, except she needs to turn around now and again.

The exterior with its small picket fences and flags is all red, white, and blue—a testament to their patriotism and Billy's service in the Marines where he was affectionately nicknamed "Rocket Billy." I did not ask why.

Billy and Barbara are a charming, energetic, pleasant couple. They also own the Little Bay Lookout, a small grocery and bait store, located on the waterfront a couple of miles from Rocket Billy's.

Breakfast is standard fare—eggs, ham, steak,

sausage, salted or unsalted fish, hash browns. Lunch offers burgers, chili, deviled crab, chicken cordon bleu, BLTs, and club, Italian sausage, oysters, and prime rib sandwiches. The crab cakes are wonderful. The barbecue and seafood bisque have been written about in magazine articles.

The food is fresh and homemade in the tiny kitchen. What opened in May 1998 as a part-time idea has become a full-time restaurant venture. And they, along with their long-time employee, Crystal Ortiz, wouldn't have it any other way! Ditto from me and their other customers!

The Sandpiper

850 RAPPAHANNOCK DRIVE
WHITE STONE, VA. 22578
(804) 435-6176

Style	Family-style
Meals	Dinner, Tuesday through Saturday
Price Range	Moderate
Superlatives	Hand-cut, char-broiled steaks, homemade desserts
Extras	Full bar

When Carole Sullivan found herself a single parent with a young daughter, she left Beckley, West Virginia, and moved near her sister in the White Stone area. She had worked as a bar hostess, waitress, bartender, and restaurant manager until opening The Sandpiper in 1982.

It was a former barbecue joint, and Carole fixed it up and started working at everything, as small business entrepreneurs usually do. She cooked, washed dishes, kept things organized, and began serving good, homemade food. Her daughter, Kelli, would go along, sleeping on two chairs put together when nap time rolled around.

The simple tan-and-green exterior is complemented inside with a burgundy theme and teal green trim. The ceiling looks like tin, and ceiling fans provide air movement as well as lighting. Sailboat prints hang on the walls.

Kelli is now an integral part of the restaurant, and a friend of hers painted the charming murals in the restrooms. Carole is quick to pass along credit for the restaurant's success to her staff. "It's a wonderful crew," she stated, adding that most of her employees have been there for years. It's always a credit to a business owner to have long-term staff, especially in a business with a high turnover like the food industry.

The roasted, sweet, red pepper soup with crab is very popular as an appetizer. There's also bacon-wrapped shrimp, onion rings, seafood chowder, and shrimp cocktail to begin the dining adventure.

The meats are hand-cut on the premises and include New York strip and filet mignon, as well as center-cut pork chops and veal liver. Sandpiper's crab cakes are all jumbo lump crab—"no filler, guaranteed." Other fresh seafood dinners are stuffed shrimp, fresh oysters, farm-raised catfish, Atlantic salmon, and a seafood platter, fried or broiled.

The kabob is a skewer with char-grilled shrimp, scallops, filet mignon, and vegetables. Shrimp Roma and shrimp scampi are also on the menu. Entrées come with a house salad and your choice of side dish.

The desserts are all homemade. One of Carole's favorites is bread pudding with vanilla sauce. Her husband, Raymond, chops the bread cubes from sourdough bread, and Carole assembles the dessert. She also makes berry, cream, and fruit pies, cheesecakes, a coconut custard pie, and sometimes other things at her whim or as a seasonal special.

White Stone Wine & Cheese

572 RAPPAHANNOCK DRIVE
WHITE STONE, VA. 22578
(804) 435-2000
WWW.RIVAHBIZ.COM/WHITSTWINE.HTML

Style	Casual nice
Meals	Lunch, Tuesday through Saturday; dinner, Wednesday through Saturday. Reservations are accepted.
Price Range	Moderate
Superlatives	*Osso buco* (braised pork shanks), roasted duck with cloves
Extras	Wine and beer

*T*here's no mistaking the French influence here. If all the French wines, the French-style bistro, and the French storefront wallpaper border escape you, incline an ear to the music. You may not know French, but you'll surely discern that the songs are not sung in English.

Owner Bruce Watson loves everything French, though he grew up in Southern California where he learned Spanish before he ever thought of speaking French. He spoke English exclusively in his hospital administrator job, but once in the boat business, Bruce dealt with French companies and mastered the language.

He took some French culinary training in Montreal and bought this little wine store in 1993. The restaurant formally opened in 2000. Lots of people come in who wish to speak French, so Bruce is often called to the tables to take orders, assist with wine selections, and chat amicably *avec les patrons.*

The ten tables have fresh flowers, little oil lamps, and burgundy-and-yellow print tablecloths under glass. The tile floor is a clean and attractive terracotta color. The walls are cream with dark green trim and a European wallpaper border. Wine bottles are everywhere, along with a selection of more than 50 beers.

Bruce holds a free winetasting every Friday between 5:00 and 7:00 P.M. Lunches are ordered at the U-shaped counter in the middle and delivered to your table. Dinners are a more extravagant affair, with Saturday's *prix fixe* French dinner with French wine a superb experience.

The menu items are in French, but the descriptions are in simple English. For example, *salade chaud de lentilles aux pancetta*—warm salad with lentils, pancetta from Italy, and baby carrots. Or, *crêpes aux fromage* – crêpes filled with soft French cheese and a light vodka cream sauce.

Entrées change regularly, and you might find *geline à la lochoise*—chicken breast stuffed with apricot chutney and herbs, baked and served on roasted Parisian potatoes with a red wine reduction sauce. Two of Bruce's favorites are *osso buco* (braised pork shanks) and the duck breast roasted with cloves.

Dessert on the menu or with the Saturday night dinner event might be *tarte framboise*—raspberry tart with pastry cream, or passion fruit petit fours.

You can go with the menu suggestions for wine or just walk around the shop and pick out a bottle to have with dinner—at the retail price marked. That's reasonable enough. *C'est vrai.*

Shuckers
213 VIRGINIA STREET / URBANNA, VA. 23175
(804) 758-1034

Style	Casual nice
Meals	Dinner, Wednesday through Sunday
Price Range	Moderate
Superlatives	She-crab soup, seafood chowder
Extras	Full bar

Carl and Brenda Cassell decided to leave the hustle and bustle of Richmond for the quiet and peacefulness of Urbanna. They would retire here, they thought. Carl is a contractor, and they also thought they would have time to work on their own house instead of always building someone else's house. With grandchildren in their future, this seemed like a good plan.

Well, energetic people are not supposed to retire. Since coming to Urbanna, Carl has continued in the contracting business. Brenda continued working as a medical sales rep. Then this little restaurant in town came up for sale, and they sort of always wanted a little restaurant.

In the fall of 2001, Shuckers opened, and with all their jobs and the restaurant, they are busier now than ever before. Developing the menu, which still changes from time to time, was a joint effort between them, their staff, the previous owners, and the customers.

Carl and Brenda included what they wanted; the staff contributed ideas; some recipes came with the business purchase; and customers offered suggestions and even gave them recipes.

The she-crab soup takes top billing as their most popular item, though seafood chowder and soft-shell crabs, when in season, are right behind. Oysters Rockefeller are another favorite. Crab dip, scallops and bacon, and potato skins with bacon and shrimp are more appetizers.

If you want to eat light, you can order salads, sides, or sandwiches. The steamed combo platter includes crab legs, oysters, shrimp, and clams with rice or potato or fries and slaw or salad. Shrimp and crab legs come steamed or raw, while clams and oysters are fried or broiled.

Shuckers combination meals are sea scallops, shrimp, crab cakes, and oysters, or you can make your own half-and-half by choosing any two of the combo meal. Delmonico and New York strip steaks can be served blackened or with sautéed onions and mushrooms.

Baby back ribs and grilled chicken breasts are often on the menu. The captain's choices are seafood lasagna and the shrimp and scallops stir-fry.

The homemade desserts, like the dinner specials, change often, but you may find their fresh cheesecake or bread pudding. At holiday time, they make coconut pies and sweet potato pies.

The Cassells are happy with their move. They like being busy, but the best part is the warmth and friendliness they have experienced from the local people.

Virginia Street Café
VIRGINIA AND PEARL STREETS
URBANNA, VA. 23175
(804) 758-3798

Style	Home-style
Meals	Breakfast, lunch, and dinner, seven days a week
Price Range	Inexpensive/Moderate
Superlatives	Clam chowder, raisin bread pudding
Extras	Full bar

Once a five-and-dime store, the space where the Virginia Street Café is located had to be completely renovated before the café's opening in 1989.

Like many restaurant owners, J. J. Wade says the place feels like a second home—sometimes even a first home. The Virginia Street Café is one large room with pine partitions about four feet high and several inches wide with real plants in them. The walls are cream, and the chairs have striped seats and cane backs. The maple floor is the original.

Eggs, omelets, hot cakes, and French toast are on the breakfast menu. The eight "Club Breakfasts" are complete meals that include juice and coffee.

From barbecue and chicken filet to a combo club, you'll find most any sandwich you could want on the lunch menu. The soft-shell crab sandwich is available only in season, but the crab cake sandwich and the oyster sandwich are offered most of the year. Among the subs are a meat loaf sub, a rib-eye sub, and a Polish sausage sub. The lunch platters—hot turkey sandwich, deviled crab, fried trout, and others—come with some combination of mashed potatoes, french fries, hush puppies, potato salad, and slaw.

A popular item at dinner is the clam chowder, made from a house recipe that has neither milk nor tomatoes in it. Oyster stew and chili are also available, along with crab balls and crab cakes in miniature. The seafood entrées include salmon, trout, crab cakes, shrimp, scallops, and oysters. Beef liver and onions, meat loaf, New York strip steak, prime rib, chicken livers, pork chops, ham steaks, fried chicken, and baby back ribs are also offered.

J. J.'s raisin bread pudding is made from scratch and is the most popular dessert she offers. She prepares sweet potato pie and carrot cake regularly and strawberry shortcake and a variety of berry desserts in season.

David's Last Chance

6209 GENERAL PULLER HIGHWAY
LOCUST HILL, VA. 23092
(804) 758-9611

Style	Family-style
Meals	Lunch and dinner, Monday through Saturday
Price Range	Inexpensive/Moderate
Superlatives	Unusual microbrews; homemade sauces, salad dressings, desserts
Extras	Wine and beer

*L*ocust Hill's post office is a small, brick structure, with the key word being "small." There's no real town center, just a handful of businesses such as a farm-and-feed store, a nursery, a florist, a nursing home, and a couple of other businesses that have a Locust Hill, Virginia, address.

While you might think this restaurant is the owner's last chance at something, the name refers to the former gas station, restaurant, and grocery store on this site. It was dry (non-alcoholic) in most directions past this spot decades ago, so the business was dubbed the "last chance" with regard to purchasing alcoholic drinks.

The building was torn down in the 1990s, and David Taylor bought the land a few years later. When he came around to naming his new restaurant, he decided to revive the old name. David's Last Chance opened March 21, 2000.

It's a bright, cozy place. The walls are a pleasant shade of green, with white trim and a grape wallpaper border. Tabletops are cream color with oak spindle-back chairs. Delightful chef prints, plates, and figurines are nicely placed around the room.

The lunch sandwiches include the Chicken Chesapeake with grilled chicken, country ham, crab, and provolone cheese; a New Yorker of pastrami, Swiss, onions, and hot peppers; and the Rappahannock with smoked turkey breast, ham, Havarti, lettuce, tomato, onions, and hot peppers. Burgers and a grilled yellowfin tuna salad are available. Like the sauces and dressings, the chicken salad is homemade.

Dinner ranges from the simple such as baked spaghetti, meat loaf, and baked crab imperial to sophisticated entrées such as veal au chance, which is tender milk-fed veal sautéed with shrimp, scallops, and crabmeat, then served in a cream sauce over fettuccini. Fried oysters, Bourbon Street steak, pepper steak, and several fresh seafood plates are also on the menu. There are vegetarian entrées and pasta dishes, chicken tenders, barbecue, and quesadillas.

David does a brisk catering and carry-out

business, so if you have a crowd, consider calling on him for everything.

While this is no longer the last chance for alcoholic beverages, it might be your only chance in the area for some of the seasonal microbrews, when they're in stock. In the fall, you might find pumpkin ale from Smuttynose Brewing Company of Portsmouth, New Hampshire. Other times, there's black chocolate stout from the Brooklyn Brewery, not from Brooklyn, but from Utica, New York.

Wines from Virginia, across the country, and around the world are available to complement any meal. Some of the wines by the glass are from Chili and Australia. Others are imported from Italy, France, New Zealand, and Mexico.

Try to save room for one of the homemade desserts. The hummingbird cake is a favorite, and I can attest to its great taste and coarse texture, a sure sign of hand mixing. This is the sort of restaurant where I consider starting with dessert and wine and working backwards, and if there's no room for salad, well, that's okay.

Galley

16236 GENERAL PULLER HIGHWAY (U.S. 33)
DELTAVILLE, VA. 23043
(804) 776-6040

Style	Family-style
Meals	Lunch and dinner, seven days a week
Price Range	Inexpensive/Moderate
Superlatives	Barbecue, jumbo lump crab cakes
Extras	Full bar

Named for its position in the delta of the Rappahannock River, this little town was originally called Unionville for two churches that united here. However, during the days of secession, local residents did not want to be affiliated in any way with the Union, so they renamed their community Deltaville.

The Galley opened in this wooden building in 1992. Judging by the number of cars outside and the cheerfulness of the folks inside, I surmised right away that this is a popular spot to get a bite to eat. In fact, I underestimated the number of patrons when I looked at the cars in the parking lot, not knowing that the Galley provides shuttle service to people docking at local marinas.

You step into a small bar area at the entrance. To the left is the dining room, which has barnboard and cream walls with watercolor paintings on them. Little oil lamps are on the tables.

The lunch specials include the catch of the day and country-fried steak. The Galley serves the sandwiches you'd expect (ham and cheese, tuna salad, chicken salad) and some you probably wouldn't, such as a trout sandwich and grilled tuna steak on a bun. Appetizers, soups, salads, and side orders are also available.

At dinner, the seafood entrées are served oven-roasted, seared, or beer-battered, and there are lots of choices. The surf and turf comes at market price, like the catch of the day. There's also a nice selection of pasta dishes, chicken, barbecue, beef, and ribs.

All the desserts are homemade.

If you're on the go, you'll be happy to learn that the entire menu is available for take-out. The Galley's barbecue sauce, billed as "World Famous," is also for sale.

Sandpiper Reef at Misti Cove

VA. 632 (GODFREY BAY ROAD)
HALLIEFORD, VA. 23068
(804) 725-3331

Style	Casual nice
Meals	Lunch, Sunday; dinner, Thursday through Saturday
Price Range	Moderate
Superlatives	Salmon, prime rib
Extras	Full bar

When you arrive at the end of Va. 632, you'll be in a small community that looks and feels like a summer camp. The building that houses Sandpiper Reef at Misti Cove—a low, gray structure with cream trim and a big screened porch—is reminiscent of a dining hall. Actually, this place was once a church camp for girls.

The restaurant's exterior gives little hint of what's inside. It's all dressed up with pink and white linens, comfortable chairs, and candles on the tables. Piano music plays in the background.

Paul and Jesse Christie bought the business in 1991. Paul is a former automobile dealer. Their motto is simply, "Good food and good service." And they deliver on both counts.

You can lead off your dinner with seafood bisque, potato wedges, a house salad, crab balls, stuffed mushrooms, or beer-battered onion rings.

Among the seafood entrées are broiled flounder, a seafood platter, stuffed shrimp, filet of salmon, and fresh crab cakes. There's a vegetarian entrée each day. The "Reef and Beef Kabob" is composed of shrimp, scallops, beef tenderloin, and grilled vegetables. Delmonico steak, filet mignon, pork chops, chicken, and barbecued ribs are among the other options. Prime rib is served on Friday and Saturday nights. If you're in a more casual mood, you can get chopped sirloin, a burger, a crab cake sandwich, or a grilled chicken sandwich. The casual meals come with french fries and slaw. The sandwiches are served on homemade rolls.

This isn't a place to hurry, so leave time and room for one of the fine homemade desserts—Key lime pie, chocolate silk pie, rum cake, bread pudding,

"Piankatank Pecan Fudge Pie," cheesecake, ice cream, or sherbet.

To find Sandpiper Reef at Misti Cove, begin at the intersection of U.S. 33, U.S. 17, and Va. 198 in the town of Glenns. Follow Va. 198 west to Va. 626 (Hallieford Road). Turn left and go a quarter-mile to Va. 632. Turn left and follow the signs to the restaurant. If you're coming by water, note that the restaurant is on the Piankatank River directly across from Fishing Bay. Also note that the water is just two feet deep at high tide, so a dinghy landing will be in order at the dock.

Kelsick Gardens

Kelsick Gardens

6604 MAIN STREET / GLOUCESTER, VA. 23061
(804) 693-6500

Style	Café
Meals	Lunch and early dinner, Monday through Saturday
Price Range	Inexpensive
Superlatives	Chicken salad, gingersnaps
Extras	Wine and beer

Gloucester native Beth Haskell went to Virginia Tech for a while and studied in the old College of Home Economics. Before finishing, she got married, "ran a catering business, then ran kids for 15 years," as she puts it.

She always wanted her own business, but not a full-service restaurant. "This seemed to be what Gloucester needed and what I could do," she said of her gourmet shop and café, which she launched late in 1992.

The flowers and the tables with dark green umbrellas on the front patio are eye-catching. Inside, the place is a lot larger than most gourmet shops with an eatery. There are seats for at least 27. The paint and wallpaper are pastel orange. The watercolor paintings on the walls are for sale. Instrumental music plays in the background. It's all quite fresh and inviting.

The same menu items are available all day—sandwiches, salads, soups, and combinations. The homemade soups might be baked potato and bean. The daily special might be a country ham salad sandwich or a Cajun catfish filet with wild mushroom and herb couscous. Heart-healthy entrées such as a "lite" quiche Lorraine are also offered.

This is a good place for children who like grilled

cheese. Every person eating here or taking some-thing to go gets a menu. You print your name at the top, check a box for "To Go" or "Here," circle what you want, write in the dessert, hand it in, and have a seat.

A word about dessert. The homemade ginger-snaps are a signature item here. There's also "Bumbleberry Pie"—a Canadian favorite that in-cludes blackberries, raspberries, apples, and rhu-barb. Tough choice.

The gourmet shop offers a nice selection of wine, baskets, crackers, teas, teapots, napkins, spices, and specialty foods.

Kelsick Gardens holds special dinners that pair food courses and appropriate wines. And it hasn't forgotten beer drinkers. Some of the special din-ners feature microbrewed beers instead of wine.

GLOUCESTER

Stillwaters on Main

6553 MAIN STREET / GLOUCESTER, VA. 23061
(804) 694-5618

Style	Casual nice
Meals	Lunch, Monday through Saturday; dinner, Tuesday through Saturday
Price Range	Moderate
Superlatives	Buffalo flank steak, smoked Gouda mashed potatoes
Extras	Full bar

Zachary Taylor Gray, a member of the Virginia House of Delegates, had this building constructed in 1923 for his son, Stanley Taylor Gray. The younger Gray opened his pharmacy in 1924 and re-tired from it in 1979. Over the next couple of de-cades, a series of restaurants came and went until Melanie and Joel Blice bought it in 1996. If my din-ner of buffalo flank steak and smoked Gouda mashed potatoes is any measure, they are here to stay.

Melanie grew up in nearby Mathews County. After several years of city life and a 16-mile com-mute that took an hour or more each way, she and her husband, Joel, decided on a slower-paced lifestyle. They are both experienced food service managers, and Melanie attended Baltimore's Inter-national Culinary College.

They agreed on the restaurant but disagreed on the first 200 names. Just before going to sleep one night, Joel asked, "What about Stillwaters? It sounds calm and peaceful." Melanie agreed and went to sleep.

There's an attractive striped awning out front and a stained-glass window above the door with the restaurant name on it. The inside is casually con-temporary. Pine floors and the original tin ceiling lend an old-time flavor. A diagonal pine-board wall across from a cream wall with Guy Buffet's art is highlighted with modern-style sconces and reflec-tive track lighting. White linens adorn the five booth tables and half-dozen or more small tables. Back-ground music ranges from jazz and blues to soft rock and classical.

Melanie and Joel created the menu together. French onion soup, vegetable chili, and sweet potato fries are found under "soups and such." Lunch salads may include Asian noodle, marinated steak, Caesar with grilled chicken and baby greens. Classic sandwiches such as pulled pork barbecue and grilled chicken club or the fresh fish sandwich are there for the non-adventurous. J.T.'s oyster po' boy, Mel's tuna salad, a grilled vegetable sandwich sound a little more interesting. The Pittsburgh cheese steak pays tribute to Joel's hometown.

Dinner is lovely. Point comfort chowder is a creamy, non-chowder soup. Roasted shallot and bleu cheese dip is served with sliced French baguette pieces. Blackened breast of turkey, grilled rib-eye steak, and the fresh buffalo flank steak are fairly standard menu items. Fettuccini alla "sea smoke" pairs tomato basil pasta with local Urbanna hot-smoked salmon and roasted red peppers.

Fresh salmon, sauté of veal, broiled shrimp and scallops remoulade, and Mediterranean-style grilled breast of chicken are also often available. Daily specials can be creative and unusual, using ingredients such as fresh andouille sausage from New Orleans.

Melanie makes the desserts, and the top two seem to be the orange cheesecake, a very creamy dessert with a hint of orange, and the chocolate pavé, a dense chocolate dessert. Chef-owned restaurants are some of the best, and this is no exception.

ORDINARY
Seawell's Ordinary
U.S. 17 / ORDINARY, VA. 23131
(804) 642-3635

Style	Casual nice
Meals	Lunch, Tuesday through Saturday; dinner, Wednesday through Sunday; Sunday brunch
Price Range	Moderate/Expensive
Superlatives	Chicken with Brie and raspberry sauce, grilled shrimp with andouille sausage
Extras	Full bar

The wee town of Ordinary has so few buildings that you could count them on your fingers and be only a couple of digits short. In fact, it has fewer buildings than there are words in these two sentences.

Some say the town was named for Seawell's Ordinary. If you look up *ordinary* in the dictionary, you'll find it listed as an adjective first; it means "customary, usual, familiar." As a noun, it means "a person, object or situation that is common." Places that serve food and drink to travelers have always been common. Seawell's Ordinary opened in 1757, four and a half decades after the original part of the building was constructed as a private residence. Thomas Jefferson's early maps show it as Sewell's Publick House. Joseph Seawell had a horseracing track on his farm, so his "public house"—or restaurant—was a busy place for eating, drinking, and gambling.

Seawell's Ordinary

The ordinary apparently closed in 1871. It served as a home until 1948, when it was opened as a restaurant again. Nine years later, the building was moved 100 feet back to make way for the expansion of U.S. 17. In 1990, realtor Eleanor Evans sold the property to her husband. It has since become a family operation, with son David now at the helm.

The interior is characteristic of buildings this age. It has lots of wood, small-pane windows, and little oil lamps. The dining room on the right has burgundy walls. The room on the left has the bar. The tables have white linen tablecloths and green napkins.

The two most popular lunch items are the chicken salad with dill, grapes, and walnuts and the shrimp and crab salad. The homemade barbecue sauce is vinegar-based, not tomato-based. The shrimp and crab salad comes on an English muffin with provolone cheese melted over the top.

At dinner, you can enjoy a seafood soup du jour or a regular soup du jour. The appetizers include a baked phyllo strudel and fried won tons. The "Ordinary Salad," which isn't ordinary at all, has mixed greens, melted Brie, toasted almonds, kiwi, and homemade sesame vinaigrette dressing. Veal, chicken, filet mignon, pasta dishes, and a low-calorie vegetarian choice of penne pasta with broccoli and sweet peppers are offered, but with the water so close, entrées from the sea predominate. The "Oysters Volcano" come with a white wine and cream sauce, diced tomatoes, capers, and pesto sour cream. Grilled salmon, blackened mahi-mahi, pan-fried Chesapeake crab cakes, and baked scallops au gratin are also offered.

Chocolate pâté is the signature dessert here. It's made with imported chocolate and premium rum, then formed into a loaf, sliced, and served on a bed of raspberry sauce.

If your out-of-state plates, your Brownie camera, and your bold shirt don't identify you as a tourist in these parts, your pronunciation of Seawell's might. It's not *See-well*, as the spelling suggests. It's *Sool*—rhymes with pool. If you say it right, surely no one will notice the other things.

River's Inn

8109 YACHT HAVEN DRIVE
GLOUCESTER POINT, VA. 23062
(804) 642-9942

Style	Casual nice
Meals	Lunch and dinner, seven days a week in summer; closed Mondays and Tuesdays in fall and winter. The restaurant is closed Christmas and New Year's Day.
Price Range	Moderate
Superlatives	Baked oysters, "Chesapeake Blue Plate," "Hazelnut Mousse"
Extras	Full bar

Gloucester Point, located at the York River and Chesapeake Bay, is about 15 miles from the town of Gloucester. It was originally called Tindall's Point for an early mapmaker. Gloucester Point was once considered a candidate for Virginia's colonial capital. But by a vote of 21 to 18, the capital stayed at Jamestown.

The River's Inn is worth finding, so pay close attention. At the first traffic light north of the bridge from Yorktown, turn right on Lafayette Heights Road. At the first stop sign, go left on Greate Road. Turn right on Terrapin Cove Road, then right on Yacht Haven Drive. There are some signs and little green arrows as you find your way.

You'll wind up at an excellent restaurant and a very pretty marina. There's a deck outside that seats more than 100 and has a different menu from the restaurant. Inside, windows along two sides look out onto the marina. Though there's room inside for about 100 people, the River's Inn has an intimate atmosphere. Mahogany barstools wind around a semicircular bar and along a wall next to it. There are fresh flowers on the tables.

Tom Austin opened the River's Inn in May 1996. You'd never guess that the place was a machine shop in its previous existence.

The most popular appetizer at lunch is "Baked Oysters River's Inn"—oysters on the half shell topped with crabmeat, country ham, cream, seasoned crackers, and a dill hollandaise sauce. There's also oyster stew, steamed littleneck clams with artichoke hearts and sautéed escargots. The Caesar salad is a comprehensive choice that includes grilled potatoes and toasted brioche; it's your option to add fried oysters or grilled duck breast. Sandwiches and entrées are also offered at lunch.

The "Chesapeake Blue Plate" is popular at dinner. It comes with she-crab soup, Caesar salad, and an entrée that combines a crab cake, crab imperial in a puff pastry, and fried oysters with Virginia ham. The herb-roasted rack of lamb with sausage is also a favorite. Everything else sounds wonderful, too. Shrimp, lobster, a variety of other seafood dishes, veal, chicken, duck, and filet mignon are among the options.

The "Hazelnut Mousse," the Key lime pie, and the cheesecake are all excellent desserts. And if you think pound cake is boring, try the River's Inn's version. It's grilled and served with butter pecan ice cream, chocolate sauce, and whipped cream.

Yorktown Pub

112 WATER STREET / YORKTOWN, VA. 23690
(757) 886-9964

Style	Pub
Meals	Lunch and dinner, seven days a week. No credit cards or checks are accepted, but an ATM is available.
Price Range	Inexpensive/Moderate
Superlatives	Crab cakes, fried fish sandwiches
Extras	Full bar

This small town was established in 1691 and saw the last major conflict of the Revolutionary War when Lord Cornwallis surrendered to George Washington. The Yorktown Victory Center provides a comprehensive presentation of the American Revolution. Walking is the main mode of movement through the town. The streets are narrow and there's much to enjoy, to read, to learn, to photograph among the historical, clapboard buildings.

The Yorktown Pub faces the wide expanse of the York River. It's a nice view from the front windows. But if you're seated in one of the wood booths or tables in the middle, you can catch something on one of the three televisions or just kick back and watch the people. Bill Cole, innkeeper at the York River Inn, recommended the pub, and I'm glad he did.

It's a cozy, rustic, busy place with hanging stained-glass lamps and lots of wood. The restaurant built here in 1956 became a pub in 1987, and buddies Rick Tanner and Dean Tsamouras bought it in May 2000. They were childhood pals in Richmond. Rick has a retail background. Dean has owned The College Deli in Williamsburg for more than 17 years.

"York River starters" sound appropriate for the region—clams, oysters, steamed spiced shrimp, fried popcorn shrimp, and clam chowder. Only Clint's famous chili steps outside the seafood category. "Sides and starters" expand the list of appetizers to include chicken wings, potato skins, cheese sticks, crab dip spread, and other things.

The chef salad and Greek salad are hearty and adequate for a meal; the house salad goes well with a meal. Seafood entrées and surf sandwiches are larger portions of some of the starters. Broiled or fried scallops, crab cakes, a combination seafood platter, fried shrimp dinner, and the pub's crab cake sandwich are some of the choices.

They offer deli sandwiches and pub specials from the grill. A Reuben on rye, prime rib sandwich, grilled breast of chicken, or the BBQ sandwich come with your choice of potato salad, coleslaw, potato chips, or fries. And you can get hot dogs, chili dogs, and chili cheese dogs.

They have fresh soups and homemade desserts. The pub is a lively place, and the town is just a neat spot to enjoy yourself and celebrate our nation's precious freedom.

Old Chickahominy House

1211 JAMESTOWN ROAD
WILLIAMSBURG, VA. 23185
(757) 229-4689

Style	Home-style
Meals	Breakfast and lunch, seven days a week
Price Range	Inexpensive
Superlatives	Chicken and dumplings, Brunswick stew, hot biscuits
Extras	Wine and beer

There's no feature of a historic house more welcoming than a big front porch with rocking chairs resting quietly and American flags waving in a slight breeze.

If there's a wait to be seated at the Old Chickahominy House—and it's likely there will be—you can sit on the porch and rock. But I opted for wandering through the part of the building that houses an antique and gift shop. American and

English antiques adorn display cases, and gifts, housewares, and toiletries fill a couple of rooms and some nooks and crannies. Most of the antiques are on the main level across the hall from the dining rooms. The Christmas shop on the upper level offers greeting cards, cookbooks, fine lotions, china, Virginia gifts, and jewelry. You can even buy a T-shirt with the restaurant's menu on the back.

When you do get called into the 18th-century-style dining room, you'll soon discover that everything here is homemade.

You'll see the name of "Miss Melinda" in a few places on the menu. She started the business in 1955. For the past decade or so, it's been run by her daughter-in-law, Maxine Henderson.

The "Plantation Breakfast" includes Virginia ham, bacon, or sausage with two eggs, grits, hot biscuits, and coffee or tea. You can also order "Miss Melinda's Pancakes" or creamed ham on toast.

At lunch, "Miss Melinda's Special" consists of a cup of Brunswick stew, Virginia ham on hot biscuits, fruit salad, homemade pie, and coffee or tea. If you'd like more of the Brunswick stew, you can buy it by the quart to go. The Old Chickahominy House is famous for its chicken and dumplings and its chicken soup as well. Hamburgers are also offered.

The Old Chickahominy House ships fully cooked boneless Edwards hams, Wigwam bone-in hams, and uncooked, country-style, pepper-coated Virginia hams. It will also ship most gifts, but not antiques or framed pictures.

Old Chickahominy House

The Trellis Café, Restaurant & Grill

403 DUKE OF GLOUCESTER STREET
WILLIAMSBURG, VA. 23185
(757) 229-8610

Style	Casual nice
Meals	Lunch and dinner, seven days a week. Reservations are strongly recommended.
Price Range	Moderate/Expensive
Superlatives	Chocolate desserts
Extras	Full bar

*T*his restaurant was recommended to me so many times via e-mail, note, and spoken word that it wasn't possible to go through Williamsburg without stopping.

An attractive place in Merchant's Square, it has patio dining out front. Inside are multiple rooms with exposed-brick walls. The various dining areas create an intimate atmosphere, and you might be surprised to learn that the restaurant can seat more than 200 people. Fresh flowers and elegant plates with The Trellis's name on them lend a classy touch.

All the food is prepared under the watchful eye of executive chef and cookbook author Marcel Desaulniers. He and John Curtis opened the restaurant in 1980.

The menu changes seasonally to take advantage of foods at their freshest. There aren't many restaurants where you'll find white trumpet mushrooms, Jerusalem artichokes, celery root, and chestnuts. Quail, wild boar, lobster, antelope, pheasant, and Texas venison are some of the special game items available at certain times of the year. Freshly baked bread comes with every meal. Stable menu items include pork medallions, sliced calf's liver, beef tenderloin, catfish, and pan-seared salmon.

Besides having a reputation that extends at least statewide, The Trellis is famous for its "Desserts to Die For," a phrase that's found at the top of the dessert menu as well as on the title page of one of Desaulniers's cookbooks. The two best-known desserts are "Chocolate Temptation" and "Death by Chocolate." Other desserts sound as elegant as they look—"Diamonds on Ice" and "White Chocolate Balloon," for example. On the lighter side, you can always order strawberries with whipped cream. If you haven't left room for dessert, make sure you exercise your final option: dessert to go.

Another cookbook by Desaulniers is *The Trellis Cookbook*. T-shirts, mugs, calendars, pepper grinders, and baseball caps are available for purchase.

The Yorkshire

700 YORK STREET
WILLIAMSBURG, VA. 23185
(757) 229-9790
WWW.YORKSHIRE-WMBG.COM

Style	Casual nice
Meals	Dinner, seven days a week
Price Range	Moderate
Superlatives	Fresh seafood, Yorkshire kabobs
Extras	Full bar

*I*n 1952, an attractive, young couple named Tom and Rose Paparis immigrated to the United States from Greece. A few years later, they opened the first pancake house in Williamsburg, The Ivy Inn. They sold it nearly a decade later and started this dinner restaurant.

Uncertain what to call their new venture, they held a name contest. More than 450 entries were received, and Yorkshire won. The place has an English pub atmosphere with wood panels below a chair rail and cream walls above it. There are booths on the outside wall and captain's chairs at the linen-covered tables. It has an old-world, European feel with soft music in the background.

The Greek heritage of the owners can be found with feta cheese on the appetizer list and the availability of a Greek salad. Crabmeat or shrimp cocktails or stuffed mushrooms with crabmeat and cheese are also good beginnings. I tried the clam chowder, which came fresh, hot, and tasty. In fact, all the food was served hot, not lukewarm, and I like that.

Fresh food is a priority. Seafood is delivered daily, and the meat is hand-cut in the kitchen. Australian lobster tail, stuffed jumbo shrimp, scallops sautéed in butter, baked crabmeat cakes, and fried oysters are often on the menu. For more variety, you can order a combination plate and get to taste different things.

David and Kathy Hoffman of Chambersburg, Pennsylvania, were dining at the next table as I was deciding what to order. "The seafood platter is delicious," Kathy volunteered, a broad smile on her face and her clean dinner platter before her. The Hoffmans came to Williamsburg on a package deal. David said the hotel clerk recommended The Yorkshire to them from the list of half a dozen or more restaurants where they could have dined.

New York strip steak, Delmonico steak, rib steak, and prime rib are cooked to your liking. The Yorkshire specialties are beef kabobs and seafood kabobs served with salad and rice pilaf. Dinners come with a salad and bread, or you can order a Greek salad if you want a salad with feta cheese.

Meals are not a rushed affair at The Yorkshire. In fact, it states on the menu: "The essence of culinary art is time; we ask your kind indulgence." You can wind up this dining experience with chocolate or cherry or crème de menthe parfait, chocolate truffle mousse cake, cheesecake, or lemon meringue pie.

As you might figure out by doing some simple math, Tom and Rose are getting on in years. Their daughter, Mary Ann, has taken reins at the business, though Rose was working the night I was there. And I know she and Tom are an attractive couple because of the family portrait on the wall behind the register.

Welcome South

8558 RICHMOND ROAD / TOANO, VA. 23168
(757) 566-8255

Style	Family-style
Meals	Lunch and dinner, Tuesday through Saturday; closed Thanksgiving, Christmas, New Year's. Reservations are accepted.
Price Range	Inexpensive/Moderate
Superlatives	Homemade soup, specialty pizza
Extras	Beer and wine

*F*rank Anderson built this restaurant, along with the motel and gas station next to it, around the late 1940s, and the family operated it until 2000. The intersection in front of U.S. 60 and Va. 30 has been affectionately called Anderson's Corner for decades.

The building is tan and cream with a couple of benches and a white rocking chair on the front porch. It's bright inside with white walls and classy, flowered print oilcloths on the tables and in the booths. The photos on the walls have been given by customers and folks who had their photos taken at Colonial Williamsburg. No famous faces, perhaps, just average, happy people. Makes me want to smile back at them.

Welcome South has "Southern and gourmet cuisine" printed on the window. According to Paulette Booth, who also happens to be a niece of Frank Anderson and grew up in these parts, they serve Southern, American, and Italian food.

Fried chicken and liver and onions are decidedly Southern, while she classifies cheeseburgers, fish, and shrimp as all-American. For the Italian taste, there's manicotti, lasagna, and great specialty pizzas—red or white—and other popular dishes.

The soups are homemade and what comes out of the kitchen depends on the mood of the cook. Cream of broccoli and chicken vegetable are frequently featured. You can order salads and sandwiches, and they offer wine and beer.

The cannolis are made from scratch. Other desserts include tiramisu, cheesecake, chocolate cake, carrot cake, and Key lime or apple pie.

Coach House Tavern

BERKELEY PLANTATION
VA. 5
CHARLES CITY, VA. 23030
(800) 291-6003

Style	Casual nice
Meals	Lunch, seven days a week; dinner, Friday and Saturday. Reservations are required for dinner.
Price Range	Moderate/Expensive
Superlatives	Crab, pound cake
Extras	Full bar

*E*stablished in 1616, history-rich Charles City County is sandwiched between the James River and the Chickahominy River. The first free black community in America was established here during the 1600s. Thomas Jefferson married Martha Skelton in Charles City County. President John Tyler was born here. Robert E. Lee spent many boyhood years here.

Charles City County is also the home of Berkeley Plantation, whose centerpiece is a three-story Georgian brick house built in 1726 by Benjamin Harrison IV and his wife, Anne. Their son Benjamin signed the Declaration of Independence and served as governor of Virginia from 1782 to 1784. William Henry Harrison, the third son of Benjamin Harrison V, was the ninth president of the United States. William Henry Harrison's grandson—yet another Benjamin Harrison—was our 23rd president.

The house at Berkeley Plantation and the 10-acre grounds overlooking the James River were opened to the public in 1938. Owner Malcolm Jamieson and his wife still live in the house, which is open daily. There is an admission fee, but you need not purchase a ticket to eat at the Coach House Tavern, a rustic old building of uncertain origin near the main house.

Sandra Capps opened a tiny café with just a few tables in 1987 and has expanded a few times since. The restaurant seats 100 and can serve an additional 200 in an outdoor tent. The slate floor in the entry and the aged beams attest to the building's longevity. There are green and white linens on the tables, and instrumental music plays in the background.

At lunch, there's French onion soup, a soup du jour, garden salad, and country-style chicken salad. A Monte Cristo, a vegetarian sandwich, and a "Coach House Club" are among the sandwiches offered. Lunch entrées include grilled tuna, pan-seared salmon, and sliced beef tenderloin.

Dinner is à la carte or a comprehensive event. You'll get an appetizer, a soup, a salad, sorbet, an entrée, dessert, and a beverage. You might start with smoked salmon or venison summer sausage, followed by "Chicken Corn Chowder," then a salad. Sorbet is delivered before your entrée, which might be crab cakes, venison medallions, or veal chops with a creamy basil sauce.

The pound cakes served at the Coach House have won numerous awards. They come in delectable flavors such as Key lime vodka and bourbon walnut.

CHARLES CITY

Indian Fields Tavern
VA. 5 / CHARLES CITY, VA. 23030
(804) 829-5004
WWW.INDIANFIELDS.COM

| *Style* | Casual nice |
| *Meals* | Lunch and dinner, seven days a week. Closed Mondays in January and February. Reservations are recommended. |

Price Range	Moderate/Expensive
Superlatives	"Steak Lyon's Den," "Sally Lunn Bread Pudding"
Extras	Full bar

*T*his plantation was established sometime between 1897 and 1903. When the fields were prepared for planting, Indian artifacts were unearthed—thus the name Indian Fields.

Indian Fields Tavern was renovated and opened by Archer Ruffin and David Napier. Ruffin became sole owner two years after the June 1987 opening. Erich von Gehren bought the restaurant in the summer of 2002. He's a chef who came to Indian Fields via Washington D.C., Chicago, and Lebanon. Chefs certainly make some of the best restaurant owners.

The building is nestled in the shade of pecan, weeping willow, oak, and beech trees. The beds of perennials are beautiful. It's a tranquil spot surrounded by fields and sky. Depending on the time of year, you'll find wheat, soybeans, or corn at various stages of growth. Inside, the cream-colored dining room with dark green trim seats about 30. Another dining room has maroon walls. There are also tables on two screened porches. Fresh flowers and classical music enhance a peaceful atmosphere.

Some of the popular lunch entrées are the chicken salad, the Reuben, and the club sandwich on homemade rye bread. Other options at lunch include the catch of the day and delicious crab cakes.

Dinner starts with appetizers such as a tartlet of duck bacon and "Jalapeño Crab Cheesecake." Sal-

ads and a soup du jour are offered. "Crab Cakes Harrison" come grilled and served over Smithfield ham with hollandaise sauce. Lamb, roast pork, shrimp, grilled filet mignon, and a special vegetarian entrée are also available.

The signature dessert is "Sally Lunn Bread Pudding." Sally Lunn was a French lady who lived in Bath, England. The recipe for her famous bread came to America with the colonists. The bread's popularity is due in part to the fact that it requires no kneading. Other desserts include chocolate bourbon pecan pie and Key lime pie.

SMITHFIELD

C. W. Cowling's

SMITHFIELD PLAZA
VA. 10 / SMITHFIELD, VA. 23430
(757) 357-0044

Style	Family-style
Meals	Lunch and dinner, seven days a week
Price Range	Inexpensive/Moderate
Superlatives	Friendly service, casual atmosphere
Extras	Full bar

*N*amed for Arthur Smith IV, Smithfield is best known for its hams. It was Captain Mallory Todd, a native of Bermuda, who made a business of curing and shipping hams from Smithfield. These amber-colored hams from peanut-fed hogs are now famous worldwide. Only hams dry-cured within the corporate limits of Smithfield can bear the town's name. Smithfield's historic district is listed on the National Register of Historic Places and is a Virginia Historic Landmark. Among its many sites are 10 buildings that predate the Revolutionary War.

If you're looking for a good place to eat in Smithfield, don't let the strip-mall location of C. W. Cowling's deter you. There's a whole different aura inside the restaurant, which opened in June 1988. It has a simple country feel. Photos of barns and local country scenes were taken by a sister-in-law of one of the owners.

The owners, Charlie and Susan Driver Webb, created the name from Charlie's initials (C. W.) and the name of a prominent local family to whom Susan is related (the Cowlings).

This is a good place to bring a pile of friends, because the menu is broad enough to please everyone. At lunch, there are more than a half-dozen salads and twice as many sandwiches. The cheddar melts come on two English muffins topped with either chicken salad, ham, seafood, or vegetables. There are also hamburgers, chili cheese dogs, chicken fajitas, Cajun dishes, and pasta dishes.

At dinner, you can get sirloin steak, chicken, catfish, shrimp, scallops, flounder, or a seafood platter. Ribs are available in the standard full rack or half rack.

You can finish your meal with fried apple pie, hot fudge cake, or a sundae served in a crunchy cinnamon shell. As with the rest of the menu, there are enough sweets for everyone in your party to find something that will satisfy them.

SMITHFIELD

Smithfield Inn
112 MAIN STREET / SMITHFIELD, VA. 23430
(757) 357-1752
WWW.SMITHFIELDINN.COM

Style	Casual nice
Meals	Lunch, Tuesday through Saturday; dinner; Wednesday through Saturday; Sunday brunch. Reservations are recommended.
Price Range	Moderate
Superlatives	Peanut-crusted pork, ham biscuits
Extras	Full bar

*N*o matter what the mode of travel—ship, stagecoach, steamboat, motor car—people passing through Smithfield have supped and slept (including George Washington) at the Smithfield Inn for nearly a quarter-century. The original house was constructed in 1752, and the inn and tavern licenses were applied for in 1759. While renovations and additions have been made by various owners across the years, the rooms retain a traditional comfort of simpler times.

The Sykes family bought the property in 1922, and one of their descendents, Joseph Luter III, now owns it with Smithfield Foods, Inc. The hams and peanuts that have placed Smithfield on the global map have been exported from this small town since a century before the inn was constructed.

The dining rooms are dressed in flowered print wallpaper, characteristic of the period architecture, with a low chair rail and painted trim. The tables

Smithfield Inn

are draped in white linens with fresh flowers, and the red carpet is elegant underfoot.

Classic, Virginia Brunswick stew is offered at lunch, along with salads, sandwiches, and entrées. The Smithfield autumn salad is a mix of wild greens with apples and pears, toasted walnuts, Percorino Tuscano cheese, and Smithfield ham. Some of the sandwiches are Cajun chicken wrap, crab cake sandwich, and prime rib sandwich. Salmon, chicken pot pie, and grilled vegetable salad are only three of the entrées.

Dinner appetizers include house-smoked brook trout and lemon cream oysters. Cream of peanut and she-crab are offered in the soup department. Light entrées might be acorn-seared scallops, roasted free-range chicken, or a medley of seasonal vegetables.

For the more hearty appetite, you'll find a surf and turf entrée, baked stuffed shrimp, pork chops,

lamb shanks, New York strip steak, and a catch of the day. One of the side dishes is ham on a sweet potato; another is a yeast roll.

Sunday brunch features more of the regional cuisine such as Smithfield ham prepared in different ways, peanut-crusted pork medallions, and a vegetable stack of several vegetables served on angel hair pasta in a garlic white wine sauce.

Apple dumplings, crème brûlée, lemon chess pie, bread pudding, and sweet potato pecan pie are usually featured.

The William Rand Tavern, named for an 18th-century owner, opens in the late afternoon, Tuesday through Saturday. It features microbrews and fine wine to go with the appetizers and sandwiches that are offered.

There are charming suites upstairs, each with a sitting room, guest room, and bathroom. The inn offers golf and romantic packages, so you don't have to drive both ways in the same day to eat here. You can drive one way, relax for an overnight or two, play some golf, enjoy some romance, and savor the history of Smithfield between road trips.

Smithfield Station

415 SOUTH CHURCH STREET
SMITHFIELD, VA. 23430
(757) 357-7700

Style	Casual nice
Meals	Breakfast, Saturday and Sunday; lunch and dinner, seven days a week
Price Range	Moderate
Superlatives	Oysters Rockefeller, Smithfield ham
Extras	Full bar

Smithfield Station

Though there's waterfront dining at Smithfield Station, patrons don't look over any great expanse of water. On the patio and inside the main dining rooms, the view extends over a narrow marina and the Pagan River, which provides access to Chesapeake Bay.

The main dining room is flooded with natural light, thanks to windows that reach to the ceiling. The pine interior is accented with dark green and mauve fabrics.

Breakfast on Saturdays is à la carte. On Sundays, there's a breakfast buffet.

At lunch, you can choose from a variety of chowders and soups. Some of the tempting appetizers are fresh oysters, steamed shrimp, and clams, served steamed or on the half shell. The menu touts "a couple of really special things we do." One is oysters Rockefeller—fresh oysters baked with spinach, Pernod and Parmesan cheese. There are close to a dozen salads and cold plates and a fried chicken breast over Smithfield ham and vegetables. You

won't be surprised to learn that the sandwiches include a crab cake sandwich and a Smithfield ham sandwich. If you're in the mood for a light meal, you have 10 or so items from which to choose, among them pork medallions and sirloin steak. There's also a fresh quiche every day.

At dinner, you'll find an even balance of chicken, pork, pasta, beef, and seafood entrées. The "Chicken Isle of Wight" is stuffed with ham, Swiss cheese, and roasted peanuts. For the person who doesn't want just one thing, there are combination plates such as steak and shrimp or steak and lobster.

The 22-room inn above the restaurant, in the lighthouse, and on the boardwalk is always open. Package deals are available for the guest rooms or suites. Boats up to 70 feet in length can be accommodated in the marina. Power and water hookups are available at most slips.

This is one place where I'd like to return—to eat and to stay.

Sting-Ray's

26507 LANKFORD HIGHWAY (U.S. 13)
CAPE CHARLES, VA. 23310
(757) 331-2505

Style	Family-style
Meals	Breakfast, lunch, and dinner, seven days a week
Price Range	Inexpensive/Moderate
Superlatives	Fresh seafood specials
Extras	Wine and beer

*I*f you're in the mood for breakfast, lunch, or dinner after leaving the northern end of the Chesapeake Bay Bridge-Tunnel, don't let the gas pumps at the Cape Charles Exxon station put you off. Cape Center, as the complex is called, is on the eastern side of the highway a few miles north of the bridge-tunnel. It's a one-stop convenience place where you can fuel up, walk the dog, picnic under pines, and stock up on most anything from ice and candy to souvenirs and lottery tickets. Tucked in the back of the big, red, barn-like building is Sting-Ray's.

By day, the restaurant deals in fast food for tourists—soups, sandwiches, burgers, subs, chicken, and such. In the late afternoon, the gourmet menu emerges—seafood, crab imperial, certified Angus beef®, rack of ribs, soft crab, shrimp, trout, and flounder.

The desserts are homemade and include Tennessee bread pudding with bourbon sauce, sweet potato pie, and Death by Chocolate—a brownie with Häagen-Dazs® ice cream, chocolate syrup, and a big pile of whipped cream. We hear it's worth the 3,000 calories.

For spicing up your home life, the store offers a variety of hot sauces with names such as "Insanity Sauce," "Capital Punishment," and "Cafe Fear Hot Sauce," which has what's described as a "near-death rating."

The Chesapeake Bay Café

21229 NORTH BAYSIDE ROAD
CHERITON, VA. 23316
(757) 331-1553
WWW.CHESAPEAKEBAYCAFE.COM

Style	Casual nice
Meals	Lunch and dinner, Monday through Saturday
Price Range	Inexpensive/Moderate
Superlatives	Crab cakes, crab and corn chowder
Extras	Full bar

*R*obert and Patricia Doughty of Virginia Beach take day trips and overnight trips around the state. I don't know them, but they have the first edition of this book. After one of their little jaunts, Robert sent me an e-mail chock full of details on where they ate, what was good, what was closed, and so on. Here's what Robert wrote late in December 2002:

I highly recommend The Chesapeake Bay Café in

Cheriton just a few miles east of Cape Charles. The Eastern Shore-style crab cakes are the best on the shore and the fact that my father was born on Chincoteague (1922-1992), and I have spent much of my life over there, kinda makes me an expert on Eastern Shore seafood-style cooking.

Joe and Gina Downes opened the café in the spring of 1998. Joe is a native of the area, who spent several years working in restaurants in the Richmond area and Deltaville before striking out on his own. The building has been a restaurant since 1936, though it was closed at the time the Downeses bought it.

The lounge has a brick wall and an eclectic collection of clocks set to different times, many of them places Joe and Gina have visited, such as Sri Lanka and Costa Rica. There's a clock for Greenwich Time, another one set on current local time, and another one that doesn't even work marked "who cares."

The dining room walls are mahogany with nautical prints. Stained-glass windows hang from the ceiling. Local artists create interesting drawings on the six 3 ½ x 5-foot chalkboards. There are 14 booths and seating for 20 to 25.

Soups and salads, specialty subs, appetizers, and fried, grilled, or broiled dishes are available at lunch with an emphasis, of course, on fresh seafood. The crab and corn chowder is a house specialty. Clam chowder, baked potato soup, and stockpot soup are also offered.

Following an appetizer of perhaps potato skins or café nachos, you select your entrée "from the land" or "and the sea" categories. Land includes chicken in a white wine cream sauce, rib-eye steak, and center-cut pork chops.

The crab cakes come highly recommended from an Eastern Shore seafood-style cooking expert quoted above. If you just aren't in the mood for a fabulous crab cake, you might consider broiled sea scallops, jumbo shrimp, fried oysters, or a house specialty such as café stuffed shrimp, seafood medley, or prime rib. There are eight specials every day—a steak, a catch, a pasta, an inexpensive blue-plate special, and others.

The dessert menu changes daily, the food is fresh, and Joe and Gina are creative, hard-working people. And the Doughtys have raved about The Chesapeake Bay Café in more than one e-mail.

Captain's Deck
U.S. 13 / NASSAWADOX, VA. 23413
(757) 442-7060

Style	Home-style
Meals	Breakfast, lunch, and dinner, seven days a week
Price Range	Inexpensive/Moderate
Superlatives	Belgian waffles, "Neptune's Special"
Extras	Full bar

*L*ocated about a third of the way up the Eastern Shore, the community of Nassawadox developed around a sawmill. Today, you can visit the Nassawadox Sawmill Museum.

Many local residents recommend Captain's Deck, particularly if you're in the mood for breakfast, which is served any time of the day. And it is surely popular for breakfast, judging by the number of cars, pickups, and panel trucks I saw in the parking lot the morning I visited.

The large, bright dining room can seat about 170. The space is surrounded by large picture windows and hanging plants. A shelf going around the room is stacked with baseball caps—hundreds of them—advertising all sorts of teams and companies. The customers keep bringing in more. The restaurant has a nautical theme, which extends to the restrooms, where orange life rings on the doors are labeled "Gulls" and "Buoys."

The breakfast menu is extensive—and colorful. For example, one item reads, "Express: Two eggs, bacon, home fries, toast, or biscuit and you're outta here." Seafood, Mexican dishes, scrapple, and omelets are also offered at breakfast. The variety might explain the popularity.

Lunch specialties include breaded veal cutlets, hamburgers, fried oysters, and hot roast beef.

Seafood entrées are popular at dinner. Charbroiled steaks, liver and onions, pizza, and chicken round out the evening menu.

For dessert, you can get pie, cake, pudding, or "Fruit Cob"—short for cobbler.

During the summer, Captain's Deck features live music on Saturday nights.

Little Italy Ristorante

10227 ROGERS DRIVE / NASSAWADOX, VA. 23413
(757) 442-7831

Style	Italian
Meals	Lunch and dinner, Tuesday through Saturday
Price Range	Inexpensive/Moderate
Superlatives	Pasta dishes, tiramisu
Extras	Full bar

When folks on the Eastern Shore crave a break from seafood, seafood, and more seafood, many of them turn to the Little Italy Ristorante, a white brick storefront just east of U.S. 13 in Nassawadox.

Shortly after noon on the weekday I visited, the parking lot across Rogers Drive was crowded with cars and pickups. A parade of take-out customers came and went. Inside, the dining room was nearly full and the aroma of Italian cooking permeated the air.

On the wall right inside the door are two United States maps and a world map. Customers can put a pin on their hometown, state, or country. Hundreds have done so. The pleasant dining room can seat about 40. It's decorated with plastic grapevines clinging to trellises and posters of Italian scenes clinging to the walls. Italian music plays in the background.

"We do have seafood, Italian-style!" contends owner and chef Franco Nocera. He and his wife, Cathy, have operated Little Italy since 1992. As a concession to their Eastern Shore customers, they offer shrimp Parmesan, shrimp scampi over pasta, and seafood Alfredo.

There are several pizzas on the lunch menu, as well as cold subs and hot subs.

For dinner, you might try baked ziti, stuffed shells, tortellini Alfredo, or one of the spaghetti dishes. There are also meat, chicken, and veal entrées, as well as half a dozen vegetable entrées.

The tiramisu is a specialty dessert.

If you're on the go, just come on in and take your order right out. For special occasions, you can get party trays of all the cold cuts, subs, and Italian casseroles offered at Little Italy.

E. L. Willis & Co.

4456 WILLIS WHARF ROAD
WILLIS WHARF, VA. 23486
(757) 442-4225

Style	Casual nice
Meals	Lunch, Monday through Saturday. Credit cards are not accepted.
Price Range	Inexpensive/Moderate
Superlatives	Seafood sandwiches, edible shell wraps
Extras	Full bar

*I*t's not too difficult to guess that a man named Willis once had a wharf here. He was Edward Willis, and he purchased land for his wharf in 1854. Today, Willis Wharf remains a real waterfront fishing village.

E. L. Willis & Co.

The old mercantile building that houses the dining establishment called E. L. Willis & Co. has served as a store or a restaurant since 1850. In both its setting and its cuisine, E. L. Willis & Co. offers a taste of the past. It's very quaint. Very Eastern Shore. To find it, you must venture off U.S. 13 at Exmore and go east on Va. 603 to Willis Wharf.

You can relax on the screened porch overlooking the marsh and watch the fishing vessels snaking through the narrow channel to the Atlantic Ocean. It's a pleasant diversion during lunch. Make sure you bring cash, as E. L. Willis & Co. does not accept credit cards.

Owner Pam Widgeon, an Eastern Shore native, has owned and run the place since the early 1990s. She doesn't advertise and so depends on loyal local business, referrals from lodging places, and travelers who seek her out—or who just get lucky while exploring the back roads.

The dining room is decorated with Pam's vintage kitchen utensils and laundry implements, such as washboards and hand-cranked ringers. You'll also note the collection of old oyster cans and the assortment of nostalgic commercial signs.

Pam makes all her own soups. But her specialty is fresh seafood. Among the offerings are crab cake sandwiches, clam fritter sandwiches (which have been mentioned in the *New York Times*), and fish filet sandwiches. Liverwurst sandwiches, ham sandwiches, and turkey sandwiches are served as well. The coleslaw and potato chips are homemade.

Pam also creates all the desserts, such as apple dumplings, rice pudding, seasonal pumpkin ice cream, and berry desserts when fresh berries are available. From the looks of what I saw, I'd recommend any one of her desserts.

EXMORE

The Trawler

2555 LANKFORD HIGHWAY (U.S. 13)
EXMORE, VA. 23350
(757) 442-2092

Style	Family-style
Meals	Lunch and dinner, seven days a week
Price Range	Moderate
Superlatives	She-crab soup, sweet potato biscuits
Extras	Full bar

There are two schools of thought on the naming of Exmore. It was purportedly the 11th rail stop south of the Maryland border. Thus, the northbound crew had 10—or *X*, in Roman numerals—more stops before reaching the state line. Others say the place was named for the village of Exmore in England.

You'll easily spot The Trawler's big roadside sign with the fishing boat logo on the eastern side of U.S. 13 near Exmore. It's an Eastern Shore landmark of sorts.

The Trawler opened in 1980. Carl and Judi Beck bought it a few years later and opened a dinner theater. Productions run 12 days each month from June through November. Marion and John Long now own and operate the restaurant.

About 250 patrons can be seated at the pine tables and booths. The spacious dining area has vaulted ceilings, exposed beams, and plank walls. A stained-glass room divider taken from a Chesapeake Bay skipjack dominates the room. Decoys, carvings of shorebirds, seascapes, clam rakes, and other fishing and boating artifacts enhance the nautical aura.

From oyster sandwiches, soft-shell crab sandwiches, grilled tuna sandwiches, and catfish sandwiches to combinations and platters of crabmeat, shrimp, scallops, and stuffed flounder, seafood dominates the extensive lunch menu. The signature items are sweet potato biscuits and she-crab soup so thick that your spoon can hardly touch bottom.

If it's dinnertime and you're not in the mood for seafood, you can order certified Angus beef® steak, prime rib, chicken cordon bleu, or just plain grilled chicken. All dinner entrées include a cup of clam chowder, a trip to the salad bar, hush puppies, sweet potato biscuits, and your choice of potato, pasta, or rice pilaf.

The desserts include pecan pie, apple pie, "Peanut Butter Blast," "Chocolate Nemesis," and others. Just don't ask for the recipes. Both *Bon Appétit* magazine and *Gourmet* magazine have requested recipes from The Trawler to publish in their pages. They didn't get them.

Formy's Original Pit Barbecue

U.S. 13 / PAINTER, VA. 23420
(757) 442-2426

Style	Family-style
Meals	Lunch and dinner, seven days a week
Price Range	Inexpensive
Superlatives	Pit-cooked pork

Ah, the aroma of pit-cooked barbecue! That's the first thing you notice as you enter Formy's.

You can't miss the place—just look for the long, white building and the big sign with the pig on it.

"We sell no swine before its time," says the menu. The pork is cooked in a secret sauce for 24 hours over a fire of oak and hickory.

All barbecue is good, some is different, that's all. The place caters mostly to the traffic on U.S. 13. Dan Field and Duane Grove purchased and renovated this Eastern Shore restaurant in May 2002. About 40 customers can be seated in the casual dining room.

You don't have to order barbecue, of course—though you'll probably want to. It's been mentioned in the *New York Times* as the "best barbecue ever." There's chicken, ribs, shrimp, fish, hamburgers, and hot dogs. Everything comes with hush puppies and two vegetables. Fresh turnip greens are available in season.

You don't even have to eat your food here. Everything—including the chocolate cake and the caramel cake—can be packaged for take-out.

Island House Restaurant

17 ATLANTIC AVENUE
WACHAPREAGUE, VA. 23480
(757) 787-4242

Style	Casual nice
Meals	Lunch and dinner, seven days a week. The Island House is closed from Christmas to the end of January.
Price Range	Moderate
Superlatives	View, seafood, homemade desserts
Extras	Full bar

Wachapreague, dubbed "the Flounder Fishing Capital of the World," is the site of some serious fishing. There are spring and fall flounder tournaments, a ladies' tuna tournament, and marlin tournaments. The town boasts four marinas, lots of charter fleets, and about 200 permanent residents.

The Island House Restaurant overlooks the

broad marshes between the Eastern Shore and the Atlantic Ocean. To find it, follow the signs from U.S. 13 onto Va. 180 into Wachapreague.

The first building on this site was a combination hotel and restaurant constructed in the early 1900s and washed away by a major storm in 1933. Z. R. Lewis and his son Randy built the first Island House in 1978. It was destroyed by fire 14 years later. Not to be deterred, the Lewises built another restaurant, this one modeled after the Parramore Island Lifesaving Station, complete down to the lookout tower. On the first floor are the main dining room and a banquet room. A dining room with expansive water views is on the second floor.

In the spring of 2003, a wraparound deck was built, and a couple of dozen patrons can dine out there. The Island House's crab cakes—"long a favorite of Jimmy Buffett," according to the menu—are delicious. Randy is a friend of the popular singer and cooks for him and his crew when they are within commuting distance.

The restaurant offers light fare (soups and salads), a soup and salad bar, a raw bar, early-bird specials (chicken, tuna, shrimp, and a crab cake platter), local seafood, and combinations.

The desserts are homemade, and some are sugar-free. I can testify that the cheesecake is absolutely wonderful.

Tammy & Johnny's

U.S. 13 / MELFA, VA. 23410
(757) 787-1122

Style	Home-style
Meals	Lunch and dinner, seven days a week
Price Range	Inexpensive
Superlatives	Fried chicken

*I*n this land of fresh and abundant seafood, subtly crisp and succulent fried chicken is a good find. However, I didn't give Tammy & Johnny's a second look as I raced up U.S. 13 north of Melfa. The red brick and orange building on the western side of the road looks like the usual fast-food restaurant. But it turns out it's a locally owned landmark. On the word of more than one loyal patron, I decided to give it a try.

"It's fresh. People can trust our chicken," states John R. "Ronnie" Edward, who owns the restaurant with his wife, Shirley. "We use 100 percent cottonseed oil and change it every day."

Ronnie and Shirley built the place in 1967 and have added onto it over the years. He's an Eastern Shore native who put in lots of years with a telephone company. Tammy and Johnny are their children. Actually, they're not children now. They're both 30-somethings who work at the family business, as do nearly two dozen other employees.

The chicken is wonderful, the flavor locked inside. The trick has to do with marinating it for 24 hours in a secret concoction and frying it for just the right time at just the right temperature—380 degrees. That's 30 degrees hotter than usual. How they do that without burning it is another family secret.

Tammy & Johnny's also offers shrimp, soft-shell crab sandwiches, burgers, and french fries.

The restaurant's following is so strong that business thrives even when the Chesapeake Bay Bridge-Tunnel is out of commission. About 50 people can be seated in the immaculate dining room at booths and utilitarian fast-food tables. The take-out counter is almost always busy. And for fresh-air buffs, there are seven picnic tables under the shade of holly trees.

Armando's

10 NORTH STREET / ONANCOCK, VA. 23417
(757) 787-8044

Style	Casual nice
Meals	Dinner, Tuesday through Sunday
Price Range	Inexpensive/Moderate
Superlatives	Artistic cuisine, specialty beverages
Extras	Full bar

Founded in 1680, the picturesque village of Onancock covers just under one square mile. It is home to Hopkins and Brothers (one of the oldest general stores in the country), Kerr Place (a gorgeous brick building dating from 1799), and several lovely 19th-century homes.

Armando's

Venturing into Armando's for the first time, your startled reaction might be: "Can I afford this?"

I'll answer with a slightly different question: "Can you afford to miss this?" Armando's is more than a unique dining experience. It's the work of an artist.

Armando's last name is Suarez, but on the menu, it's simply Armando, with a little heart for the *o*. The menu explains how this native of Argentina ventured to New York City in 1970 and dabbled in everything from hair styling to jewelry and leather design before ending up in the little town of Onancock. In 1988, he opened a gourmet pizza and croissant sandwich shop in an abandoned grocery store as part of Onancock's downtown revitalization. Fascinated with the design of the building, which dates from around 1940, he remodeled extensively, exposing old brick and preserving an old skylight. He converted the parking lot into a patio courtyard. Bored with just pizza and sandwiches, Armando expanded to a full menu of original creations in 1991.

The wide range of beverages served here—cappuccino, espresso, international coffees, special teas, imported beers, a fine array of wines—is unusual among Eastern Shore eateries. Armando's features a martini bar as well with more than 30 martinis. The "Golden" is a blend of orange juice, vodka, Grand Marnier, and champagne, and the "Silver Bullet" has vodka, Bombay Sapphire, and Chardonnay. Several martinis are rimmed with sugar, and garnishes include lemon or lime twist, various fine olives, almonds, anchovies, roasted garlic, or marachino cherries marinated in brandy.

The extensive menu makes pleasurable reading while you sip Perrier or Irish coffee and let Armando prepare your meal from scratch. The veal piccata, for example, is described as "an artistic expression of pure genius: scallop of veal gently sautéed with garlic and those incredible shiitake mushrooms in a velvet sauce of lemon, butter, and citrus zest. What makes it so ingenious? The elegant simplicity of it all."

Shrimp Danielle, crab crêpes, and lobster ravioli are some of the entrées, along with a variety of chicken and veal dishes.

Armando says moving to this small town on the Eastern Shore is the best move he's ever made. The many diners who fill the place inside and out just might agree.

Wright's Seafood Restaurant and Crab Galley

WRIGHT ROAD
ATLANTIC, VA. 23303
(757) 824-4012
WWW.WRIGHTSRESTAURANT.COM

Style	Casual nice
Meals	Dinner, seven days a week from Memorial Day to Labor Day
Price Range	Moderate/Expensive
Superlatives	Water view, stuffed flounder, seafood platters
Extras	Full bar

The small town of Atlantic is located a few miles south of Chincoteague Island on the ocean side of U.S. 13, the main highway down the Eastern Shore. Most of the farmers in this rural area raise chickens, so you'll see quite a few chicken houses.

In fact, what is now Wright's Seafood Restaurant and Crab Galley started as a sandwich shop in an old poultry processing plant. That was nearly three decades ago, when the place had two tables. Now, it has two kitchens, three dining rooms that can seat a total of 350 patrons, and a banquet room that extends over the water on pilings.

The only things that haven't changed are the panoramic view and the location. From U.S. 13, take Va. 175 toward Chincoteague, then turn south on Atlantic Road. After about half a mile, turn left on Wright Road (Va. 766), which is a winding road flanked by fields. Suddenly, you'll come upon a long, low building with yellow vinyl siding. You're here.

Like most of the restaurants profiled in this book, Wright's—where the owners claim that "everything is always just right"—is a family business. Carol and Lewis Wright and their daughter Theresa McCready manage the daily operations. Lewis runs one kitchen and Theresa is in charge of the other.

In the "Crab Galley" dining area, neatness doesn't count. In another room, white tablecloths and napkins lend a semiformal air. In yet another room, you'll find old Liberty ship hatch covers embedded with sand, shells, and starfish, a fascination for children and adults alike.

The menu served in the "Crab Galley" features à la carte items and several all-you-can-eat choices. The main menu has more than two dozen fresh seafood entrées, along with prime rib, steaks, baby back ribs, chicken, and pork chops.

If you're a thirsty traveler, you'll particularly appreciate Wright's iced tea, which will be delivered to your table in a carafe. It's great for those in need of instant refills.

Garden and Sea Inn

4188 NELSON ROAD / NEW CHURCH, VA. 23415
(757) 824-0672

Style	Fine dining
Meals	Breakfast, for lodging guests only. Dinner, Saturday April through Thanksgiving. Reservations are recommended. Dinner is available other nights by reservation only; call for information.
Price Range	Expensive
Superlatives	Shrimp, scallops, oysters
Extras	Wine and beer

New Church is the first community south of the Maryland state line. It was established in the early 1700s when the Reverend Francis Makemie organized the institution that gave the town its name—a new church.

The Garden and Sea Inn is an oasis of country tranquility just a block west of busy U.S. 13. While there is no dress code, one feels compelled to dress up a little—a shirt with a collar, at least. It's a lovely place, and they maintain a casually inviting atmosphere.

The inn and restaurant, located in a Victorian gingerbread house of coral, green, and beige, has been owned by Tom and Sara Baker since 1994. Tom trained at the Culinary Institute of America and has worked at some of the finest restaurants in Virginia. Sara runs the inn, which includes eight guest rooms between the main house and another building on the landscaped property.

Garden and Sea Inn

Gourmet meals are served either in the main dining room or on the enclosed porch. Apricots in brandy sauce, wonderful soups, and salads whet your appetite. Entrées vary among a shrimp, scallops, and oyster dish; filet mignon; grilled salmon; boneless rack of lamb; and other fresh seafood and meats.

Desserts are fabulous, and there are several from which to choose. It might be better if there were just one, as it's tough to select either chocolate pecan pie, crème brûlée with blueberries, Girl Scout chocolate mint cookie cheesecake, or one of the others.

Guests come from far and wide to savor Tom Baker's culinary art with or without the fine wines.

AJ's on the Creek

6585 MADDOX BOULEVARD
CHINCOTEAGUE, VA. 23336
(757) 336-5888

Style	Casual nice
Meals	Lunch and dinner, Monday through Saturday
Price Range	Moderate/Expensive
Superlatives	Chowder, fresh seafood, steaks
Extras	Full bar

Chincoteague Island measures seven miles by one and a half miles. Although the first white man arrived here in the 1670s, the 1800 census reported a population of only 60. The little town of Chincoteague was the first in Virginia to have a public school; the superintendent was paid $50 per year in the early days. Today, Chincoteague is noted for its fresh fish, its craftsmen, and its wild ponies. Each year, ponies from neighboring Assateague Island are brought here to be auctioned. The pony swim takes place in July.

Commercialism has left its mark on Chincoteague. The island is awash with places for tourists and anglers to dine. But ask Eastern Shore locals where they go, and most will say AJ's.

The main dining room seats around 100. It's light, bright, and airy—upscale yet relaxed. Colorful prints and carvings of egrets, herons, and shorebirds accent the room.

Sisters Lisa and April Stillson bought the place in 1985 when it was a fast-food joint called McDuffy's. They named it for their other partner,

Anthony John Stillson, who also happens to be their father.

April is in charge of the kitchen. She taught herself to cook by watching cooking shows on television, and the results are remarkable.

At lunch, you can get seafood chowder, burgers, sandwiches, clam strips, and platters. The crab cake sandwich and the fried shrimp basket are excellent.

Two of the popular appetizers at dinner are fried artichoke hearts and oysters Rockefeller. The raw bar menu includes clams, oysters, and salmon. The house specialties are the catch of the day and flounder smothered in seafood. April's seafood bouillabaisse, crab Alfredo, and mussels marinara give the local sea bounty an Italian touch. Several pasta dishes and several veal dishes—veal and shrimp, veal Marsala, veal piccata, veal Oscar—are offered, as are steaks, lamb chops, and surf and turf.

"We were young and foolish," says Lisa of the sisters' decision to buy the restaurant when they were in their mid-20s. But they've done well. Perhaps their personal-service motto—"Every customer is the most important one"—has had something to do with their success.

Chincoteague Inn
100 MAIN STREET / CHINCOTEAGUE, VA. 23336
(757) 336-6110

Style	Casual nice
Meals	Lunch and dinner, seven days a week from March through October
Price Range	Moderate/Expensive
Superlatives	View, outdoor bar
Extras	Full bar

*T*he Chincoteague Inn, overlooking Chincoteague Channel, is just what you'd expect of a vintage waterfront restaurant on an island that's a mecca for fishermen. It's very salty (in the nautical sense) and very, very casual.

The inn has weathered cedar siding and a weathered wraparound deck with an anchor chain for the railing. From the open-air bar, you can watch a fleet of charter fishing boats. Old Key West and Ernest Hemingway—and maybe Jimmy Buffett—spring to mind. Part of the building is around 100 years old. One of the first commercial structures on the island, it started as a dock before a small restaurant was added.

Paul and Jane Tatum have owned it now for around 20 years. Even though the Tatums reduced the size of the dock by adding the outdoor bar, fishermen still bring their catch to sell to the inn. Inside the restaurant, the atmosphere ranges from the salty to the delightful. The lounge is dark, and the main dining room is as bright as all outdoors.

The entrées run the gamut from scallops, crab cakes, oysters, flounder, and lobster to seafood Florentine, lobster tail with Delmonico steak, and soft-shell crabs fixed a number of ways. The Chincoteague Inn is most definitely a seafood place. What else would you expect here? Still, chef Walt Van Hart, Sr., ranks his prime rib au jus as "supreme." His seafood specialty is the "Bay Platter," which combines baked fish filet, baked scallops, and shrimp on a stick. And some patrons will tell you that the inn's crab imperial is the very best of all.

Index of Towns

Index of Restaurants